A new scandal about misuse of "power"
haunts "Pinch" Sulzberger and the "Times"

LIBEL
by New York Times

Gay Marriage didn't just happen in Massachusetts,
It was engineered by the New York Times

By J. Edward Pawlick

Mustard Seeds, Inc.
P.O. Box 812844
Wellesley, MA 02181-0026
www.mustardseeds.com

1 2 3 4 5 6 7 8 9

Second Printing

ISBN 0-9746670-0-5

Unarmed truth and unconditional love will have the final word in reality. That is why right, temporarily defeated, is stronger than evil triumphant.

— Martin Luther King Jr.,
Accepting Nobel Peace Prize, Dec. 10, 1964

Dedication

To My Grandchildren

This book is dedicated to all my grandchildren, including my "black"grandchildren.

Those "black" grandchildren will not be welcome anywhere in America if Arthur O. Sulzberger, Jr. ("Pinch"), Publisher of the *New York Times*, is allowed to use blacks as his own personal toy as he did Jayson Blair — talking down to him and using him as a token to make himself and the *Times* appear "tolerant" and "inclusive."

I am not concerned about my daughter and my black son-in-law, but I am hopeful that their children will be treated the same as other Americans.

They will not be welcomed by the "haters" among the blacks because they are not "black" enough. The haters among the whites will not welcome them either. The only way that they should be welcomed is as fellow citizens, not by the color of their skin. The blood flowing in their veins will be Belgian, Black, German, Irish, Italian and Jewish. That is a recipe for the perfect American unless the race-haters have their way.

And what will be their status under the law as compared to their white cousins? Will they be special for some reason? If so, why?

My previous book in 1998 was also dedicated to these grandchildren who were not yet born at that time. It foresaw that people like Sulzberger would be using them for their own advantage, in many cases attempting to assuage their own guilt for being rich while others are poor. The book explained why the Civil Rights Act of 1964 is taking us in that direction.

I am confident that our country will change in that the majority of its people are of good will. They may not understand what is happening now but they're beginning to. When they do understand, they will call for change from racists like Pinch Sulzberger.

There are quotation marks around the word "black" because the use of that word to describe anyone who has any negroid blood, even of the slightest amount, has historically been used by those whites who believe they are superior to such a person, as Pinch Sulzberger does today. He wishes them to be in a separate and distinct category, obviously subservient to him, where he can observe and categorize them. He even separates them into distinct legal categories, which requires us to make such divisions on an individual basis and categorize every citizen by their race, although assigning such a category is impossible where a person is, for example, white, Chinese and black.

The problem is highlighted by the real-life troubles of Pinch's father, Punch. Many people have no idea who their father and mother are, much less their distant ancestors. This is true for Punch's illegitimate child for whom he paid support while denying that he was the father. Punch obviously had no idea whether he was the father. From the way he describes the mother, probably she has no idea either.

Punch's sister advised her daughters to follow the same relaxed standards of sexuality. If everyone does so, this means it will be impossible for most people to positively identify their parents, unless we require DNA tests of the father for every newborn.

CONTENTS

PART III — Decay of New York Times and Supreme Judicial Court

VISIT OUR WEBSITES

For more information about
"Libel by New York Times" and
"Freedom Will Conquer Racism and Sexism"
visit our website at www.mustardseeds.com

Our daily news site, "Massachusetts News," is found at
www.massnews.com

PART I

The Lawsuit

Section I

It's Not Difficult to Recognize Libel

In order to recover for libel, a plaintiff must show a falsehood which damaged his reputation in the community.

It's "libel" when written and "slander" when spoken. Together, they are known to lawyers as "defamation."

A judge may use his drastic power to stop a libel case from going to the jury only if the defendant can show that the plaintiff has "no reasonable expectation of proving an essential element of [the] case," according to the Supreme Judicial Court of Massachusetts. That state law is binding on a federal court.

The federal judge in this case, Patti B. Saris, wrote in a previous case that, when deciding whether to grant a motion to dismiss a case, "the Court accepts as true only the allegations set forth in the complaint." In other words, if there is a dispute as to the facts in the case, the jury must make the decision, not the judge.

The article from the *New York Times* was on Judge Saris' bench in her Boston courtroom when she made the quick decision on August 21, 2003, dismissing the libel suit against "The New York Times Company."

You'll find the article on the next page of this book exactly as it appeared at the top of page 22 in the National Sunday Edition of the *Times* on April 7, 2002, plus an easy-to-read typewritten copy.

1

Can You Find the Libel?

Below is the article that appeared in the Sunday National Edition of the *New York Times* on April 7, 2002. It went to 1.6 million subscribers across the entire country, one-half-million more copies than the daily edition of the *Times*. It had a particularly large circulation in Massachusetts.

On the pages that follow in this chapter is the text from the article. It was obtained from the *New York Times'* website, www.nytimes.com.

April 7, 2002, Sunday

NATIONAL DESK
Drive to Ban Gay Marriage
Is Accused of Duping Signers

By PAM BELLUCK

BRAINTREE, Mass., April 5 — Outside a Stop & Shop in this suburb south of Boston a few months ago, Richard Leeman was stopped by a man with a clipboard who asked him to sign a petition to ban the practice of slaughtering horses for people to eat. Mr. Leeman, a retired insurance executive, planted his signature on the paper.

But Mr. Leeman recently discovered that the petition he signed was apparently not to protect horses, but to ban gay marriage in Massachusetts, something Mr. Leeman says he would never support.

Across the state in Pittsfield, Marie Coe, a homemaker, says the same thing happened to her. So does Christine Bogoian, a vitamin saleswoman in Worcester, in central Massachusetts.

"People were tricked," Ms. Bogoian said. "I never meant to sign the marriage petition, and now I'm told that my name was on the marriage petition and not on the horse petition."

Organizers of the horse campaign say hundreds of people were duped into signing the marriage petition when they thought they were endorsing a horse-slaughter ban. They say bait-and-switch tactics left the horse initiative 2,574 signatures short of the 57,100 it needed to be placed on the ballot in November.

Organizers say the culprit was the company hired to collect signatures by the backers of the marriage initiative and, separately, by the Save Our Horses campaign. Save Our Horses says the firm, Ballot Access Company of Phoenix, was getting paid more per signature for the marriage initiative. They say it used the horse petition to lure people to unwittingly sign the marriage petition, which signature collectors affixed to the same clipboard, under a cover sheet of a horse decorated like an American flag.

The horse proponents have sued to get their measure on the ballot after all.

Backers of the marriage amendment, which got 76,607 signatures — more than enough to advance toward its goal of getting on the ballot in 2004 — deny the accusations. Ballot Access Company officials did not return phone calls, but James Lafferty, a spokesman for the amendment's sponsors, Massachusetts Citizens for Marriage, said the company had denied the accusations.

In a letter to the state this week, Massachusetts Citizens for Marriage said the "horse people" had political motives and "some opponents were signing our petition in order to later claim that they had been 'tricked.'"

State officials say they have never heard of a case anywhere in the country where voters have asked to have signatures moved from one petition to another.

The horse initiative is one of a growing number of efforts to eradicate the slaughter of horses for food. The number of horses slaughtered in this country, 62,379 in the 2001 fiscal year, increased for the first time since the mid-1990's, apparently because mad cow disease scared beef eaters in Europe and Asia into eating more horse meat.

A bill in Congress would prohibit horse slaughter for human consumption; another would ban interstate transportation of horses to slaughterhouses. California banned horse slaughter for human consumption in 1998.

After the petition drives started in Massachusetts last September, people complained to the secretary of state's office about switched petitions.

"We found that there were some irregularities and that people may have signed a petition they didn't want to sign," said Ann Donlan, a spokeswoman for the attorney general's office.

In recent weeks, Save Our Horses has mailed questionnaires to Massachusetts voters, asking them to check a Web site to see if they signed either petition.

Susan Wagner, a horse advocate from Bedford, N.Y., who formed Save Our Horses, says hundreds of people have mailed the cards back claiming they were hoodwinked, and she believes the total will exceed the 2,574-signature shortfall.

Lowell Finley, a California lawyer for the group, said signature collectors have said they were coached to use the horse petition to snag marriage signatures. One signature collector, Jason Hampton, said he and others were given clipboards with horse cover sheets, but more marriage petitions than horse petitions underneath.

Secretary of State William F. Galvin, the defendant in the lawsuit, said horse advocates face an uphill battle because they did not file their complaints by December, the statutory deadline. Horse proponents say those deadlines do not apply.

Marriage amendment backers, citing the support of gay rights groups for the horse advocates' claims, say the complaints are politically motivated. But horse supporters say they just want to get their measure on the ballot.

"It goes against rah-rah America," said Ms. Bogoian, a plaintiff in the lawsuit. "It goes against everything we stand for to ruin a petition like that."

2

Why Was Judge Saris Worrying?

It was clear to Judge Saris, as it would be to anyone, that the *headline* for the story which was "**Drive to Ban Gay Marriage Is Accused of Duping Signers,**" was "libel" by itself.

It was a false statement. No one anywhere had "accused" the supporters of the "Protection of Marriage Amendment" of "duping" voters.

The *article* underneath the headline was also libel. But it was done by innuendo. "It didn't exactly say they were criminals," was what the lawyers at the *Times* were prepared to say. (The lawyers had undoubtedly read the article before it was published.)

If cries were raised about the article (which the lawyers were sure would never happen), they were ready to point to the paragraph in the story that contained a statement from the horse people that the "culprit" was the company that employed the signature gatherers. The lawyers would say, "See, it was the signature gatherers who were accused, not the plaintiffs."

The article was meticulously written to skirt the edges of libel without going over the edge. But the *Times* did, in fact, go much too close to the edge. As we will see, innuendos can be libel.

Whether the article was carefully written by the reporter or not, it didn't really matter in the final analysis, because she didn't see the headline before it was published. A headline is always written at the last minute. It must exactly fit the space that is allotted to it by the copy editor on the day it is published.

Someone was not warned. The headline threw away all the careful writing in the article. The headline was clear and explicit. The *New York Times* newspaper was guilty of "libel."

New York Was Watching Very Closely

The lawyer in charge of all this for The New York Times Company was Assistant General Counsel George Freeman at headquarters in Times Square, New York. He received a copy of everything that happened in the Boston court during the progress of the suit. That was noted on documents that went to the court. The message was thus given to Judge Saris that the New York headquarters was watching everything she did.

Although The Company was telling the judge that the *Globe* was totally independent, the reality was completely different, as she could easily see.

Was Atty. Freeman the one who missed the boat and failed to catch that headline? Did it really matter if he did miss it? If any "nut" did bring a libel suit, The Company had the federal and state courts in Boston well-saturated with friends.

The only defense for the *headline* that The Company lawyers could argue was that its first word, "Drive," was too ambiguous for anyone to believe that it included the supporters of the Amendment, particularly the plaintiffs.

This is where Patti Saris ruled even before she sat down in her chair in a courtroom at the federal courthouse on Boston Harbor. She held that the Boston Globe is independent of any control by Pinch Sulzberger, Publisher of the New York Times. Therefore she was going to dismiss the case for libel, despite the fact that the Sulzbergers have always been obsessive about knowing and controlling everything that is published in their newspapers.

Not Its First Story about the Amendment

The April 7 article in the *Times* was not the first one that "The New York Times Company" had published in its chain of newspapers about the Protection of Marriage Amendment and the "fraud" of its supporters.

In fact, the story was getting a little boring to us in Massachussetts. The *Boston Globe* had already written three articles about "horses and fraud," beginning with its very first coverage of the Amendment on November 21, 2001. However, it had not been successful in turning the majority of the citizens against the Amendment (although the paper was a very important influence upon those politicians on Beacon Hill who opposed the measure).

Because of the *Globe's* failure to affect the citizens, someone at The Company decided that the full power of the *Times* newspaper must be brought to bear on a hearing that was scheduled by the Legislature for Wednesday, April 10, at the State House in Boston.

Therefore, a story was scheduled for the national edition of the Times for the Sunday before the hearing, even though <u>*nothing new had occurred since the first Globe story of November 21*</u>.

Naturally, a large story in this prestigious newspaper would have a considerable impact in Massachusetts. The Sunday edition had a circulation of 1.5 million across the country, which was a half-million above the daily distribution. (But even this was not enough to accomplish its purpose, as we shall see later.)

The reporter, Pam Belluck, attempted a "fair and balanced story" by attacking the plaintiffs only through the use of innuendoes. Her charade failed when the headline writer read the story and then wrote that it accused the plaintiffs of "duping" voters. According to Webster's, "dupe" means to "trick," "deceive," "cheat."

The headline writer understood that the plaintiffs had not only been accused of fraud, they were guilty of the charge.

<u>Even though the plaintiffs were never formally accused by anyone in the story, the innuendoes were so strong that the headline writer at the *Times* wrote that they had been so accused.</u>

The Reporter Did Make Mistakes

Although the article was dated Friday, April 5 (the day when it was filed by Belluck), it started by telling what had happened to an unhappy signer "a few months ago." But the incident which Belluck was reporting did *not* take place "a few months ago" as she claimed. If it happened at all, the alleged signing had to have taken place sometime between September and November 2001, which was at least four months previous. The average person telling this story would say, "late last year," or "last fall" or something similar.

Not a big point, but it is odd. It causes one to wonder why Belluck stretched the timeframe. The answer could be that she knew she had nothing new to report. She felt guilty rewriting a story that had appeared many times before. She didn't want to reveal to the reader how old and stale the story was. (What would she have answered if we could have asked her that question during discovery proceedings? She, a *New York Times* reporter, must have been embarrassed about re-writing a story from the *Globe*.)

The headline summarized the story accurately and clearly. It said that the people in charge of the Protection of Marriage Amendment, i.e. the plaintiffs, were accused in the story of tricking and deceiving voters.

The Company said in its brief to Judge Saris that the first word in the headline, "Drive," is ambiguous and no reader would possibly understand it to mean the plaintiffs. But who else could it mean? Certainly not the people hired to obtain the signatures. It clearly meant the people who had written and proposed the Amendment, who were on record as such in the Secretary of State's office and were actively coordinating the statewide efforts to pass it, i.e., the plaintiffs.

The Company also, as expected, did argue in its brief that the article clearly said that the "culprit," according to the horse people themselves, was "the company hired to collect signatures." But then Belluck added at the end of that sentence that those "crooks" had been hired . . . "by the backers of the marriage amendment." Again, a nasty innuendo. Innocent but nasty. She gets her point across.

Belluck skipped a paragraph before using that exact phrase once again in paragraph 8 where she reported, "Backers of the marriage amendment ... deny the accusations."

ACCUSATIONS!?! What "accusations?"

So the headline writer was correct. Accusations had been made. Why did Belluck write what she did? *Obviously, she understood that accusations* **had** *been made.* And she wrote that the accusations were denied by the plaintiffs.

Those innuendoes were masterfully done, but she went too far.

Any reader can see that Belluck's intent was to accuse the plaintiffs. She did not use any quotes from them. She merely paraphrased them and made them say whatever she wished them to say.

The article portrayed the plaintiffs as nasty people who would not care about the slaughter of innocent horses. The article ends on a flag-flying note with the horse people saying exactly that: "It goes against rah-rah America. It goes against everything we stand for to ruin a petition like that."

Judge Saris Was Worried

Judge Saris was particularly worried by the headline. She knew it was defamatory on its face. There is no other way to describe it.

She could say about the article that it didn't cross over-the-edge and specifically name the plaintiffs. She would be wrong, but she wouldn't be laughed at.

All of the reporters at the *Globe* had done a credible job of obfuscation by innuendo in their stories about the Amendment, thus painting the plaintiffs with libel while denying that they were doing so. They undoubtedly had a lawyer read every story they wrote. Belluck at the *Times* also did a good job of painting "fraud" all over the plaintiffs. But someone at the *Times* forgot to tell the headline writer or have the final copy and headline checked by a lawyer. The reporter wasn't around to help because she had filed the story on Friday and was gone for the weekend.

Judge Saris was Editor of the *Harvard Crimson* while in college and must know something about newspapers. It is common knowledge that headlines are not written by the reporters, but by copy editors or headline writers. This headline obviously was not written by the reporter.

When the copy editor wrote the headline, he did so after reading the story. He then summarized it in the headline. He did an excellent job.

How then could Patti Saris dismiss the case?

3

Did Judge Saris "Solve" Her Problem?

When Judge Saris retreated to her chambers at 3 p.m. on August 21, 2003, she knew there was libel in the article, but she was afraid of angering The New York Times Company. She immediately wrote the Order, which is printed here in full.

ORDER
August 21, 2003

After hearing, I **ALLOW** the Motion to Dismiss of The New York Times Company. Plaintiffs have filed an action for defamation, claiming that the newspaper libeled plaintiffs with its story headline, "Drive to Ban Gay Marriage is Accused of Duping Signers" on April 7, 2002. Defendant argues that when the article is read as a whole plaintiffs were not defamed. It points to the paragraph:

Organizers say the culprit was the company hired to collect signatures by the backers of the marriage initiative and separately, by the Save Our Horses Campaign. Save Our Horses says the firm, Ballot Access Company, of Phoenix, was getting paid more per signature for the marriage initiative. They say it used the horse petition to lure people to unwittingly sign the marriage petition, which signature collectors affixed to the same clipboard, under a cover sheet of a horse decorated like an American flag.

After reading the article, I agree that any ambiguity about the entity that is accused of duping signers is clarified when the article is read in its totality. Foley v. Lowell Sun Pub. Co., 404 Mass. 9, 11, 533 N.E. 2d 196, 197 (1989) (holding that a publication must be viewed "in its totality in the context in which it was uttered or published").

[It is not necessary to read the following portions of the Order at this time. They will easily be understood later in the book.]

The allegations against the Boston Globe are dismissed because it is a corporation separate from the New York Times Company. See Exhibit A to affidavit of Terry Klein. (Docket No. 9).

Defendant has withdrawn the Special Motion of Defendant The New York Times Company to Dismiss pursuant to M.G.L. ch. 231 ß59H.

ORDER

The action against the New York Times Company is DISMISSED with prejudice. However, the action is DISMISSED without prejudice with respect to the claims against the Boston Globe.

Judge's Order Was Silly and Specious

As we saw in the previous chapter, the Order was silly and specious. When the article is "read in its totality," as the headline writer did, and with the headline prominently above the article, as all the readers do, all courts would agree this was libel.

4

Judge Saris Made a Fool of Herself

The plaintiffs didn't want a lawsuit. They didn't set out to "expose" The New York Times Company. Their primary goal was to pass the Protection of Marriage Amendment, not to recover the $1.7 million they lost because of the unlawful actions of The Company.

But by the spring of 2003, it appeared that all other doors were being slammed shut against them in their attempt to bring this disgraceful episode to the attention of the public. They were upset about stories in two newspapers, one story in the *Times* and twenty-one in the *Boston Globe*.

However, the judge refused to even consider the twenty-one stories in the *Globe*, saying that although it was owned by The Company, it was a separate, independent subsidiary that was not <u>controlled</u> by The Company.[1]

It's plain that <u>all</u> of the stories in both papers were part of <u>one</u> illegal effort to kill the Protection of Marriage Amendment. In order for the jurors to fully understand the lawsuit, the story in the *New York Times* newspaper must be viewed in the total context of The Company's effort.

---

[1] The judge dismissed the suit against The Company "with prejudice," which means it cannot be filed again in any court, state or federal. However, the claims against the Globe were dismissed "without prejudice," which means the plaintiffs are free to file a suit against the Globe in either state or federal court. In practical effect, this means the judge threw the case back to the state courts. Plaintiffs and the Globe are all residents of Massachusetts and a federal court would not have jurisdiction if The Company were not also a defendant. In theory, the judge did not damage the plaintiffs because if they do file in a Massachusetts court, it will still be possible to include the New York Times story in that trial to show the intent of The Company. But the judge's decision and attitude made it clear that this would be a difficult effort in any Massachusetts court, state or federal. The plaintiffs thought it better to continue the battle at this time on the stage of public opinion and to challenge The Company where the discussion will not be limited to dark courtrooms but to have the discussion in full view where everyone in the country can see what The Company is really about.

This was all terribly frightening to the people at Times Square because they didn't want the public to realize that this world-famous newspaper was being used as a club to bully (and libel) little people who happened to disagree with them.

They needed desperately to separate the two newspapers. They therefore argued to the judge that the Globe is run by a separate, independent subsidiary with no shared control or management from The Company at Times Square.

They told Judge Saris in their brief: "Plaintiffs present no basis for disregarding those corporate entities, nor could they."

But the plaintiffs had no desire to "disregard" the corporate entities; they merely wanted to join the trial of the two corporations for a speedy and just resolution, whether they were related or not.

The Rules of Court, which each federal judge has sworn to uphold, say in Rule #1: "They shall be construed and administered to secure the just, speedy, and inexpensive determination of every action."

The Company Is Like "Joe's Bar & Grill"

What really occurred makes The Company sound very provincial and unsophisticated. It's a common occurrence for every lawyer. We've all seen it happen. It's just like "Joe's Bar & Grill." Joe incorporates his tavern but doesn't follow any of the rules and even takes his personal money from the cash register.

What is different in this case is that you don't usually see this happening in a multinational, billion-dollar company. The controlling-owners of this huge conglomerate are four elderly members of the Ochs/Sulzberger family, all siblings. They still run it from their hip pockets, not always as their lawyers instruct.

As you glance over some of the problems that the lawyers faced, just consider what the plaintiffs would find if Judge Saris had allowed them to question these people. It's no wonder they were terrified.

The *Boston Globe* is published by a separate corporation, known as the "Globe Newspaper Company," according to The Company. But that separate corporation is not found anywhere in the pages of the *Boston Globe*. In addition, there is no telephone listing for such a company anywhere in the state of Massachusetts. (This is not to say that it does not

The Boston Globe

MANAGING EDITOR
Mary Jane Wilkinson/*Administration*

DEPUTY MANAGING EDITORS
Lucy C. Bartholomay/*Design & Photo*
Robert L. Turner/*Editorial Page*
Michael J. Larkin/*News Operations*
Peter S. Canellos/*Washington*
John Yemma/*Sunday*
Mark S. Morrow/*Projects*

SENIOR VICE PRESIDENTS
Gregory L. Thornton/*Employee Relations
and Operations*
Mary Jane Patrone/*Sales & Marketing*
Yasmin Namini/*Circulation*
Alfred S. Larkin, Jr./*General Administration
and External Affairs*
George A. Barrios/*Chief Financial Officer*

VICE PRESIDENTS
Robert T. Murphy/*Information Technology*
Harriet E. Gould/*Employee Relations*
Stephen Cahow/*Production*
Peter O. Newton/*Advertising*
William F. Connolly/*Administration*
Robert Powers/*Marketing Services*
Christopher M. Mayer/*Circulation Sales*
Susan Hunt Stevens/*Circulation Marketing*
Scott B. Meyer/*Strategic Planning*

Charles H. Taylor
Founder & Publisher 1873-1921
William O. Taylor/*Publisher 1921-1955*
Wm. Davis Taylor/*Publisher 1955-1977*
William O. Taylor/*Publisher 1978-1997*
Benjamin B. Taylor/*Publisher 1997-1999*
Laurence L. Winship/*Editor 1955-1965*
Thomas Winship/*Editor 1965-1984*

A NEW YORK TIMES COMPANY
NEWSPAPER

*Although the Company told Judge Saris that
the Boston Globe is totally separate from its
New York City headquarters, the bottom two
lines of this directory, which appear every day,
tell a different story.*

exist on paper, but it is not an active, viable entity for management purposes. Everything is controlled by The Company.)

The custom of the newspaper world is to note its owner at the bottom of the Editorial page. The following is printed (in capital letters) on the bottom of the *Globe's* Editorial page.

A NEW YORK TIMES COMPANY
NEWSPAPER

It strains one's imagination to contemplate how this defendant could possibly be so bold as to inform the Court that the *Boston Globe* is not "run" from the New York City headquarters of The Company, much less refuse to answer the Complaint, and how Judge Saris could accept that. Every day of the year, the *Globe* tells the world the opposite, as shown above. This alone would forbid an impartial judge from ruling as Ms. Saris did.

At the bottom of page B2 of the *Globe* every day, a box prominently displays the following:

A SUBSIDIARY OF
THE NEW YORK TIMES
COMPANY

As if those words are not strong enough, a graphic element is included to make it crystal-

The Boston Globe
Directory

News Desks

Local	(617) 929-3100
National/Foreign	(617) 929-3125
Business	(617) 929-2903
Living/Arts	(617) 929-2800
Sports	(617) 929-3235
Editorial Page	(617) 929-3025
Switchboard	(617) 929-2000

Submit a news tip to:
localnews@globe.com

Editors and writers can be reached via e-mail as listed below individual stories.

Spotlight Team tip line:
(617) 929-7483

The Globe ombudsman:
For reader comments and complaints

By phone:
(617) 929-3020
Or leave message: (617) 929-3022
By e-mail: ombud@globe.com

Globe Online
On the Internet:
http://www.boston.com/globe
By e-mail: bosfeed@globe.com
By phone: (617) 929-7900

Advertising

Classified	(617) 929-1500

Mon-Fri 8 a.m.-8:30 p.m., Sat-Sun 1-8:30 p.m.

E-mail:classified@globe.com
Place a classified ad online at:
www.bostonglobe.com/classifieds

Home Delivery

TOLL FREE:
For delivery by 6 a.m. weekdays
8 a.m. weekends and holidays

(888) **MY GLOBE**
(888) 694-5623

Delivery by US mail
(617) 929-2215

Subscriber Assistance Hours:
Mon-Fri 6 a.m.-5 p.m., Sat-Sun
8 a.m.-noon. Our automated
voice response system is
available 24 hours a day at the
phone number above. We can
also be reached via our website:
www.bostonglobe.com/subscribe.

Weekly subscription rates,

7-day $7.75; Thu-Sun $5.75
Mon-Sat $4.50; Sun. $3.50
Rates may vary by area

Questions about your bill, call toll free:
1-888-MYGLOBE (888) 694-5623
Hours: Mon-Fri 6 a.m.-5 p.m.
Military, student, and mail
subscription rates upon request.
e-mail: circulation@globe.com

The Boston Globe Store
1 School Street, Boston
By phone: (617) 367-4000
www.globestore.boston.com
Front pages, photographs, Globe gear

A SUBSIDIARY OF
The New York Times
Company

Although The Company told Judge Saris that the Boston Globe is totally separate from its New York City headquarters, the bottom right hand corner of this directory which appears every day tells a different story.

clear; a portion of the well-known and distinctive *New York Times* "flag" (which appears at the top of the front page of the newspaper) is also shown. The reader sees a very large "T" in Olde English type which causes the above statement to connect the *Globe* even more closely with the *Times*.

The definition of a "subsidiary" is: "a company controlled by another company which owns most of its shares," according to *Webster's Dictionary Unabridged.* The entire definition of a "subsidiary" in *Merriam-Webster's Collegiate Dictionary* is: "one that is subsidiary; esp: a company wholly controlled by another."

The Company said in its brief, it is "undisputable" that the only defendant in the case is The Company inasmuch as the plaintiffs never obtained service upon the *Boston Globe*. (That is true. For reasons that will become clear to you, the plaintiffs named The Company as the only defendant and had the Complaint served only on The Company at its New York offices, which also house the *New York Times* newspaper.)

To make it more duplicitous, The Company's lawyers informed the Court that the "Publisher" of the *New York Times* <u>newspaper</u> *is* The Company. Despite that, the newspaper states in every issue that Arthur Ochs Sulzberger is the publisher of the paper. Even The Company's lawyers are uncertain who owns what. They constantly disregard the legal niceties of the "corporate entities" which they are paid to watch.

In addition, an undated Press Release (apparently from the year 2000) from "Boston Globe Services" reported that there were two new executives for the "New England Newspaper Group," a division of The Company. At the end of the Press Release it stated, "The [New York Times] Company ... publishes The New York Times, [and] The Boston Globe ..." So even top executives in this empire are uncertain as to who publishes what.

In addition, the website for the *Globe* is copyrighted not by the mysterious and shy "Globe Newspaper Company" in which Judge Saris put so much faith, but by The Company. Apparently this is done by its "New York Times Digital" "business unit," which appears to have total ownership of the *Boston Globe* work-product except for the daily print edition. This has become even more obtuse because "Digital" has just begun posting an exact copy of the valuable front page of the print product on the Internet.

Nowhere in either of the two newspapers is there any notice to the public about what entity or person owns that newspaper.

(The Company says it is divided into six "business units." They are: The New York Times, which we assume is the newspaper; New England Newspaper Group, of which the *Globe* is a part; New York Times Digital; Regional Newspaper Group; Broadcast Group and The International Herald Tribune. We are not told how many corporations are included within those six "business units" or whether each "unit" is a separate corporation.)

This is all very familiar to every lawyer and very similar to Joe's Bar & Grill, Inc.

What should be decisive in this lawsuit is not the personal desires of the defendant, but the workload of the Court and that justice be served. The defendant Company was saying that the plaintiffs should have brought two lawsuits, one in federal court against the defendant and another against the *Globe* in a Massachusetts state court.

Defendant would like to say that the plaintiffs are attempting to pierce the corporate veil, but that is not true. The plaintiffs were merely seeking to have all the litigants before the Court at the same time to ensure justice.

The real crux of this decision is not the wishes of the defendant, but the Federal Rules of Civil Procedure.

As you glance over these problems that the lawyers faced, just consider what would have happened if the plaintiffs had been given the right to ask questions of this corporation.

How embarrassing it would have been for them.

Repetition of a False Story Is Libel

Judge Patti Saris does not appear to know much about libel. The defamation in this case was *not* just one article in a newspaper. It was repeated and republished over and over with never a correction. These facts show libel, even malice.

The awesome power of The Company was used to frame the debate among the citizens and put the plaintiffs on the defensive at the outset,

The New York Times

Founded in 1851

ADOLPH S. OCHS, *Publisher 1896-1935*
ARTHUR HAYS SULZBERGER, *Publisher 1935-1961*
ORVIL E. DRYFOOS, *Publisher 1961-1963*
ARTHUR OCHS SULZBERGER, *Publisher 1963-1992*

ARTHUR OCHS SULZBERGER JR., *Publisher*

JOSEPH LELYVELD, *Executive Editor*
JOHN M. GEDDES, *Deputy Managing Editor*

Assistant Managing Editors
SOMA GOLDEN BEHR   ANDREW ROSENTHAL
TOM BODKIN   ALLAN M. SIEGAL
MICHAEL ORESKES   CRAIG R. WHITNEY

GAIL COLLINS, *Editorial Page Editor*
PHILIP TAUBMAN, *Deputy Editorial Page Editor*

JANET L. ROBINSON, *President, General Manager*
SCOTT H. HEEKIN-CANEDY, *Senior V.P., Circulation*
JYLL F. HOLZMAN, *Senior V.P., Advertising*
MARC Z. KRAMER, *Senior V.P., Production*
DENISE F. WARREN, *Senior V.P., Planning*
LIAM J. CARLOS, *V.P., Chief Financial Officer*
ALYSE MYERS, *V.P., Marketing Services*
JAY I. SABIN, *V.P., Labor Relations*
DENNIS L. STERN, *V.P., Human Resources*
MICHAEL G. WILLIAMS, *V.P., Chief Information Officer*

THOMAS K. CARLEY, *President, News Services*

Although Judge Saris opined that the corporate structure of the New York Times Company is clear, even its lawyers don't know what it is. They told us during our suit that "The Company" is Publisher of the Times newspaper, even though the paper says every day of the year that Pinch is the publisher.

almost like denying that you beat your wife. After a while, you almost give up because you hear the untrue statements from so many directions that you can never really answer them all and refute the lies. You are always playing defense. Those are serious *criminal* charges and should not be uttered lightly. In Massachusetts, such a charge is libel *per se*. Nevertheless, the insinuations were reported over and over with the full power of The Company.

There are three possibilities why these newspapers of The Company engaged in their libelous conduct: 1) they were part of a plan with the opponents to discredit plaintiffs by charging them with fraud, or 2) they were not part of a plan but published the stories in order to assist such a plan or 3) the newspapers were negligent and careless and the libel was committed because of poor reporting. No one will ever know the answers to those questions because the plaintiffs were not allowed to take "discovery" and question reporters, editors or anyone else, such as the lawyers and others at the horse headquarters.

The "fraud" charges were published, and re-published by the *Globe* in the first stories it wrote about the Amendment in November 2001,

January 2002, March 2002 and April 2002. The *Globe* never printed a corrected story. The theme was carried forward by the *New York Times* newspaper on April 7, 2002, only three days before an important legislative hearing. This was done for the purpose of re-publishing the allegations in a different, highly respected, high-impact newspaper.

Repeating a libel indicates not just libel, but also shows malice, according to Prof. Rodney A. Smolla. He is the author of a two-volume text on libel that has been updated every year since 1986 by West Publishing Company, the largest and most respected legal publisher in the country. Prof. Smolla says:

> When in such a republication or follow-up story no new investigation is undertaken, despite the appearance of new reasons for doubt, actual malice may exist with regard to the sequel even if the first story was protected.

Certainly, between November 2001 and April 2002, there was enough time and there were enough questions about the accuracy of the accusations by the "horse" people so that the defendant should have checked into the story before running it again and again, unless their intent was to damage the plaintiffs.

The textbooks, *Corpus Juris Secundum* and *American Jurisprudence 2d,* state this black-letter law as follows:

> Every republication or repetition of the defamatory matter by the defendant constitutes a cause of action which is separate and independent from the cause of action arising out of the original publication.
>
> Proof tending to show that the defendant repeated or republished the defamation complained of is admissible to show malice.

Innuendo Can Be Libel

Innuendos and implications can be libelous. The defendant's reporters realized that innuendos could cause them legal trouble and they attempted to protect themselves and never "cross the line." But they were eminently unsuccessful.

They attempted to walk right along the edge of libel without committing it. But it didn't work. The Company was not protected even if there was only one publication of the libel. However, the libel against these plaintiffs lasted many months with many re-publications.

The attempt by The Company to avoid libel by the use of innuendos is apparently not unique to just them. Prof. Smolla discusses how newspapers often will libel persons by innuendo, all the while claiming that their facts are all accurate and they are not defaming anyone. Smolla says that the media is constantly attempting to push the courts into holding that libel by innuendo simply cannot exist:

> The issues surrounding defamation through implication have, for several years, been among the most hotly contested in defamation litigation across the United States. Media defendants have made defamation through implication a major litigation battlefield, precisely because so many newspaper articles, magazine pieces, and television stories today present very damaging portraits of individuals, while nevertheless couching those reports in language that goes right to, but not quite over, the edge of an outright factual statement.

Smolla writes that a balanced view is the soundest approach and apparently everyone agrees with this belief:

> Statements in context in a defamation suit ought not be construed in a strained or extreme manner to benefit either a plaintiff or a defendant, but should rather be interpreted as the average person would most naturally understand them. ...
>
> Defamation law should be grounded in common sense, in how ordinary readers read and ordinary viewers view.

As we read the above by Prof. Smolla, we must remember that his discussion concerns just a **SINGLE** libel. However, our case involved repetitions over a period of time.

The facts in this case should be decided by a jury, not a judge.

The two-volume Practicing Law Institute book, *Sack on Defamation* by Robert D. Sack agrees with Prof. Smolla and says:

> A publisher is, in general, liable for the implications of what he or she has said or written, not merely the specific, literal

statements made.

When Can A Judge Take a Case Away from a Jury and Summarily Dismiss It?

In 1999, the opinion from one of Judge Saris' cases was included in a compilation of important opinions from federal district judges known as the Federal Supplement. In it, she wrote about summary judgment. She said that when ruling on whether to grant it, "the Court accepts as true only the allegations set forth in the complaint." But, in order to rule as she did in this case, Judge Saris "accepted as true" the exact opposite of what was stated in this Complaint.

There was talk a few years ago that summary judgment was favored in libel cases. This was squelched by the Chief Justice of the U.S. Supreme Court, Justice Warren Berger, in 1979. He wrote that in order that it be possible for the plaintiff to show "actual malice" by the defendant (as is required of public figures), the plaintiff must be allowed to conduct discovery of the defendant before summary judgment can be entered.

5

Wait Judge, There's Worse News

In addition to her other worries, Judge Saris has a serious ethical problem.

Did you notice that in the last paragraph of her Order, she said that The Company had "withdrawn" the "Special Motion of Defendant The New York Times Company to Dismiss pursuant to M.G.L. ch. 231 ß59H"?

We never received any notification that the "Special Motion" had been withdrawn. A search of court records reveals nothing to show that it was ever withdrawn.

How did this mysterious occurrence happen, and why is it important?

I cannot tell you how this mysterious thing occurred, but I can say that Judge Saris could not have dismissed the suit if the mysterious event had not occurred.

What Is a SLAPP Suit?

When The Company filed its brief which argued that the suit should be dismissed, it also filed a "Special Motion," which is really a type of suit, known as a SLAPP suit. That meant that if the suit was dismissed and the "Special Motion" granted, this small nonprofit organization and its President would be liable to pay for all The Company's lawyers fees and costs.

The New York Times Company didn't just want to "win." They wanted to continue pummeling these "little guys" and teach them a lesson!

The SLAPP suit is a new invention which began in California. Its original purpose was to stop large developers from ruining little home-owners who were trying to protect their neighborhoods by informing other citizens at town meetings or in letters to the newspapers that the developer had a bad reputation, etc.

This law is found in most states today and was passed by the Massachusetts legislature in 1994. Since then, it has been interpreted by the Supreme Judicial Court of Massachusetts to no longer be used just to protect little people; often, it is used to *hurt* the little person. It has been broadened to protect persons in many situations (not just small landowners) where they believe that free speech is in danger. The law has had a tremendous effect in the state. The lawyers are universal-ly afraid of SLAPP suits being used against them. It's difficult enough to have to tell a client they lost a case, but if the lawyer must add the bad news that they now have to pay thousands of dollars to the lawyers on the other side, it is not a fun experience for the losing lawyer.

It is doubtful in Massachusetts whether a newspaper is allowed to sue under the law but no one knows for sure. The California courts held that they can, but no other state appears to have done so. The rul-ing in a landmark case like this would almost certainly be appealed by the losing side and the First Circuit Court of Appeals might possibly send it to the Massachusetts Supreme Judicial Court for a ruling. All of this would require huge attorney fees to argue such a landmark case, with these plaintiffs having to pay the attorney fees of the New York Times Company if they lost. These could easily amount to $500,000 if this were appealed all the way. This is an excellent example of where the little people have, in effect, been denied their access to the courts because most lawyers would be afraid to touch a case such as this. It shows why many lawyers strongly cautioned us against bringing the suit and why the lawyers for the *Times* were gleeful about pointing it out to us.

I was not terribly concerned because the law would not apply if we could show that The Company's request did not have "any factual sup-port or any arguable basis in law" and they had caused "actual injury" to the plaintiffs.

How Did Judge Saris Commit A Serious Violation?

So why did Judge Saris insist in her Order that the Special Motion had been withdrawn?

She did so because the federal courts are more careful to protect the rights of the plaintiff in this regard than are the state courts. Before such a drastic remedy can be used against the plaintiff in a federal court, the plaintiff must be allowed full discovery against the defendant. (Since plaintiffs in this case are "public figures" under the U.S. Constitution, they must show "malice" by the defendant.) Of course, in our case, **no** discovery had been allowed. Therefore, the suit could not be dismissed until discovery by the plaintiff had been permitted.

How did Judge Saris know that The Company had withdrawn its SLAPP suit? It does not appear anywhere on the record. It goes without saying that one of the worst things for any judge is to communicate in any way with one of the parties without the other party being present.

How could Judge Saris say that The Company had withdrawn its SLAPP suit when there was no notification to us and nothing appears on the record?

Did she just make it up?

She could not dismiss the suit unless the SLAPP suit had been withdrawn. Was she that desperate to please The Company that she would commit a serious violation of ethics for them?

6

Should "The New York Times Company" Be Allowed to Violate Freedom of Speech?

This lawsuit is about Freedom of Speech.

The New York Times Company should not be allowed to impinge Free Speech, no matter how powerful they are.

This suit is **not** about politics or the *merits* of a particular Amendment to the Massachusetts Constitution, although that is what The Company would have you believe.

In a sense, it *is* about politics — the best of politics, i.e. the functioning of our state government. Although the issue was not formally raised in the suit, it is quickly apparent to anyone, even Judge Saris.

The United States Constitution at Art. IV, Section 4, guarantees to the residents of every state a "Republican Form of Government." The SJC told the Governor in its advisory opinion of December 20, 2002, that the state Legislature violated the Constitution when it refused to vote on the Protection of Marriage Amendment. The Governor did the same by not calling the legislature back for a vote. The SJC has indicated it does not have the power to require a vote. This leaves the citizens without any redress and without a Republican Form of Government, in violation of Article IV, Section 4, a circumstance which could not have happened except for the power of the New York Times Company.

The suit is about the illegal power of The Company to deny the citizens their rights under the U.S. Constitution to have a functioning, legal government in the state. If they are to have a Republican Form of Government, the Massachusetts Constitution must be obeyed by that

Pinch Sulzberger schemed to have Margaret Marshall appointed Chief Justice of the Massachusetts Supreme Judicial Court so that he could begin to impose gay marriage across the nation. He has been obsessed with homosexuality since his teens.

Government. It must do what is required, as was envisioned by the framers of art. 48 of the state Constitution, and provide a robust, public debate, allowing all the citizens, to thoroughly _discuss_ and _debate_ the merits of **every** proposed Amendment.

It does not matter whether The Company agrees with this particular Amendment or not. It cannot use libel to stop the voters of the state from voting on any Amendment. What a terrible precedent this is.

In Judge Saris' courtroom, we were deciding many issues:

• Can a small, nonprofit corporation and its supporters be falsely attacked over and over with an intent to defame and damage it in the eyes of the citizens and thus make it difficult for the corporation to operate and raise money?

A democratic form of government is guaranteed to the residents of every state by the U.S. Constitution in Article IV, Section 4. We have lost this in Massachusetts where the Legislature and the Governor collude to violate the state Constitution and the Supreme Judicial Court says there's nothing anyone can do about it. Some citizens note that there is still time to sue the legislators who voted to violate the Constitution on July 17, 2002 if they continue their illegal actions.

• Can an ordinary citizen express her opinions about an important subject of public concern, or are the rich and the powerful allowed to falsely attack her and her supporters _**personally**_, with accusations of fraud?

Strong Public Interest in Punishing Libel

The rich and powerful believe that when the U. S. Supreme Court decided the suit against the *New York Times* in 1964, it gave the rich and powerful a carte blanche to say anything they wish without restraint. But that is not true.

Justice Hennessy of the Massachusetts Supreme Judicial Court made that clear in 1975: "The suggestion has been made that the First Amendment provides absolute protection for the press, protection extending even to knowing publication of falsehoods, but this suggestion has been rejected and is not the law."[1] This was clearly stated by the U.S. Supreme Court in 1990.[2]

The Supreme Court said its recent cases demonstrated their passion about the free and uninhibited discussion of public issues. But it made clear there is another side. It quoted Shakespeare's Othello:

---

[1] Stone v. Essex County Newspapers, Inc., 367 Mass. 849 (1975)
[2] Milkovich v. Lorain Journal, 497 U.S. 1 (1990)

Who steals my purse steals trash. ... But he that filches from me my good name Robs me of that which not enriches him, And makes me poor indeed.

The Court emphasized that preventing libel was an important function of any government in a civilized society:

[W]e have regularly acknowledged the "important social values which underlie the law of defamation," and recognize that "[s]ociety has a pervasive and strong interest in preventing and redressing attacks upon reputation." ... Justice Stewart in that case put it with his customary clarity:

"The right of a man to the protection of his own reputation from unjustified invasion and wrongful hurt reflects no more than our basic concept of the essential dignity and worth of every human being, a concept at the root of any decent system of ordered liberty. ...

"The destruction that defamatory falsehood can bring is, to be sure, often beyond the capacity of the law to redeem. Yet, imperfect though it is, an action for damages is the only hope for vindication or redress the law gives to a man [or woman] whose reputation has been falsely dishonored."

Both Have Right to Endorse or Oppose Marriage Amendment

The Company's newspapers have a strong editorial position in favor of homosexual marriage. As a result, it led the fight to oppose the Marriage Amendment, as was its right and its *"duty"* under our democracy.

However, all newspapers are aware that "news columns" are different. One does not expect to find opinion there. That is expected on the "editorial" and "opinion" pages. The liberal Justice William Brennan expressed that truism in 1990 in the U.S. Supreme Court case mentioned above:

[S]igned columns may certainly include statements of fact, they are also the "well recognized home of opinion and comment." ... Certain formats - editorials, reviews, political cartoons, letters to the editor - signal the reader to anticipate a departure from what is actually known by the author as fact. ... ("The reasonable reader who peruses [a] column on the editorial or Op-Ed page is fully aware that the statements found there are not 'hard' news like those printed on the front page or elsewhere in the news sections of the newspaper").

The Company expressed its opinion about gay marriage in a *New York Times* newspaper editorial on March 18, 2000:

> In time, Vermont's example will show the rest of the country that same-sex unions are not a threat to traditional marriage and deserve the name of marriage as well as the law's full protection.

A *Globe* editorial had as its headline, "An Ugly Amendment," on July 16, 2002, the day before the Legislature violated the state Constitution. The *Globe* first "covered itself" by saying that the Legislature should have a vote (which, of course, did not happen). Then it wrote:

> However, legislators must focus on the merits — or, in this case, the ugly demerits — of the proposal. They cannot vote simply to pass the decision along to the electorate. The Constitution, by giving them veto power over constitutional Amendments, demands a vote of conscience, not a rubber stamp. Legislators should see this measure as the mean-spirited attack on a minority that it is and reject it.

That type of *editorial* comment is expected in a democracy *when* it is clearly indicated to be opinion.

In its news pages, both the *Globe* and the *Times* ignored the proposed Amendment at its inception in September 2001, hoping it would die if its presence was not acknowledged by them. This is regarded by the plaintiffs as legally acceptable "hardball."

But the Amendment did not die and go away. It remained vibrant and vital. It was approved by the Attorney General as a proper ballot question for November 2004. (This was upheld by a unanimous SJC on appeal in June 2002.) It obtained 20,000 more voter signatures than required during the fall of 2001, causing it to be certified by the Secretary of State to the Legislature in January 2002 for a vote. (The vote in the legislature requires approval by only 25% of the legislators in order to be passed on to the voters.)

The majority in the Legislature violated the Constitution on July 17, 2002. They refused to allow a vote on the measure by the 25% who wanted to approve it, thus making it totally impossible for the measure to obtain a 25% approval.

Plaintiffs have been on the opposite side of the issue from The Company since May 2000, being the sponsors of the Protection of Marriage Amendment under the initiative procedures of art. 48 of the Massachusetts Constitution. The Amendment would codify the existing definition of marriage (one-man-and-one-woman) as it has always been.

Plaintiffs believe, as is their right even if they are wrong, that the traditional family structure in this state has been the foundation of our society and any change in that definition will seriously weaken and damage that structure. They believe a change would damage the purpose of marriage, i.e., the protection of children, by causing them to become of secondary importance, instead of the primary purpose of marriage. They agree with the Vermont Supreme Court which stated in its own ruling in 1999 that its case could "destabilize" the institution of marriage and affect it in "unpredictable" ways. The Vermont court acknowledged it had no idea what would happen as the result of its tampering with the basic foundation of society.

The institution of marriage is currently being challenged on many fronts by many *sincere* people, not just homosexuals. These include:

•Those feminists who sincerely believe that marriage, as

Sen. Birmingham was visibly jolted by jeers and cries of "No!" that thundered at him from the hundreds of pro-marriage spectators in the gallery after he quickly postponed the Marriage Amendment in June 2002.

an institution, is damaging all women.
- Men who want to practice bigamy and have several wives.
- Polyamorists who desire group arrangements.
- Heterosexual couples who do not want to bother with rules.
- Those men who wish to prey on women without incurring any responsibility for them or their children.
- Homosexuals who wish to get married or who are gay activists.

The purpose of marriage has always been to provide a mother and a father for as many children as possible. Because it involves humans, it is a flawed institution. One alternative possibility is for the state to raise the children, as occurs in socialist countries.

Whatever one believes, whether it was an evolutionary force or a Judeo-Christian God or some other god or gods, whoever or whatever it was who made us, the plaintiffs believe that most people would agree that "he," "she" or "it" created both man and woman for the purpose of procreating and raising children.

Article 48 of the Massachusetts Constitution was written in 1918 with the intent that there be a robust discussion of proposed amendments; but if the New York Times Company, whether alone or in concert with others, publishes untrue statements which by innuendo attempt to link the plaintiffs to criminal, fraudulent activities; and if the defendant then publishes many inaccurate, false statements of the method of amending the Constitution, which portray that the plaintiffs are engaging in additional fraud by misstating the law, then the defendant has libeled the plaintiffs and destroyed the process.

Company Determined to Stop Passage of Amendment

The Company was determined to stop the Protection of Marriage Amendment by any means. The allegations of fraud against the plaintiffs were originated by the sponsors of another initiative petition who were attempting to forbid the sale of horsemeat for human consumption. That petition did not get enough signatures and the Marriage Amendment was blamed for its problems.

That falsehood continues today and will do so in perpetuity to the damage of the plaintiffs, who are constantly branded as purveyors of fraud, even in the courts of Massachusetts. For example, when Gov.

State troopers warn a homosexual activist to stop harassing the people.

Picketing at the State House continued even after the illegal vote on July 17. This shows the President of Massachusetts Citizens for Marriage, Sally Pawlick, in front of the State House holding a sign, Let the People Vote on Marriage.

Swift asked the Supreme Judicial Court for an opinion in December 2002, the Court invited all interested parties to write a brief.

One such brief included a copy of the omnipresent *Times* story. That story was used to authenticate this statement which appeared on the first page of the brief presented to the SJC: "We are familiar with the substance of [the Amendment] as well as the signature gathering and lobbying undertaken in connection with [it]." The brief then devoted more than five of its 18-pages to "possible fraud in the signature gathering process." This brief, which is now on file in the vaults of the Supreme Judicial Court, has many pages in the Exhibit section about the "fraud." However, the plaintiffs have never had a chance to rebut the accusations.

Sally has no idea who on the SJC has read about her "fraud." Who has been exposed to this libel of her? It certainly was made possible *only* because of the *Times* story. This type of unfair tactic has undoubtedly influenced the Justices on the SJC and its staff.

Bay Windows Explains Why "Company" Is Passionate

The homosexual newspaper, *Bay Windows*, revealed a portion of the truth in an editorial in its August 15, 2002 paper, which celebrated the "victory" of July 17, 2002. The editorial was probably written about August 12. But after hearing of the suit in the SJC which was filed by Sally on August 16, their August 29 edition had a much more balanced story.

The editorial on August 15 was ecstatic about the "victory" over the Amendment. It reported, however, that the average homosexual had not been interested in the marriage brouhaha. It was like pulling teeth to get them to contribute to the effort, one activist reported.

Sally told the press at the time, "This [editorial] confirms what we have been saying. This is not primarily about homosexuality. It's about a powerful, extreme liberal agenda to change our sexual morality. These liberals are seeking a socialist state similar to Sweden or Cuba, in which children are the responsibility of the state, not their parents.

"That's why the national, liberal organizations are so interested in what is happening in Massachusetts. They are hiding behind homosexuals and others to achieve their objective.

"They wish to diminish the institution of marriage which has been the bedrock of our country since its founding. When the state was first founded, everyone knew what 'marriage' meant, so it was never written down. But now it's obvious to everybody that we must do so." None of that was printed by the *Globe*.

There is nothing wrong with the *Globe* pushing their agenda as long as it is not false.

The "horse" trick was broadcast far and wide by the *Boston Globe* and the national edition of the *New York Times*. They never reported that paid signature gatherers became necessary because the other side was training blockers, who would harass the voters, and violate their Constitutional right to vote, at every major mall throughout the state. When the decision was made to hire professionals because of concerns for the safety of the volunteers, the plaintiffs hired a reputable organization, which was already in the state working for both the horse people and a Libertarian candidate for Governor, Carla Howell.

(*Bay Windows* reported at the time that the signature-gathering company had a good reputation. In its issue of Nov. 15, 2001, it wrote, "Using paid signature gatherers is not unusual in the political world and Derrick Lee has built a million-dollar company around the con-

A State House security officer directs would-be spectators to move back from the entrance to the House Gallery in Boston, Wednesday, July 17, 2002. It was filled by people wanting to witness a vote on a citizen-initiated ballot question which would ban gay marriages. Over 500 arrived to show their displeasure with the legislature.

cept, according to the Phoenix Newtimes.com., an online newspaper. He is also, according to an April 13, 2000 profile in that paper, highly respected and considered politically influential in Arizona politics for getting the job of collecting signatures done, and getting it done right." But it also reported that he's had a "handful of petitioners who've pleaded guilty to forgery" and it cited four examples of them from 1997-2000.)

After all the effort and expense by the horse people — including the expensive mailings and a lawsuit by a high-priced lawyer from California against the state, demanding that their petition be put on the ballot — the horse people reported the names of only a handful of people who said they were tricked (out of a total of 76,607 people who were certified as signers). They found only this tiny number even though they had been working at it since before November 2001. (For the first time, we discovered in defendant's brief that they reported 100 alleged "victims" to the Attorney General, but neither this fact nor the names were ever released to the public to our knowledge.)

It must be noted that almost 45,000 letters from the horse people were sent to signers of the Marriage Amendment about the same time as the *Times* article appeared. Was this really an effort to find signers who had been deceived by the "fraud" of the plaintiffs or was it a tremendously effective attack against the Amendment? Was it an attempt by someone to discourage all the supporters of MCM? It is estimated that the mailing cost $40,000.

No citizen should be treated as Pawlick and the other supporters of this initiative have been. It goes beyond the pale to be libeled in a brief in the SJC without being able to respond.

It was very difficult and very expensive for MCM to compete with the power of the *Globe* and keep the citizens informed of the truth. The opponents thought that the plaintiffs couldn't win. But the plaintiffs did "win." Sen. Birmingham has publicly stated that he was defeated in the gubernatorial primary because of his illegal actions on July 17. The matter also hurt the final Democratic candidate, Shannon O'Brien, although she did not agree as openly. The *Globe* cited it as one of the "social issues" that killed her election, but it didn't state that they had pushed her into supporting those issues.

It was the "power" of the *Globe* and its libel that made the opponents so bold as to keep violating the law and challenging the order of the Supreme Judicial Court. The *Globe* reported the advisory opinion of December 20, 2002, with this headline, "SJC declines to weigh in on gay marriage ballot debate." The message that everyone received was that the SJC had **vindicated** Sen. Birmingham! This was totally false but went unchallenged by anyone except for MCM.

On March 6, 2003, the *Globe* was still writing in a front-page story (about new laws on gay marriage that were introduced by legislators two months earlier in December) that the Amendment was killed in July 2002 by a "procedural maneuver" by Sen. Birmingham that "avoided a vote on its merits."

Avoided a vote on its merits? A procedural maneuver? He broke the law on purpose.

Plaintiffs believe that we, as a society, can either accept those who practice homosexuality or extol them. The vast majority of Massachusetts citizens would choose to accept them. It will not be the end of this type of demand if it is extolled. There is a professor of ethics, Prof. Peter Singer, the Ira W. DeCamp professor at Princeton's "Center for Human Values," who argues that sex with animals is normal and should be allowed and encouraged for those who desire it. Bigamy and group sex are already knocking on the door for acceptance.

A few of the more than 500 supporters of the Amendment stood outside the State House on their way inside on July 17, 2002.

Even those at the North American Man/Boy Love Association, and others in intellectual circles, who argue that sex with children is a positive experience, are very much alive and would like to lower the age of consent to twelve-years.

Should the citizens be excluded from this crucial debate by the rich and powerful at the New York Times Company with their false charges of "fraud?"

PART II

Libels by the
New York Times

Section II

Who Were the Mysterious "Blockers"?

Who were the mysterious "blockers" who caused nasty scenes everywhere they went — surrounding signature-gatherers at the malls and frightening voters so that they hesitated to approach the noisy disturbances? The people at Massachusetts Citizens for Marriage (MCM) still don't know the identity of the blockers.

But they do know who sent them. That will be explained in this section.

The blockers were violating voting rights that are guaranteed by the U.S. and Massachusetts Constitutions.

As a result, it became necessary in the malls to use male professionals to gather the signatures. A local gatherer, who saw the blockers in action, said he wouldn't even consider asking his employees to work for the Protection of Marriage Amendment. It would be a brutal experience with all that harassment — and very <u>un</u>profitable, inasmuch as they would be paid only for each signature they gathered.

Therefore, MCM used an out-of-state firm that was already in Massachusetts working for Carla Howell, the Libertarian candidate for Governor, and for Save Our Horses, the group trying to stop human consumption of horsemeat. Our people had to be extremely patient because the blockers were trained to incite a "push" or a "shove." That would enable them to yell, "Hate and violence against gays!" The *Globe* was anxious for that headline. But it never got the chance.

The people at MCM and the signature-gathering company made sure there weren't any incidents despite some extreme provocation. The supporters of marriage tried to ignore the unlawful actions and just move on to get the measure passed. Later, when "fraud" charges were trumpeted against them by the two newspapers of The New York Times Company, it became important whether the petition gatherers were guilty of fraud, as alleged, or whether they had performed well under terribly stressful conditions. The consensus was they had performed admirably.

Blockers Appeared on Day #1

The blockers were well prepared. They appeared on day #1 at the major malls across the entire state.

However, the news about them and about voters being bullied in violation of the law was not reported in either of The Company newspapers during September, October and most of November. When it finally was reported by the *Globe* on November 21 — what a "spin!" The thrust was that the *supporters* of marriage were getting "ugly."

That was the first story the *Globe* wrote about the Amendment. They finally reported it at that time only because they had come to realize that the blockers had failed in their attempts to stop the Amendment. The *Globe* could ignore the story about marriage no longer. It was not going to just fade away. The *Globe* had to acknowledge it and begin their attack.

Luckily, MCM had been able to get pictures of the blockers with the help of a camera hidden in a van, although that had been very difficult to do, as it was both time-consuming and costly.

Right to Gather Signatures at Malls Is Protected by
United States Constitution and Massachusetts Constitution

The right to solicit signatures was stated clearly by the Massachusetts Secretary of State in a Memorandum dated August 30, 2001. There was no new law revealed in the Memorandum, just a good recitation of what everyone already knew. It is reprinted here.

Solicitation of Signatures in Public Places

Both the United States and Massachusetts Constitutions protect the right to solicit signatures on ballot question petitions in a reasonable and unobtrusive manner in open public areas. This includes the public areas of municipal property as well as the common areas of privately owned shopping centers. Distribution of printed material in connection with signature solicitation is also protected. The right of signature solicitation (along with other free-speech activities) on municipal sidewalks, in parks and in similar open public areas is clear.

7

Obnoxious, Illegal Blockers Appear

Who dispatched the blockers during the fall of 2001 to confront both voters and signature-gatherers?

Those people were trained and sent by MassEquality, an organization formed especially to block the Marriage Amendment. It is still very much in existence, still fighting for homosexual marriage in Massachusetts.

One important member of MassEquality was, and still is, the American Civil Liberties Union. One of their lawyers, Norma Shapiro, says she is proud of her role. She trained many of the blockers, in addition to participating on squads herself. She told *Bay Windows* that her volunteers were trained to talk politely, not to interrupt people while they were speaking and to remind potential signers to read what they're signing. "I have real confidence in the people that we've trained. I don't believe there's been anything confrontational to the point where anybody's been upset about it," she said.

The pictures of blockers tell an entirely different story.

The presence of the ACLU was clearly explained less than a year later by an exuberant *Bay Windows* editorial which exalted in the "victory" after the legislature violated the state Constitution on July 17, 2002.

However, that editorial also expressed disappointment. The *homosexuals* had <u>not</u> shown much interest in the subject of marriage. One activist reported it was like pulling teeth to get the homosexuals to contribute.

The Real Force Behind Opposition

The real force behind the opposition to the Marriage Amendment, according to the editorial, was not the average homosexual. It was extreme feminists, socialists, libertines and others, such as NOW, ACLU, Anti-Defamation League, the Libertarian Party, homosexual activists, the AFL-CIO, plus all the "swingers" everywhere who were pushing the agenda for a weakening, or an elimination of the institution of marriage.

These people won't even discuss the issue of children because they think it obvious that children should be raised by the state in a socialist environment like that of Sweden or Cuba. Others are blissful as long as someone else has to deal with the fruit of their sexual activity. They believe that sex is necessary and important for everyone, and should be encouraged at an early age. They are pushing for the age of consent to be lowered to 12, which would mean that parents could not control their child's sexual behavior and the "swingers" could get more of it.

The professional "behavior" people, the psychiatrists, psychologists, social workers and others, are riddled with those who have such beliefs. The American Psychological Association published a study which indicated that pedophilia can have a positive influence on a child but backed down after Congress denounced them in 1999 by a vote of 355-0.

The APA struck again a few months later with an article saying that fathers are not "essential" for children. Fathers may even be detrimental because of the male tendency to consume "resources in terms of gambling, purchasing alcohol, cigarettes, or other nonessential commodities," which "increase women's workload and stress."

The authors admitted they had a strong political agenda saying, "We acknowledge that our reading of the scientific literature supports our political agenda." Their "agenda" was to create socialist states. Sweden was their model. They also said that their concern was with the "backlash" against "the gay rights and feminist movements." They believe that any attempt to reintroduce the father into the American culture through the use of marriage is, "an attempt to reassert the cultural hegemony of traditional values, such as heterocentrism, Judeo-Christian marriage, and male power and privilege."

The article was the lead story in the June 1999 issue of the *American Psychologist*, which is the only publication sent to every member of the APA and which is used routinely to espouse the viewpoint of the leadership.

The APA hasn't changed their minds. They're just lying low until the heat blows over.

These groups, together with their allies, were lurking in the background of the push for homosexual marriage in Massachusetts while the homosexual activists were pushed to the front in prominent, important positions where they reveled at being in the limelight and having more power than they had ever dreamt about. The New York Times Company continued to be a crucial ally although it was not mentioned by *Bay Windows*.

"Gays and lesbians cannot win these fights on their own," the editorial said. "They must have strong and committed straight allies, such as labor unions and the ACLU."

Lurking in the Background

When legislators voted on July 17, 2002 not to allow a vote on the Marriage Amendment, an underground chant was heard in the chamber, "This is a union vote. . . This is a union vote. . . This is a union vote." The Representatives and Senators reported that union lobbyists had visited every one of them and gruffly ordered that they prevent a vote on the Amendment, even though such a move was illegal.

Another force against the Amendment was the Libertarian Party of Massachusetts. They were so stridently in favor of domestic partnerships in 2000 that homosexual lobbyists urged them to be more quiet because they were only agitating the general populace. The Libertarians were the "only group that has seriously pushed a pro-gay marriage bill in Massachusetts," according to Arlene Isaacson, Chairwoman of the Massachusetts Gay and Lesbian Political Caucus and the lobbyist for the AFL/CIO-affiliated teachers union in the state. She told *Bay Windows* that it was not a good idea because it "would go down to a flaming defeat."

NOW is a deep-rooted leader of the coalition. They still have a strong belief, dating from their founding in 1966, that the institution of marriage is damaging to women. These feminists said in 1968, "Any real change in the status of women would be a fundamental assault on marriage and the family. People would be tied together by love, not legal contraptions. Children would be raised communally; it's just not honest to talk about freedom for women unless you get the child-rearing off their backs. We may not be ready for any of this yet, but if we're going to be honest, we've got to talk about it. Face it, raise the questions."

The formation of NOW was also the beginning of modern hedonism. Its leaders thought they were entitled to the same sexual freedom that they believed men enjoyed. Germaine Greer expressed this sentiment when she stated that she would never have to be one man's woman. "I could have lovers in every town," she said. And she did.

NOW Is No Longer a Rallying Force

Everyone knew that feminist support from NOW would be the kiss-of-death, so it was forced to stay in the background.

This was evidenced by the visit of President Patricia Ireland to Boston in 2001. The *Globe* headlined the occurrence: "On campuses, fewer rallying for feminism." Even at Wellesley College, only 40 students came to listen to Ireland. A Brandeis sophomore reported she had lost a few male friends over the issue. It was apparent even to the *Globe* that "NOW" and "feminists" were no longer popular items with anyone except the *Globe* and other extreme liberals. The number of stories about NOW in the *Globe* went from 90 in 1998 to 31 in 2000 and 25 in 2001.

But you have to give these extreme feminists some credit. The people at NOW have not lost their vision even after more than thirty years. They still have the same objective in sight. They've only changed their tactics. They couldn't capture that stronghold in a frontal attack, so they have made a simulated retreat and are trying from a different position.

Most people don't realize that the main reason Betty Friedan lost control of NOW in 1970 was because she did not want to let the lesbians take over. After Kate Millett revealed that she was a lesbian, the pressure on the Movement became intense. At a march on December

12, 1970, some women began distributing lavender armbands, which signified a support for the lesbian cause.

When they handed one to Friedan, she let it drop to the ground. A biographer of the movement says, "[T]his was the turning point, the moment when the women's movement took on a life of its own, moved beyond Betty Friedan's 'civil rights' structure, leaving the creator of NOW, respected, admired, feared, and sometimes hated, behind. [The others] would come to feel that Betty's approach had dealt only with 'symptoms,' that only those willing to explore the significance of 'women loving women' would come to grips with the underlying causes of women's oppression." In contrast, Gloria Steinem supported the lesbian cause.

Betty Friedan also noted in *The Feminine Mystique* that sex at an early age was found in underdeveloped civilizations. In America, it was found in the slums. She wrote: "[A] certain postponement of sexual activity seemed to accompany the growth in mental activity required and resulted from higher education and the achievement of the professions of highest value to society."

In other words, free and open sex was not something new and modern. It was not a sexual "revolution," but merely a regression back to a less advanced society.

But this wasn't what the leaders of the Women's Movement were saying. They were saying that every male practices free sex; therefore, females should also.

The figures that Friedan quoted were from the Kinsey Report which showed that men who went to college had a totally different outlook on women than did the rest of the men in the population. "[E]arly sexual preoccupation seemed to indicate a weak core of self which even marriage did not strengthen," according to Friedan. "[T]he key problem in promiscuity is usually 'low self-esteem,'" she said.

But the Movement pushed for a return to free and easy sex, and it still is pushing that agenda.

In Massachusetts, the *Globe* gave immediate, important publicity to a new group started by a straight, twentyish couple who are living together without the benefit of marriage. They call it "Alternatives to Marriage Project." They represent everyone who is opposed to the

Marriage Amendment. They say on their website:

"The ATMP advocates for equality and fairness for unmarried people, including people who choose not to marry, cannot marry, or live together before marriage. We provide support and information for this fast-growing constituency, fight discrimination on the basis of marital status, and educate the public and policymakers about relevant social and economic issues. We believe that marriage is only one of many acceptable family forms, and that society should recognize and support healthy relationships in all their diversity."

They say they are open to everyone. "The Alternatives to Marriage Project is open to everyone, including singles, couples, married people, people in relationships with more than two people, and people of all genders and sexual orientations. We welcome our married supporters, who are among the many friends, relatives, and allies of unmarried people."

They reject the many studies which show that married people are happier and healthier than unmarried ones. But that misses the entire point. There would not be an institution of marriage if people were just trying to be healthy and happy. The purpose of marriage is to protect, nurture and love the children who are usually born from such a union.

The first question, of course, is who funded these two young people to start this group?

Aggressive, Obnoxious and Dangerous

The blockers in Massachusetts in 2001 encouraged people to telephone a report wherever they saw signatures being gathered. "We need to know where the signature gatherers are in order to dispatch volunteers to those locations," the group said on its website at MassEquality.org. A hotline number was advertised. "This is the most important job that we have. If we can't find them, we can't block them." When someone called, they immediately dispatched "truth squads" to "educate" the public about the issue.

They claimed they were lowering the number of signers by 80%. They obviously did have an effect because most people try to avoid any confrontation. However, the nasty attacks caused some supporters to become more active and passionate. Many thought it sad to see a handful of discontents trying to block the democratic process.

There were many blockers at the Natick Mall doing different things but two of the blockers are obvious and prominent. This young man (facing camera) stood very close, arguing loudly with anyone who disagreed.

This young woman would not allow a conversation to take place without standing close and also arguing very loudly. When the older woman tried to ignore her, the blocker just talked even more loudly.

The young woman-blocker watches as another blocker (left with beard) argues with a signer (on the right) while the signature-gatherer (facing the camera) tries to calm him down.

The blocker from the previous page next accosted this signer.

Blockers say on their website that they reduce signers by 80%. When allowed to do this type of illegal activity, it is easy to see how they would achieve their goal of destroying voting rights and making a mockery of our election process.

This lone woman, Elenore Courtney, was so intimidated when six blockers from the Campaign for Equality surrounded her at Assumption College, Worcester, that she was afraid to return the next day until reporter Ed Oliver offered to go with her with his camera. The outsiders did not return. Courtney had called the Worcester Telegram to take pictures the first day without realizing that they are also owned by The New York Times Company.

Two blockers (the woman on the left and the blonde man) stand beside a man as he tries to sign the Protection of Marriage petition outside the K-Mart at Holyoke. (The man on the right is the petition gatherer.)

As he begins to sign, the woman continues her harangue.

The blonde blocker appears to be attempting to bump the clipboard of another man who is trying to sign the petition. If this caused a mark on the sheet, it would disqualify the entire sheet of names.

The blonde woman blocker attempts to intimidate a petition gatherer by writing down his license plate. Because cars of petition gatherers have been vandalized, it was necessary for the gatherer to spend time following this woman.

Reports from signature-gatherers in the field were that the "truth squads" were aggressive, obnoxious and dangerous.

An unpaid, volunteer petitioner, who asked that his name be withheld, reported after he had been coordinating signature-gathering efforts for three weeks:

"They try to head the public off at the pass. They get between the public and us before we can talk to them. They are not only intimidating the public, but now <u>we</u> are being intimidated. Any time people enter your personal space, put their face close to your face, or spit at you or try to hit you with a petition board, we feel a certain amount of concern for the safety of those out there gathering signatures.

"Generally there are three to seven people in a 'truth squad,' male and female. They come in shifts. They never identify themselves and always work in teams. If we are there eight hours, they are there with us the whole eight hours.

"One of my friends two days ago was in Greenfield gathering signatures. A member of a 'truth squad' went up to him and spit in his face and screamed so loud that the manager came out to see what was happening.

"I personally have been grabbed by one of the blockers and moved out of the way so that they could talk to someone. I had to tell the guy, 'Look, that's assault and battery. I realize this is a heated debate, but let's not physically touch each other.' I told him I would have to call the authorities and he left immediately.

"When using a quiet voice doesn't work, they just start to scream and yell that we are the 'religious right' and that we have targeted the gay community, that we don't care about people, that we are lying about the petition so people will vote for it. One of their main arguments is that single women and children will lose their healthcare benefits.

"Three of them went up to me and a friend when we were gathering signatures in Springfield. They were handing out flyers. They were crowding us. They would surround us and tell people not to sign the petition, that it was going to take healthcare benefits from their children, things like that. It's made it extremely difficult to gather signatures because when you bring up children, people become confused.

Our hidden camera captured blockers being helped by the
Worcester Police Department which sent two cruisers to Shaw's market
on Route 9 at the apparent request of the blockers.

The manager of Shaw's market tells MassNews that the store did
not call the police nor talk to them after they arrived.

This all happened despite the fact that Massachusetts law is clear:
the signature gatherers had a Constitutional right to be at this location.

*At the right (with a dark blazer) stands the man (apparently from the ACLU) who ran training
sessions every night for the radical homosexual organization, MassEquality, which teaches
"blockers" how to violate the rights of voters. He is watching two signature-gatherers sit outside
Shaw's market talking to a gentleman who is interested in signing the petition. The "blocker"
stood in his position for about an hour, just watching and listening.*

*Two squad cars from the
Worcester police arrive, apparently at the request of a second
ACLU employee, standing at the
left and facing the camera. The
police said they had a report of
disorderly conduct. The Worcester
police later told MassNews they
have no oral or written report
from these officers.*

The police and the two ACLU activists continue to block the table for 30 minutes. The purpose of the blockers, says MassEquality on their website, is to "convince" voters not to sign the petition.

The signature-gatherers pack up their material after being ordered by the police to leave. The store says it made no call to the police and the police refuse to reveal the name of the person who did.

The police and the ACLU employee talk things over after everyone else has left.

"If you have a camera, they will stay a foot or two away, but if you don't, they will surround you on three sides and block you from talking to people. People coming out of the store don't know what we are doing, so it just creates a massive amount of confusion."

'Phenomenally Successful'

A fund-raising email from MassEquality, that was circulated by homosexual groups said, "If we can ramp this effort up statewide, we have an excellent chance at slowing down the signature drive enough to stop the ballot campaign before it starts."

The email boasted that efforts to block signatures have been "phenomenally successful."

The email mentioned that the "truth squads" were organized to work four-hour shifts. "All you need to do is hand out leaflets and talk to passers-by. Everyone who has worked in a Truth Squad says it's an empowering and 'downright fun' experience."

One carload of signature-gatherers was driving from the North Shore to Worcester when they noticed that two cars were following them. They stopped and the other two cars also stopped. When they questioned the pursuing cars, they were told that the people in the following cars were private investigators who had been hired by the opposition. They were followed into Worcester where some passengers were dropped off, and they continued to be followed all the way across the state into Holyoke.

Blockers were at Holyoke and Shrewsbury supermarkets that day, as well as the Square One Mall in Peabody. In the Natick Mall, the blockers harassed from noon until two p.m. when they were asked by mall executives and security to leave for disorderly conduct. At Square One, the mall security told them to stay ten feet from the table. So they left.

The original training of the blockers was done in June by the National Gay and Lesbian Task Force from Washington, D.C. This and other national homosexual groups receive millions of dollars from people like Tim Gill, founder of the software giant, Quark. Just that one man gave $10 million to homosexual organizations. (He gave $225,000 to GLSEN which conducted the Fistgate scandal at Tufts University in 2000. See Chapter 24.)

The blond blocker shown on page 54 is often seen inside the State House, talking with many there.

These dollars pour into the coffers of the homosexual activists, which explains their appeal to many politicians. The person who inherited millions from the Hormel meat company, James Hormel, the homosexual appointed by President Clinton as Ambassador to Luxembourg, is the founder and benefactor of the largest homosexual organization in the country, the Human Rights Campaign. Most of the big money for these causes is coming from other high tech moguls. Kathy Levinson donated about $500,000 per year and David Bohnett gave about $2 million.

Unions Involved Again

The United States Attorney in Boston was asked by MCM to investigate a move by the AFL-CIO of Massachusetts and MassEquality to distribute the home addresses of pro-marriage leaders. Six of those targeted were women.

"This is designed so that pro-homosexual union members and homosexual extremists can harass us and our families," said an MCM spokesman.

He had been told by many union members that they objected to the AFL-CIO's pro-homosexual stance at the national level. The members had no voice in the making of that position and no recourse to stop it.

"I don't understand why the AFL-CIO is in this to begin with, but I do understand that passing around our home addresses is part of an effort to threaten and intimidate us," said the spokesman.

Later on, the names of <u>all</u> the signers of the Amendment were placed on the Internet site of MassEquality. They claimed this would allow the signers to discover if their names had been placed on the petitions without their knowledge. But later events proved that the opponents were getting almost no response and the entire exercise was another method of attempting to intimidate the signers.

Training sessions for blockers were held by MassEquality at the Hotel and Restaurant Workers Union Hall, 58 Berkley St. in the South End of Boston.

8

Local Signature-Gatherer Saw
Nasty Blockers in Action

The local signature-gatherer, who wouldn't endanger his employees after watching the nasty blockers, was Robert Wilkinson. He was already gathering signatures against bilingual education and for Libertarian Carla Howell's proposal to eliminate the state income tax (which did surprisingly well at 45.4% and frightened all the politicians in the state). The following is what Wilkinson told the lawyer for Save Our Horses, Lowell Finley, according to this sworn affidavit from Finley:

"[A spokesman for Massachusetts Citizens for Marriage] told Mr. Wilkinson that they wanted to contract with Mr. Wilkinson's company to collect additional signatures on the Marriage Amendment petition, Petition E.

"Mr. Wilkinson declined. He had been spending time on the street supervising the collection of signatures on other petitions, and knew from what he saw and heard there that the Marriage Amendment was controversial. He saw that many anti-Petition E activists were stationed at the shopping malls where most of the signature gathering was going on, and heard them urging voters not to sign Petition E [The Marriage Amendment].

"He knew from his experience with past signature drives that controversy makes it harder to collect signatures and therefore makes a controversial petition a bad business venture ... ."

This would explain why MCM probably had to pay more for each

Joshua Friedes, right, director of the Religious Coalition for the Freedom to Marry, addresses a news conference Tuesday, Feb. 6, 2001 in Boston, speaking out against a proposed legislative bill that would define marriage in Massachusetts as "a legal relationship between one man and one woman." Gay and lesbian activists said they believe it to be "the most anti-gay family bill" ever filed in the Massachusetts legislature. Friedes is seen here with Rev. John Streit, dean of Saint Paul's Cathedral in Boston (left), and Beth Jacklin (center).

signature than did Save Our Horses.

The affidavit of Wilkinson was used in a lawsuit brought by Save Our Horses later in 2002.

It's obvious that MCM could not benefit by engaging in *anything* that was fraudulent. Extensive monitoring by MCM failed to uncover any fraudulent activity.

Sightings

Some interesting "Sightings" from Massachusetts News at the time told why the opponents were unleashing the blockers.

Massachusetts Is Seen As Important

The man who is leading the opposition in Massachusetts, Atty. Josh Friedes, told *Bay Windows*, "At this moment the majority of people are opposed to equal marriage rights."

Friedes sees Massachusetts as an important battle, which could decide whether the nation continues with marriage as a basic core of our society. He calls the Bay State "ground zero." He was elated with a poll done by MCM even though only 39% say they support gay marriage. He didn't report that 50% oppose it or that the Amendment is approved by 60%, while only 34% oppose it.

Another activist agrees. Sue Hyde, based in Cambridge for the National Gay and Lesbian Task Force, Washington, D.C., tells *Bay Windows* that gay activists have an abysmal record in successfully combating voter initiative campaigns. "We're 0 for 5," she observes, listing Hawaii, Alaska, California, Nevada and Nebraska as those states where such ballot initiatives passed.

After they failed to stop people from signing the petition last fall, Friedes told *Bay Windows* on Dec. 6 that if they are unable to mount a challenge to the signatures and the Amendment goes to the legislature, this is the time for them to make their presence known to legislators. "We have to now confront the reality," he says, "that it's possible that this ballot initiative may be certified and we have to act now in order to insure victory in 2004."

Opponents to Marriage Appear Desperate

Opponents of the Protection of Marriage Amendment continue to appear desperate. They know that the vast majority of citizens are against them. Most people support the Marriage Amendment.

"If the developments across the country are any indication, supporters of same-sex marriage [in Mass.] may be facing an uphill battle," according to the gay newspaper, *Bay Windows*. It points out that 35 states already have laws similar to the proposed Amendment in Massachusetts. Some 70% of the voters in Nebraska have approved a similar measure in 2000 and 60% already approve it in Massachusetts.

Nobody Counters Gay Groups

There is not one single group *anywhere* in the entire country that is working solely to counter the efforts or money of the national homosexual groups — much less one that is rich.

One activist told *Bay Windows* that the National Gay and Lesbian Task Force was "doing amazing work already. I think that if we organize and really mobilize and take our lead and learn from the mistakes

that some of the states have made, like California, I think that we have
a fighting chance. It's like 50-50 right now, so it could go either way."
That's the organization that still has Sue Hyde on the ground in
Massachusetts. It conducted training sessions for activists in Worcester.

The opponents wish to stop the people from voting because they
have a better chance of winning if lawyers and judges make the decisions. The feminists have many lawyers in high positions in the courts.
Therefore, they would like lawyers to decide the issue and not the citizens.

One of the lawyers at GLAD, Mary Bonauto, told *Bay Windows* she
didn't think the matter "should be on the ballot at all" because it is a
civil rights issue. But others pointed out that this concerns the *writing*
of the Constitution. When a country writes a Constitution, it does not
invite only lawyers to do so. But Atty. Bonauto desires that to happen
because she knows it is the only way her side will win.

According to *Bay Windows*, Atty. Bonauto "takes issue with MCM's
attempt to _circumvent_ the judicial system by putting the issue of gay
marriage to voters."

Bonauto said: "I'd _like_ to think that the majority of Massachusetts
citizens will reject that."

Vermont Activists Urged to Help in Massachusetts

The following email was sent to homosexual activists in Vermont,
asking them to join the "truth squads" in Massachusetts.

Much of the information in this email was blatantly false. None of
the typos in the email have been corrected by us.

GLAD is an acronym for Gay & Lesbian Advocates & Defenders.

Subject: MASS needs our help
I received this from the folks at GLAD -
URGENT: PLEASE FORWARD THIS EMAIL AS WIDELY
AND QUICKLY AS POSSIBLE
We Need Your Help in the Next Five Weeks in Massachusetts
to Stop the Defense of Marriage Ballot Initiative. The
Massachusetts Citizen's Alliance is sponsoring a defense of marriage

ballot initiative. This initiative would change the Massachusetts constitution to prohibit not only gay and lesbian marriage, but also to deny gays and lesbians even the most basic of domestic partner benefits, such as health insurance, bereavement leave, and hospital visitation rights.

If our opponents collects enough signatures, the initiative will go on the ballot in 2004, where it stands a very good chance of passing. They have hired an out of state petition drive firm to collect the 100,000 signatures they need. They have until Thanksgiving to collect the signatures.

Our coalition of gay and civil rights groups, the Campaign for Equality, is organizing a "Decline to Sign" campaign to block this paid signature drive. Whenever we find a paid petitioner in front of a grocery store or in a mall, we send a "Truth Squad" consisting of two or three people to stand near the circulator and urge people not to sign the petition.

So far, our effort has been PHENOMENALLY successful. Whenever a Truth Squad is out there near a paid circulator, we've seen the circulator's signature totals drop by as much as 80%. If we can ramp this effort up statewide, we have an excellent chance at slowing down the signature drive enough to stop the ballot campaign before it starts.

WE NEED YOUR HELP RIGHT AWAY. We have only six weeks to stop this hate campaign.

1) Send an EMERGENCY contribution today. We must raise $75,000 in the next two weeks if we are to be successful with the "Decline To Sign" campaign. We have pledges for about one-third, but are just beginning to organize fundraising for the ballot campaign which will need $2.5 million—if we are unable to stop their signature drive. We need 1000 people to give $100 in this emergency. If you can give more—thank you

If you can give less—we are grateful. You may donate by mail to

Campaign for Equality, 398 Columbus Avenue, Suite 198, Boston, MA 02116.

Please make your check out to the Campaign for Equality and

write >"Decline to Sign" on your check.

2) Help us find the paid circulators. We need lots of people - in every city and town in Massachusetts - to check stores in their local areas to see if there are paid circulators working in the one or two likely spots, and report in to us any that are sighted. This is the most important job that we have. If we can't find them, we can't block them.

3) Join a Truth Squad—only a few hours would help. We will provide training and put you in a team with other experienced Truth Squadders. All you need to do is hand out leaflets and talk to passers by. Everyone who has worked in a Truth Squad has said that it's an empowering and "downright fun" experience. We need your help for as many or as few hours as you can spare. The best times for collecting signatures are Saturday and Sunday noon to 8 PM, followed by Thursday, Friday and Monday 4 PM to 8 PM. Those are the times we need to target. Scouting store fronts: we need as many people as possible to go out on Thursday, Friday, Saturday, Sunday and Monday between 11AM and noon, to check store fronts in their areas and call in sightings. We will give you a list of stores in your area to check.

Truth Squads. We are organizing four hour shifts as follows: Saturday and Sunday - noon to 4PM and 4PM to 8PM. Thursday, Friday and Monday - 4PM to 8PM. We have only five more weeks to stop the signature drive. If you can help, please contact us. Contact www.massequality. com and then click on DTS where it lists volunteer training times, etc. [GLAD NOTE: If that fails, contact GLAD for information.]

PLEASE VOLUNTEER YOUR TIME AND/OR MONEY TODAY. THANK YOU.

Section III

Masterminds of "Fraud" Hoax Are Uncovered

The plaintiffs had hardly heard of "Save Our Horses" before November 16, 2001, which was almost the end of the signature-gathering period.

They knew that the horse people were trying to pass a law forbidding the slaughter of horses for human consumption. They did not know of any trouble. They knew that both of them were using the same signature-gathering company. Everything changed on November 16.

On that day, the Attorney General issued a short, innocuous News Release saying he had received complaints from "several," unspecified people. (The word "several" is defined as "more than two but not many; of an indefinite but small number," according to Webster's.)

These several, unnamed people alleged they had been cheated. They had attempted to sign the petition being circulated by Save Our Horses, but claimed the signature-gatherers handed them the petition for the Protection of Marriage Amendment instead.

The *Boston Globe* jumped with glee all over this News Release. It used that single item over-and-over for month after month, to screech accusations of "fraud" against the plaintiffs.

The Release said only that "some spot checks" by the Attorney General had found that those claimants "MAY" have signed a petition they did not support.

But that didn't stop the *Globe*.

Attorney General Tom Reilly really had no choice but to issue the

News Release. The homosexuals, who were his political allies, were very angry that he had obeyed his legal duty and certified earlier in 2001 that the Amendment was a proper question for the ballot. "I know I will never let him forget it," wrote Jeff Epperly, Editor of *Bay Windows* at the time.

Therefore, when the political activists went back to Reilly in November 2001 and asked him to issue a News Release advising voters to be careful and alert as to what they were signing, he naturally responded in an attempt to appease this group. But he reported neither a "wave" nor an "onslaught" of complaints as *Bay Windows* claimed, only that he had received "several" complaints and that people always should be careful when they sign any petition.

(Reilly's decision that the Marriage Amendment was proper for the ballot was upheld the following spring by a unanimous Supreme Judicial Court. An appeal had been taken from his decision by GLAD, a homosexual non-profit law firm of five lawyers and nine support staff. They work solely in New England, mostly in Massachusetts, with an estimated budget of $1 million. They are the ones who brought the gay marriage lawsuits in Vermont and Massachusetts. The acronym stands for "Gay & Lesbian Advocates & Defenders."

(Reilly was still being grilled about this on June 25, 2002, at the annual meeting of the Massachusetts Lesbian and Gay Bar Association, where twenty homosexual lawyers questioned him about many issues. At that meeting, he was asked, according to *Bay Windows*, why he had not issued a stronger News Release about the accusations of "fraud and forgery" "which Reilly's office did little to investigate, outside of issuing a press release cautioning voters to read petitions carefully before signing them." The Attorney General responded that his office did not feel the allegations justified taking the measure off the ballot. Fraud and forgery, he said, are "difficult to prove when you've signed a petition." But many of the activists were still not satisfied.)

News Release Was Important to No One but *Globe*

The people at MCM didn't take the allegations of "fraud" any more seriously than did the Attorney General. They had always realized that the opponents had people signing the petitions as spies, in order to accomplish myriad nefarious tricks. And they knew that the *Globe* was, at the very least, close friends with that clique.

They had no knowledge, at that time, that Save Our Horses was a stalking horse for homosexual marriage.

The people at the *Globe* made this into a seismic event. They repeated these spurious charges from several, unknown persons over and over for many months until the charges became an accepted truism. Then they threw the weight of the *New York Times* newspaper behind the phony charges on April 7, 2002, with an obviously libelous headline on top. The plaintiffs and others at MCM knew they were seeing a dirty, corrupt side of the world, and of The New York Times Company, that nobody would believe existed. Nobody.

Still, the supporters kept winning the battle and The Company had to instruct the *Globe* to pile on, with more and more lies and libelous stories.

It will be difficult for the reader to sense the utter disbelief and frustration that the people at MCM felt as they slowly realized how dishonest and nasty the *Globe* was. They had always understood that the paper opposed the Amendment. They expected "hard ball." But this?!?

It became crystal clear there would be no dispassionate, intelligent discussion of the Protection of Marriage Amendment — ever.

My personal involvement with MCM was from a distance until the legislature violated the law on July 17, 2002. My main focus was publishing *Massachusetts News*, an Internet newspaper with a monthly print edition of 250,000 copies, which was founded in June 1999. The 24-page, four-color tab newspaper was mailed randomly to citizens around the state, in addition to the paid subscribers. We were publishing a conservative newspaper which covered many subjects, but we found that we had to devote more and more time and space to refute the lies about the Protection of Marriage Amendment.

When the *New York Times* reporter, Pam Belluck, called MCM with the news that they were joining the attack against MCM (the reporter didn't state it that way, but we knew what was coming), we realized we had to find out who was behind this hoax about "horses" and "fraud."

9

Globe Created the Hoax about "Fraud"

As it became apparent that the blockers had been <u>un</u>successful in their battle to kill the Amendment, the New York Times Company became desperate.

That's the reason the *Boston Globe* began the "fraud" scam on November 15, 2001.

On that day, they published a letter from Jane Detwiler, Natick. She said she had signed the Marriage petition for a volunteer while at her son's soccer game. She was not deceived in any way but discussed it later with friends, was unhappy that she signed and was seeking to have her name removed.

The next day, Attorney General Tom Reilly issued his News Release warning all signers to, "Carefully read the actual piece of paper you are being asked to sign."

Inasmuch as the *Globe* prints only a tiny fraction of letters received, you know that when one is published, it serves their purpose in some way. Because Judge Saris did not allow discovery, no one will ever know when Detwiler wrote the letter, how long it was held before being printed or whether she was part of an organized plot.

The town of Natick was especially suspicious because there is a Unitarian Church in the next town with a group made up of "gays and straights," known as Interweave. That group was very active on the streets with in-your-face activities.

MCM Agreed With Warning

A spokesman for MCM responded that he agreed wholeheartedly

with Reilly's warning that everyone must be certain what they are signing when approached by any petition gatherer.

The spokesman said, "This new tactic shows our supporters that they must be ready for a long fight because the people on the other side will do anything to win. They do not want an intelligent discussion of the issues.

"We've been aware for some time that some of the people who are a part of the organized opposition to our petition have signed the petition in order to cry 'foul' at some point in the process. Therefore, we anticipated this type of complaint to the Attorney General's office. We do not know the number of people in opposition to us who have done this on purpose, but it is probably more than one or two. We have warned our petition gatherer to be very careful when obtaining the signatures to avoid any possibility that his people may be confusing people.

"The people who are gathering signatures for us are the same ones who have been doing this for both Carla Howell [Libertarian candidate for Governor] and the people opposing the slaughter of horses. If any or all of these signature gatherers have been deceptive, they will be condemned by everyone, including us.

"By the same token, the people who are making false accusations should also be condemned.

"The Attorney General gives excellent advice when he admonishes everyone, 'Carefully read the actual piece of paper you are being asked to sign.'"

Now that the blockers had failed, the *Globe* would use the News Release from the Attorney General as the new, nasty and illegal method of attacking and destroying MCM and its supporters. This article was the first in the series of five that would paint them with "fraud."

There would be no discussion about marriage, or family and children in a changing society. This would become only an issue about homosexuals.

But first the opponents would carefully examine the signatures which were now at the Secretary of State's office to see if they could wear-down MCM. A challenge of the signatures would cost MCM hundreds of thousands of dollars in lawyer fees and handwriting experts, plus the staff's time.

Signatures Carefully Examined

A team from the ACLU appeared in the Secretary of State's office on the first day that the petitions for the Marriage Amendment were available for examination, Wednesday, December 12.

They were there to begin an attempt to invalidate the signatures even though only a handful of petitions were yet available to the public. There were fourteen on the team on the following day.

"They are already circling like vultures," said a spokesman for MCM. "Their threats and intimidation didn't work during the campaign. Now their lawyers will try to nit-pick the petitions to death."

The ACLU had a handwriting expert conduct a preliminary examination of the petitions. It's common knowledge that when paid circulators are hired to gather signatures, there will always be one or two of them who will be less than honest. Almost every petition drive is forced to hire these paid persons to supplement the volunteers. The need for paid persons was particularly acute with the Marriage Amendment because there was so much illegal harassment by the blockers.

Any firm has one or more signature-gatherers who will take a name which was mistakenly placed in the wrong town and put it in the right town. This is obviously not legal, and a handwriting expert could testify that some of the signatures were written by one person, the signature gatherer.

The bad news for the opponents was that this petition went 20,000 signatures over the required amount. When any ballot effort does that, it is difficult to expect they will find anywhere near that number of fraudulent signatures.

But the challenge could be used as a public relations tool, with the help of the *Globe*, to make it look as though the entire campaign was fraudulent. It could be a method of harassing MCM and forcing them to spend large amounts of money for lawyers and their own signature experts.

If challenged, MCM would need many people at the Secretary of State's office to watch the ACLU people to make sure that the petitions were not removed or had "stray marks" put on them which would

Pinch Sulzberger's plan for gay marriage started in Boston in 1999 when Richard H. Gilman suddenly showed up at the Globe to oust the Taylors from control of the paper where they had reigned for 126 years. Inasmuch as Pinch Sulzberger planned to use the Globe to impose homosexual marriage across the nation, he sent this Times senior vice president from New York to be his Publisher in Boston. Gilman is shown here talking to Globe employees on the day he arrived from New York.

invalidate the entire petition.

Since the opponents of the marriage petition had acknowledged many times that they expected to lose if the matter were decided by the voters, they were desperate to do anything to stop the ballot initiative.

Having Second Thoughts

Bay Windows reported that the anti-marriage activists were having second thoughts about challenging the almost 80,000 certified signatures that were collected.

But the MCM spokesman said, "I believe they will go ahead regardless. If they can get a lot of money and volunteers, they will swamp us with as much 'busywork' as they can in an attempt to thwart the will of the voters. They want us to spend tens of thousands of dollars in lawyer fees."

The opponents were also faced with the news that over 120,000 people had signed the petitions. Although the signatures weren't all certified, it indicated that the Amendment had broad popular support.

Bay Windows had reported earlier that the anti-marriage coalition would be "scrambling to find hundreds of volunteers within the next couple of weeks to conduct a possible signature challenge."

"They threw their best political punch," said MCM's spokesman.

"They got to harass our people at the shopping malls and supermarkets. They bullied people trying to sign our petitions and followed them to their cars. Nothing was done to stop them. And still they lost because the bulk of the signatures were gathered by people in their neighborhoods, places of worship and even at town dumps.

"Now they are going to rant about fraud and false signatures in a final desperate mission to thwart the will of the people. They should admit they have lost in their efforts to stop the people from deciding and try to begin an intelligent discussion about the issue."

A Major Production

The *Bay Windows* article predicted a major production. The co-chair of the Massachusetts Gay and Lesbian Political Caucus, Arlene Isaacson, warned, "In order for a successful signature challenge to take place, they need several things: donation of a large conference room in downtown Boston; money; and at least 20 to 40 people every day — morning, noon and night — seven days a week."

MCM said they expected the full force of the opposition to hit in the coming weeks. Another local homosexual newspaper, *Innewsweekly*, reported that the opponents were "set to embark on a massive signature challenge that Isaacson says could cost 'hundreds of thousands of dollars' and would require a cadre of volunteers to work around the clock for at least two months. She adds that there is no doubt in her mind that the effort would keep the question off the ballot. 'This would begin next week, and continue into January. It would be office work. People will have to take time off, but we will train anyone,' said Isaacson. 'And, it's going to be a very expensive process because we need to hire attorneys, hand-writing experts, coordinators, etc.'"

Know They Will Lose

Isaacson admitted they would lose if the voters were allowed to decide. This is how *Bay Windows* reported it:

"Right now, Isaacson said, 'It is absolutely essential to run a signature challenge if we can because otherwise we risk a distinct possibility that the radical Right will win this issue on the ballot even though they did not honestly gather enough signatures.' There are two problems with all this, Isaacson said: 'Our civil rights should not be up for popular debate,' and if they have to be, 'it should at least be done legally. It is so clear that the radical Right has egregiously and unethically obtained signatures.'"

MCM strongly disagreed with this assessment and said Isaacson and her group helped coordinate the harassment and intimidation with their "truth squad" attempts to disrupt the orderly gathering of signatures.

"What legitimate reason could they have to follow people who had signed the petitions to their cars and copy down their license plate numbers? They obviously were trying to intimidate the persons who had signed the petition."

'Wave' of Bait and Switch?

The *Bay Windows* article reported a "wave" of bait-and-switch allegations concerning the signature gathering, but they reported only one woman, Janet Drake of Framingham, who made such an allegation.

They reported another woman, Karen Ahlers of Ashland, a lesbian, who said she "went up to where the [signature gatherer] was" and proceeded to ask people not to sign. When she got into a predictable altercation with the man, she became upset.

Both of these women were from the Framingham area which had the Interweave group in its Unitarian Church.

They also reported a third woman, Marina Whall, who drove around the city looking for signature gatherers and was successful in at least making some people "pause" before signing. She said she belonged to "Interweave."

This was a "wave" of allegations!?

10

Two Prestigious Lawyers
Were Masterminding the Hoax

After the plaintiffs finally realized that Save Our Horses was out to hurt them, they believed that the troublemaker was Susan Wagner. She was the spokesperson for the group and lived in the borough of Queens on Long Island. It appeared that she was lending a hand to their opponents. But why would she want to damage the people at MCM? Where did she get her money?

Wagner was the only person ever mentioned by Save Our Horses until the group started its silly lawsuit against the Commonwealth in the spring of 2002. She was generating the publicity about the "fraud." The failed SOH campaign had caused her an embarrassing, personal blot in her attempt to get the horse petition on the ballot. The new lawsuit would be another excellent chance for more publicity to put the blame on the Marriage Amendment people.

(Many wondered whether Wagner was trying to protect herself from the unknown backers who had given her the money to finance the effort. She had obviously done a poor job for them. Was it the gambling interests which would be after her?)

Sure enough, the *Globe* picked up the lawsuit and wrote a long story on March 26, "Horse Lovers Say They Were Duped." The suit hadn't even been filed when the article was published, which meant that the *Globe* was in close contact with the group and had been given the suit ahead of time. (When the suit was dismissed by a judge less than a month later, that important story received no mention at all by the

Globe.)

When the suit was filed, some other names began to surface. All those names meant nothing until April 7 when the *New York Times* story came crashing through to a million-and-a-half readers. This was no longer a joke. The tiny staff of *Massachusetts News* dropped its other stories and did some investigating about Save Our Horses.

The answer to the mystery was simple. The reporters at *Massachusetts News* quickly discovered that two Boston lawyers were masterminding the hoax, although Wagner was obviously going along with it.

The "offices" of the group were discovered by Sally Pawlick in a franchise for "Mail Boxes Etc." on Route 9, 1257 Worcester Road, Framingham. This location on the outskirts of Boston was as close as possible to the Framingham exit of the MassPike and a quick trip back to New York. The "offices" were in mailbox 284, also known as "Unit 284." It was just about large enough to hold a few dozen, standard-size envelopes and some leaflets from Stop & Shop.

The two lawyers were from the prestigious 100-year-old, 170 lawyer, Boston firm of Palmer & Dodge. They were Neil P. Arkuss, a partner, and George Ticknor, chairman of their finance department.

Why So Hostile to MCM?

But why were these two lawyers so hostile to MCM?

Massachusetts News learned that they both lived in Concord, Massachusetts, where they, and their wives and neighbors, were involved in an art center which occupied an entire building, the town's former high school. All the original signers of the Save Our Horses petition were involved in the art center.

The people at MCM knew that Concord is a very liberal town. Back in 1999, it had had a meeting at the high school to promote "safety in the schools," even though they had not had any problems. The local paper wrote that one organizer believed the school was "fortunate, so far, that as communities, we have not had a problem" with harassment or violence against homosexuals. But they held the rally anyhow, just in case.

The supporters also knew that the art center did not recognize "mothers and fathers" and required that students refer to parents as "adult partners." But were these people such ideologues that they would stoop to this nasty, and unlawful, sort of behavior? They were the type who prided themselves on being "tolerant" and "inclusive."

It was a safe assumption they were supportive of animal rights and had signed on as a group with Save Our Horses in order to "protect" the horses from harm. (Some also wondered if the law firm represented gambling interests.) When the horse effort was failing and a couple of people reported that someone had tried to switch their vote, they realized they could use this as a weapon against the "homophobes" at MCM.

They apparently thought it humorous to anonymously defame those with whom they disagreed.

This also explained why the horse people were so careful to go right to the edge of libel when talking about the supporters of the Amendment. Their leaders were two lawyers.

Somebody had thought that by hiring a few professional signature gatherers, they could just sit at home and ignore it. That is not the way you run a ballot campaign if you plan to win.

Arkuss Used Publicity Skillfully and Deceitfully

Arkuss had kept the matter simmering for many months with little teasers to the press, saying that he had new information. And he kept dribbling out letters to the signers of the Marriage Amendment advising them of the "fraud" which had taken place against them and others. He sent the letters across the state in an attempt to demoralize the signers. But he didn't understand that he was also stirring them up, not just demoralizing some.

When it became clear that a legislative hearing would be held about the Marriage Amendment on April 10, he let loose on March 23 a barrage of 19,613 letters to signers of the petition. (Keep in mind that the hearing date was not announced, at least to the public, until about March 23. How did he get advance information of its timing?) The letters arrived in over 19,000 mailboxes of supporters just a week before the Marriage Amendment hearing. Arkuss had previously sent letters to 6,000 signers on February 21 and 2,438 on March 15.

The only offices for "Save Our Horses" in Massachusetts were inside one small mailbox in this franchise of Mailboxes Etc., located on Route 9, only a short distance from the Turnpike exit at Framingham.

The horse "office" was one of the mailboxes shown on this wall. The photo on the right shows "Unit 284, 1257 Worcester Rd.," the home of "Save Our Horses" in Massachusetts.

In addition, he placed the story in the *New York Times* for April 7, three days before the hearing.

His machinations did have results, but not as much as he expected. About 15 state legislators, out of 200, attacked the Amendment in a media "circus" at the State House. Committee members Rep. David Torrissi (D-Lawrence, N. Andover) and Rep. Paul Demakis (D-Boston) kept raising the "fraud" against the horse petition.

The lesbian activist, Arlene Isaacson, went on at length about alleged fraud and deception in the signature-gathering effort. She said there were hundreds of victims of bait-and-switch tactics. She said she had affidavits from signature gatherers who had been trained to use these tactics.

When a *Massachusetts News* reporter asked Isaacson if he could see the affidavits to which she was referring, she nervously said, "I'll be right back," and never returned.

Reps. Torrissi and Demakis also raised the resignation of Executive Director Bryan Rudnick from MCM in February after the signature campaign was successfully concluded. Reports at the time said Rudnick resigned in order to prepare to go to law school.

The two committee members wondered aloud why Rudnick "suddenly" left and implied it may have been related to the allegations of fraudulently obtained Marriage petition signatures although they did not reveal how the two could possibly be connected.

Sally Pawlick pointed out to the legislators that almost two years in the first job after college was a long time and to expect two additional years after that from Rudnick was too much.

Many have wondered how Arkuss managed to get a computer database of the signers which had obviously been manipulated at great expense by someone who planned to use it a lot. Who would have given it to him except the opposition?

Supporters Had Thought Complaint Might Be Legitimate

When the horse story first surfaced, the people at MCM thought the inquiry might be legitimate.

So they went to the field and investigated. After all, the signature gatherer, Derrick Lee of Phoenix, Arizona, had to hire many people. It

All slander against the supporters of the Marriage Amendment originated from the horse people at the "Emerson Umbrella Center for the Arts" in Concord. The attack was led by the lawyer-husbands of two resident artists. They, plus two of the staff, four resident artists and other family members comprised the original 13-signers of the horse petition.

was almost inevitable he would hire some "bad apples." They attempted to see if they could help in any way.

They had hired Lee at the last moment when it became clear that the blockers were going to make it dangerous for ordinary citizens to be soliciting signatures at the large malls. Lee was

The Center no longer recognizes mothers and fathers and teaches children to refer to parents as "adult partners."

already in the state working for the horse people and for Carla Howell, the Libertarian candidate for Governor. The people at MCM hired him because they found him already here and working.

Even the homosexual newspaper in Boston, *Bay Windows*, said at the outset that Lee had a good reputation. But Lee had undoubtedly never encountered blockers like his people had to endure in Massachusetts.

The California lawyer, who was flown in to bring the Save Our Horses lawsuit against the Secretary of State, said that the signature gatherers were coached to use the horse petition to snag "marriage" signatures. But only one signature gatherer materialized after that claim. The article in the *Times* said only that "he and others were given clipboards with horse cover sheets, but more marriage petitions than horse petitions underneath." There was nothing there about misleading people.

It became more and more clear to the supporters that no one at Save Our Horses wanted to talk with them. This brouhaha was merely an effort to hurt the Amendment. But why? Was the entire horse effort a "front" for homosexual activists?

The supporters believed this would all go away eventually. The horse people would either prove that some of the signature gatherers had deceived people or they wouldn't. But it was not that easy. Even after it became clear to everyone that their campaign was dead, they kept spending tens-of-thousands of dollars. For what, other than to damage the Marriage Amendment? Where was all this money coming from?

As for the *New York Times* which publicized the affair, the people at MCM had thought the paper would be coming up with something new and startling, not just a rewrite of a four-month old story from the *Globe*. After all, this was the National Edition of the *New York Times* carrying a major story that was sent across the entire country to 1.5 million subscribers.

When the *Times* announced it would be writing about the horses, only three days before the hearing at the State House on April 10, the people at MCM were concerned. They thought that the paper knew something they didn't and would put their top people on the story, but obviously the paper didn't do that. The story was just a rewrite of the *Globe* story. It appears that no one from the *Times/Globe* even left their offices to investigate. (Or perhaps they already knew that Save Our Horses was just a mail-drop.)

The *Times* reported that the horse people were 2,574 signatures short of getting on the ballot. Then it wrote that "hundreds" of people had mailed the cards back "claiming they were hoodwinked." But it said the organizer "believes" that "the total will exceed the 2,574-signature shortfall."

After almost five months of searching, the *Times* and the *Globe* reported the names of only five people who said they were tricked.

Some were left wondering whether the horse offices in Framingham could even hold a large number of postcards.

They wondered why the *Times* and *Globe* did not question who was providing all the money to perpetuate the horse hoax. (That would have been an interesting question for MCM to ask in their lawsuit. No wonder The Company wanted the suit dismissed.)

How Did Sen. Birmingham Become a Lawyer at Palmer & Dodge?

Is it merely coincidence that Senator Tom Birmingham, the Senate President who violated the state Constitution in 2002 and lost his bid for Governor as a result, began working at Palmer and Dodge in 2003? It's cause for wonder about the powerful forces that did not want us investigating any of this.

The *Globe* editors exhibited great hostility against Birmingham in July 2003 after he had been out of office for six months. A front-page story about state financial troubles started with strong innuendos that the Senator had spent "tens of thousands" of state money for his gubernatorial campaign in 2002. The innuendos were wrong and the paper's ombudsman said the paper had not been fair. The story painted the *new* Senate President as a "good" person although his spending record was about the same as Birmingham's.

Dirty Tricks Originated in Concord

All of the 13 original signers of the horse petition were residents of Concord. They included the following:

— Atty. Arkuss, his wife, Nancy, who is a Resident Artist at the Emerson Umbrella Center for the Arts, and apparently their son, Brett, all of the same address.

— Atty. Ticknor, his wife, Susan C. Getsinger-Ticknor, who is a

Resident Artist at the Center, his apparent son, H. Malcolm and her apparent son, Alex, all of the same address.

— Marijane Raymond, Resident Educator at the Center.

— Maxine Payne, Resident Artist and Staff Member at the Center.

— Corrine Kinsman, an active artist at the Center's "Concord Players" and "Concord Youth Theatre."

— Priscilla Parrott, Resident Artist at the Center, member of First Parish Unitarian Church.

— Suzanne Winsby, Resident Artist and Staff member at the Center, member of Unitarian Church.

— Allison Aley, member of Social Action Council at Unitarian Church.

Horse Petition Was Foolish and Dangerous

The horse petition would have been a foolish and dangerous law. If those who signed to "save" the horses had known the facts about the initiative, many would not have done so.

The originator of the proposal was Susan Wagner of Equine Advocates on Long Island, which is within walking distance of Aqueduct Racetrack. She says she worked in the racing industry for 14 years until she formed this organization in 1996. Many wonder whether she still works there and is receiving money from the racing industry in order to keep them from getting the bad publicity which has gone to the greyhound racetracks.

Where else would she have gotten all this money?

Wagner says on her website that "over 100,000 American horses are being slaughtered here and in Canada annually." She has "rescued" only a few dozen of those half-million horses in the past six years and takes enormous credit for it.

The law she would have had us pass would have done little to correct the problem. It would have prohibited the slaughter of horses only if they were destined for human consumption. It would not have stopped the slaughter for dog food or other purposes. All 100,000 horses could still be slaughtered every year.

In addition, it would have put innocent people in the grasp of a poorly written law. It included people who "give away," "offer to give away," or "transport" horses where the person knows "or should know" that the animal was going to be slaughtered for human consumption.

If a horse is going to a slaughterhouse in Canada, how would anyone know the final use of the meat?

The penalty is one year in jail for each horse.

Susan Wagner's website is at www.equineadvocates.com.

Palmer & Dodge Refused to Talk

Sally Pawlick wondered at the time. "We have been very quiet while this slander has been going on. But this news is especially disappointing. Why can't these people play according to the rules? Their calumny is disheartening, to say the least. How would they like it if a large headline in the *New York Times* went across the country falsely accusing them of fraud?"

She said she would like to ask them, "Why are you doing this to us? Have you no sense of decency or honesty?"

I immediately sent a polite note to the managing partner of Palmer & Dodge, inquiring whether the firm knew about this nefarious activity by the two lawyers which appeared to violate the law and damage many good citizens, including my wife. The managing partner never responded.

The following letter was sent to Atty. Neil P. Arkuss by MassNews Publisher/Atty. J. Edward Pawlick. A response was never received from Atty. Arkuss.

Neil P. Arkuss, Esquire
Palmer & Dodge
One Beacon Street
Boston, MA 02108

Dear Attorney Arkuss:

You are an experienced and distinguished lawyer in the prominent law firm of Palmer and Dodge.

This newspaper has been following the lawsuit brought by you as the lead plaintiff for "Save Our Horses" against the Secretary of the Commonwealth. As you know, I am also a Massachusetts lawyer.

You stated in a sworn affidavit for this lawsuit on April 10, 2002 that "thousands of signatures" of registered voters were "fraudulent[ly] diverted" from the horse petition to the petition for the Protection of Marriage.

The Chair of your organization, Susan Wagner, swore in an Affidavit that, Save Our Horses has received written responses from over 1,000 voters in all parts of Massachusetts, stating that they had intended to sign only Petition A [the horse petition], and that they had not intended to sign Petition E [the marriage petition] but were listed as signers of Petition E."

No One Has Seen 'Written Responses'

As you must be aware, no impartial person has ever seen the 1,000 "written responses" which you and your friends allege.

A box of something was brought to the hearing before Judge Thomas E. Connolly a few weeks ago, but no one has ever seen the contents of the box. The "responses" were not shown to the lawyers from Atty. Gen. Reilly's office who represented the Commonwealth. They were apparently not given to the judge. When I talked with your trial lawyer, Atty. Daniel I. Small, today, he informed me that they are probably in the custody of Susan Wagner.

Atty. Small assured me that they do exist, but to be honest with you, that is an enormous amount of paper and I doubt, in any case, that he would have closely examined all of them.

As you are aware, this suit by you has caused great personal damage to all the supporters of the Marriage Amendment. It appears to many of them that this slander and libel against them is intentional on your part.

What Is the Truth?

After you filed your lawsuit against the Secretary of the Commonwealth in March, the President of "Massachusetts Citizens for Marriage" urged the Secretary to "conduct an investigation" in order "to examine the evidence" which you claimed in your lawsuit.

She said, "We request that you begin this investigation immediately and complete it as quickly as possible. As you know, the statements made to the media by 'Save Our Horses' have never contained either names or facts. Over the past five months since last November, they have complained repeatedly that a substantial number of people signed our petition while thinking they were signing the horse petition. We have waited vainly for over five months for any proof of those charges. But none has been forthcoming. Nevertheless, now that a suit has been filed against you, still without any proof of the charges, we must request that your office undertake an immediate and thorough investigation of this matter."

The names of the thousand or more people you claim have made written responses to you have still not been revealed. But your friends, who are the opponents of the Marriage Amendment, still use your lawsuit to disparage all who signed the Marriage Amendment even though Judge Connolly has dismissed your suit.

Your Reputation Is At Stake

You have made serious charges against the Marriage Amendment, which many believe was done on purpose. It is time for you to prove those charges. If some of the signature-gatherers who were hired by both you and Mass. Citizens for Marriage did indeed defraud anyone, both of you would be upset — and rightly so.

We request that you allow Massachusetts News to examine those written responses. If that is not satisfactory to you, I would request that you suggest an impartial person of unquestioned integrity to do so.

Please be kind enough to inform me how this examination would occur.

Sincerely,
J. Edward Pawlick
Publisher, Massachusetts News
Attorney at Law

11

Horse Suit Thrown Out by Judge Connolly

The suit by Save Our Horses was dismissed on April 24, 2002, by Judge Thomas E. Connolly in Boston's Superior Court.

This was reported the next day, April 25, by *Massachusetts News*. But the *Boston Globe* has never reported that the suit was dismissed despite the large story published only a month previously when the suit was filed. The matter just dropped out of sight. The *Globe* knew it was dismissed. Their Associated Press wire had a story about it.

The *Globe* didn't want to admit that they knew the fate of the lawsuit when it wrote a story on April 25 about a legislative hearing, titled, "Same Sex Marriage Ban Dealt a Setback." (This story was the last of the five libelous ones that were listed in the Complaint in the MCM lawsuit.) The only information about the lawsuit that the *Globe* put in the story was that the horse people had "sued the state." They didn't say what happened to the suit.[1]

The suit had been dismissed before that story was written. Are we to believe that the *Globe* didn't know it? Don't they look at their A.P. wire? They have _never_ reported to this day that the suit was dismissed.

After five months of publicity and fanfare, only six people presented affidavits in the lawsuit saying they were tricked and five more returned cards from the mailings to signers, out of more than 75,000 voters who had signed the petition.

---

[1] Here's the full paragraph from the *Globe*:
"The ballot question has attracted considerable controversy recently. Workers trying to gather the 57,100 signatures required to get it on the ballot have been accused of misleading some voters, telling them they were signing a petition to protect horses from slaughter instead. Members of the Save Our Horses campaign have sued the state because their signatures had been diverted to the marriage question, keeping their own initiative off the ballot."

Two of the six affidavits made absolutely no sense.

Christine Bogoian, the woman who had her picture prominently in the *New York Times* story said in her affidavit:

"A young black man asked me to sign an initiative petition against horse slaughter. I said yes and signed what I thought was the horse slaughter petition. While I was walking away, the man asked if I wanted to sign a petition against same sex marriages."

But if she had already been tricked into signing the marriage petition, why was she asked to sign it again when she was walking away?

The same question needs to be asked of Richard Leeman, who was in the first paragraph of the *Times* story. His affidavit in the lawsuit said: "A man in his 40's or 50's asked me to sign an initiative petition about horse slaughter. I said yes, and signed what I thought was the horse slaughter petition. The petition was on a clipboard the man was holding. I saw only one clipboard. After I signed, the man asked me to sign a petition about marriage. I told him no and walked away."

The horse people were so desperate for affidavits that they even submitted one from a Framingham woman, Janet Drake, who said she was not tricked. That woman first surfaced with her allegations the previous year in an article in *Bay Windows*. Her affidavit said, "I said I did not want to sign that petition, I wanted to sign the horse petition. Finally, the man gave me the horse petition, with the letter 'A' in the lower right, and I signed it."

Judge Considers Case for One Week

The judge considered the case for a week before dismissing it. The hearing had taken place on April 19.

Judge Connolly had not appeared to be impressed at the hearing and pointed out that it was the horse people who hired the signature gatherers. "Assuming fraud took place," he said, "it would be by employees of the company. It is the fraud of the people you hired, not fraud by the Commonwealth."

At least one representative from the radical homosexual legal group, GLAD, was present at the hearing, lending credence to the claim that the horse issue was manufactured by opponents of the Marriage Amendment in order to smear the measure.

One of the plaintiffs, Anita Constantine-Gay, denied that she is a lesbian. She told *Massachusetts News*, "My signature was stolen. I agreed to sign a petition to save horses. Instead, I was tricked into signing one, which was hurtful to decent people. That is the source of my outrage." She said she "flipped out" after she learned through a gay activist web site that her name was on the marriage petition. She said she learned about the website through the *Boston Globe*.

The horse people presented nothing new at the hearing to bolster their claim that thousands of people intending to sign their petition were defrauded.

California Lawyer Argues for Horses

Arguing for Save Our Horses, Attorneys Lowell Finley, from California, and Dan Small said that the paid signature gatherers had tricked people into signing the Protection of Marriage petition, instead of the horse petition.

They said that the wrong message would be sent to the voters if the fraud succeeds. They also said that there was still time for the legislature to consider the horse petition if the court forced the issue.

The attorneys produced an affidavit given to them the day before by State Sen. Diane Wilkerson. She said that there was still time for the legislature to act on the horse petition if the court ordered the Secretary of the Commonwealth to certify it.

But the judge was not impressed with that either. He noted that Wilkerson's affidavit only said it was "possible" that the legislature had enough time to act on the petition should he force the certification.

"Possible is a wide range," said Connolly, who said that it was only one legislator's opinion. "I'd like to have the Senate President or Speaker agree with that statement."

The attorneys said their evidence consisted of affidavits from:

• "Victims" of signature fraud.

• Voter witnesses to "fraud."

• A paid signature gatherer who says he was trained on how to obtain signatures fraudulently, although he didn't do so.

• A direct mail expert, who said the one thousand alleged responses to 28,000 questionnaires sent out by the horse group looking for victims, represents a much larger number of people who were victims.

Secretary Was Concerned but Not Convinced

Arguing for the other side, Assistant Attorneys General Richard Weitzel and Peter Sacks said that the defendant, Secretary William Galvin, was obviously concerned by the allegations of fraud but was bound by constitutional restrictions. He must enforce the basic rule, with no room for compromise, that the initiative petition must bear 57,100 certified signatures.

The lawyers said that the horse people were relying on "statistical analysis" as evidence of fraud. A projection based on the number of responses to a questionnaire mailed out by the horse people is unreliable evidence, they said.

Each signature on the successful marriage petition was certified and represented the will of the voters, said the defense. Each signature on the marriage petition allegedly obtained through fraud would have to be withdrawn on an individual basis, necessitating evidence in the form of sworn courtroom testimony from each of the alleged 2,574 victims.

The Secretary felt the evidence was not competent or sufficient, and there was a lot of hearsay based on statements from the Save Our Horses director. The one thousand alleged responses were not signed, and there was no assurance they were from actual voters. Solid evidence was required.

The time factor was also critical, they said. The plaintiffs waited until the last minute to force this matter, even though they had been making allegations since November. The legislature should not have to jump through hoops, but should give any ballot question meaningful consideration over a reasonable period of time. Two weeks is not sufficient.

After the hearing, Assistant Attorney General Peter Sacks told *Massachusetts News*, "We do not feel that plaintiffs met their burden to show that enough people were defrauded. Plaintiffs have offered some reason to believe that some people were defrauded. To prove that anyone has been defrauded, we would need to see actual evidence."

Sacks said actual evidence would have to come on an individual basis in courtroom testimony.

Horse petition attorney Lowell Finley told *Massachusetts News*, "We're pleased how the argument went. The judge is obviously giving the matter careful consideration. We're hopeful for a positive outcome."

12

Horse Trial Showed That "Fraud" Was a Hoax

The hearing that took place before Judge Connolly on April 19 failed to convince him, or anyone, that there was evidence of "fraud" in the gathering of signatures for the Protection of Marriage Amendment.

Although the judge didn't explicitly say it, the entire event was clearly seen after the trial as a hoax, a scam, if you will, concocted by the New York Times Company, with the intent of defeating the Amendment.

Attorney General Reilly also indicated that he didn't agree with the charges of "fraud" that had been created out of his News Release. It was clear that he disagreed with the *Times'* and *Globe's* spin of the News Release. It really was an innocuous document, as we said. The Attorney General didn't read much into it.

There was no question that The New York Times Company was guilty of deceit and libel for attempting to make the Release into something different. The harassment from Save Our Horses mostly ended after April 19. The Company tried a new method of assault against the Amendment after that. But they will continue forever the claim of questionable signature gathering if they are permitted to do so.

Immediate Investigation Requested by MCM

Just before the *New York Times* story broke, Sally wrote a letter to Secretary of State William Galvin, encouraging him to begin an immediate investigation into the charge by Susan Wagner and Save Our Horses that unfair practices were being used by Sally against them.

Galvin did not institute an investigation that would result in any charges against Wagner, but he did have the Attorney General investigate the charges that were contained in Wagner's suit against him and the Commonwealth.

As a result, the Attorney General and the Secretary of State repudiated the claims of Save Our Horses.

Sally wrote: "It is common knowledge in any political campaign that false charges and smears are always hurled, by those who are prone to do so, during the final week before the election. They hope that the candidate will not be able to respond in time.

"Inasmuch as this is exactly one week before our 'election,' which begins next Wednesday, April 10, with a Legislative hearing about our Protection of Marriage Amendment, the recent actions by 'Save Our Horses' fit the pattern exactly.

"It appears that our opponents — of which 'Save Our Horses' is now most prominent — hope to hurl baseless charges in order to create smokescreens at the Wednesday hearing.

"We ask that you conduct an investigation to examine the evidence which 'Save Our Horses' asserts in support of their lawsuit which was just filed against you.

"We request that you begin this investigation immediately and complete it as quickly as possible.

"As you know, the statements made to the media by 'Save Our Horses' have never contained either names or facts.

"Over the past five months since last November, they have complained repeatedly that a substantial number of people signed our petition while thinking they were signing the horse petition. We have waited vainly for over five months for *any* proof of those charges. But none has been forthcoming.

"Nevertheless, now that a suit has been filed against you — still without any proof of the charges — we must request that your office undertake an immediate and thorough investigation of this matter.

"We sincerely believe that any deliberate effort to manipulate our election process should be prosecuted fully.

"We support punishing those who deceive the public, whether it is by some form of trickery in collecting signatures or by making unsubstantiated and false charges to the media.

"But the time for speculation concerning this deceptive practice has long since passed. If 'Save Our Horses' has proof of any fraudulent practice, they should present it to you immediately. We do not understand why this was not done during the critical period of certification of the petitions by your office.

"Most of the signatures on our petitions were gathered by unpaid volunteers outside churches and shopping malls across Massachusetts.

"At the time this charge first surfaced, we contacted the contractor and asked if such practices were being used by him. The contractor denied using any of the deceptive techniques described by the horse group to the media. We also dispatched members of our staff to various locations to observe the contractor's employees. Our employees saw no evidence of any of the deceptive practices described by the horse group to reporters.

"Mr. Secretary, we ask that you carefully examine the charges and the documentation, which we assume, will be made public, at some point in the future, by 'Save Our Horses.'"

Please Check These

Sally requested an examination of the following:

• "The relationship between those who have complained about this alleged deception and organizations such as the National Organization for Women (NOW), American Civil Liberties Union, the Campaign for Equality, Citizens for Participation in Political Action, the Freedom to Marry Coalition and Foundation, the Human Rights Campaign Fund, the Gay and Lesbian Advocates and Defenders (GLAD), the Massachusetts AFL-CIO, Massachusetts Lesbian and Gay Bar Association, National Gay and Lesbian Task Force, Norwood-Walpole Citizens for All Families, Partners Task Force for Gay and Lesbian Couples, Religious Coalition for the Freedom to Marry, the Vermont Freedom to Marry Task Force and other organizations opposed to the Protection of Marriage Amendment.

• "The results of the mailing to signers of the Protection of Marriage Petition by 'Save Our Horses' asking signers if they (1) intended to sign the horse petition, (2) did not intend to sign the Protection of Marriage

Tens of thousands of these letters were sent to people who had signed the Marriage Petition, telling them that they may have been tricked into signing. This letter went to Sally and me at our home. Note that someone had gone to the expense of computerizing the database so that every family received only one letter. They also enclosed a return envelope with a first class stamp attached.

petition and did not know why their name appears there or (3) intended to sign both the horse and Protection of Marriage petitions.

• "The scope, cost and information about who funded the recent 'Save Our Horses' mailing to our signers and the relationship between the funding of this extensive mailing and the National Organization for Women (NOW), American Civil Liberties Union, the Campaign for Equality, Citizens for Participation in Political Action, the Freedom to Mary Coalition and Foundation, the Human Rights Campaign Fund, the Gay and Lesbian Advocates and Defenders (GLAD), the Massachusetts AFL-CIO, Massachusetts Lesbian and Gay Bar

Association, National Gay and Lesbian Task Force, Norwood-Walpole Citizens for All Families, Partners Task Force for Gay and Lesbian Couples, Religious Coalition for the Freedom to Marry and the Vermont Freedom to Marry Task Force or any other organizations opposed to the Protection of Marriage Amendment.

"It is estimated by experts that the recent mailing to our supporters by 'Save Our Horses' cost them approximately $1.31 apiece, unless they are in collusion with those who opposed the Amendment. The very fact that a computer was used to manipulate the list of signers so that not more than one letter was sent to a household (even though more than one person had signed the Petition) indicates that they undoubtedly worked with someone who provided them with a corrected mailing list."

13

Pinch's Illegal Strategy on Gay Marriage Flew in the Face of Democracy

Pinch Sulzberger's silly charges of "fraud" were a total failure. In addition, *Massachusetts News* pointed out that the charges were libelous, in both the *Globe* and now the *Times*.

Therefore, in May 2002, Sulzberger's people suddenly switched strategies. No longer talking about "fraud" after the spring of 2002, they went to a new lie on May 2. The *Boston Globe* reported at that time that one man, Senator Thomas Birmingham, had the power to kill the Marriage Amendment all by himself, because he was the person in charge when the legislature considered Amendments.

They were desperate. This was the only way Pinch could possibly win. He would coerce the legislature into violating the state Constitution and breaking the law. But Senator Birmingham couldn't accomplish that all by himself without any help. He needed "cover" in order to do so. Therefore, the *Globe* kept repeating the new lie, that this one person had the legal power to discard a referendum petition which had been signed by 130,000 citizens after great effort and expense.

This also had an added benefit for Pinch: It made the activists for the Amendment, such as Sally Pawlick, MCM, and others, look like liars when they attempted to point out the truth, that the scheme was highly illegal. This new lie by the *Globe* was not as clearly libelous as the "fraud" charges had been, but it was certainly a question of fact for a jury (not a judge) to decide in that this was also a lie which damaged the reputation for honesty and accuracy of the Amendment's supporters.

The main problem for Pinch was that Senator Birmingham, who is a lawyer, knew that the scheme that the *Globe* had hatched for him was not really viable. He knew that such power did not reside in him; he could accomplish this only if he would break the law and violate the state Constitution.

In the May 2 article in the *Globe*, he was quoted, "I'm exploring ways to stop it, but I also think that we're sent here to vote on things." The story said he was aware of "the constitutional process for the Legislature to deal with such proposals" and he was "leaning toward allowing the measure to come up before the full Legislature."

Pinch's *Globe* didn't agree that a vote should be allowed. Its news article explained:

"[B]irmingham will have full control over the agenda. Some gay leaders want Birmingham to use that power to ensure that the amendment never reaches the voters, where they fear it would pass. ... <u>As Senate president, Birmingham could choose to not schedule a proposed amendment for a vote</u>, which would scuttle the measure." [Emphasis added]

That was not true, of course. If he had that power, he could also "choose" to take a gun and shoot Sally Pawlick and any legislator who voted for the Amendment. Both would be breaking the law.

This went way beyond "interpretation" in a news story. It presented a legal opinion without any attribution whatsoever.

But Pinch's people kept assuring the citizens that this was a perfectly moral and legal thing to do.

Flies in the Face of Democracy

It doesn't take a genius to see that this philosophy flies in the face of a democratic government. Senator Birmingham knew that it was the Democratic Party, plus the liberals and Progressives, who had led the way in 1918 for the voters to have the power of the referendum. They were all very enthusiastic. The inspiring saga of that Convention would make a fascinating novel or movie.

Anyone who reads the record of the debates that occurred back then is struck by the goodwill of all those diverse delegates, liberal and conservative, as they strove to make their state a better place. They had vastly different viewpoints as to how to accomplish their common goal.

They had not sought consensus. They had argued and debated with passion for two years and had finally come up with a plan about which they could all be excited. In the end, the conservatives joined in passing the referendum plan they had all crafted.

Like John Adams and the other founders of our country, they were under no delusion about human beings. They knew that humans, bar none, are weak and corruptible. That's why they gave us a government of laws, not men, with many checks and balances.

They entrusted it to us in 1918, knowing all of our weaknesses. But this scheme in 2002 by Pinch Sulzberger was returning us to pre-1918 and its smoke-filled rooms.

All the delegates spoke with great enthusiasm in 1918 about their belief that the people should be involved in the process of initiating amendments. Before then, an amendment required the approval of a majority of both the House (160 members) and the Senate (40 members). This meant that 21 members in the Senate could block any amendment. They were commonly referred to as "twenty-one willful men." Everyone agreed that this had to change, but many feared giving the power completely to the people by referendum.

So they came up with a compromise. The two bodies would sit together with only 25% of the joint session being necessary to approve an Amendment which was initiated by a petition of the voters. It would then go on the ballot for the voters to decide by a majority vote. It is ironic that one delegate said that this procedure would alert the citizens to the issue because it would require a "real debate" in the Legislature. But in 2002, under the leadership of Pinch Sulzberger, not only didn't it get a "real" debate, it got no debate at all.

The delegates couldn't foresee everything because the same delegate said: "I do not believe we need to consider seriously ... a defiance of the provisions of the amendment by either of these two branches of the [legislature]."

This indicates that although they did have problems in 1918 with the Legislature, they could not even _conceive_ of the problems that we face today in Massachusetts.

<u>They believed that no one could be _that_ crooked.</u>

14

What Were the Libelous Stories from Pinch's Boston Globe?

Was Pinch's campaign against the Protection of Marriage Amendment successful?

No! It was never successful in its primary purpose of changing the beliefs of the citizens of Massachusetts. However, it was very successful in providing "cover" for the politicians of the state so that they became emboldened enough to refuse to follow the state Constitution.

After all, the *Boston Globe* said it was legal. In addition, when the Supreme Judicial Court ruled on December 20, 2002, that the politicians' shenanigans had violated the Constitution, the *Globe* reported exactly the opposite. Almost everyone in Massachusetts still believes that lie.

The article that appeared in the *New York Times* newspaper was damaging but Pinch got really serious in the fifteen articles printed by the *Boston Globe*.

After all, Sally Pawlick and the others at MCM were threatening an important goal of Pinch's for the entire United States.

His goal had been clearly stated:

> In time, Vermont's example will show the rest of the country that same-sex unions are not a threat to traditional marriage and deserve the name of marriage as well as the law's full protection.

His opinion of the Amendment that had been proposed in

Massachusetts was also clear:

> Legislators should see this measure as the mean-spirited attack on a minority that it is and reject it.

Horses and Fraud Stories Ran First

The horses and "fraud" libel ran five times from November 21, 2001 to April 25, 2002, one of those times in the National Sunday Edition of the *New York Times*.

Pinch finally ended that line of attack after I pointed out in *Massachusetts News* that the April 7 story in the *Times* was libelous. We had no desire to sue Pinch Sulzberger; we wanted him to stop this uncivilized behavior. All we desired was a fair chance for the citizens to vote on the Amendment. Either up or down, it was their choice. But we would tolerate no interference from outside bullies.

(If anyone wishes to read any of the following stories in their entirety and determine if I report them accurately, they can be obtained very quickly and easily from the *Globe* website for $1 to $3, depending upon the quantity you buy.)

November 21, 2001 "Battle over gay marriage petition gets ugly."

The first story that appeared in the *Globe* having anything at all to do with the Marriage Amendment came near the end of the signature-gathering period, on the front page of the Metro section. It set the stage for defeating the Amendment by accusing it of fraud. It maliciously gave the impression that its supporters were lying and using deceptive practices, particularly in regard to those who wanted to sign the horse petition and had been "tricked" into signing the plaintiffs' petition. The hoax about horses was promoted by the *Globe* as a true story even after it became clear that it was a hoax. The only reason the hoax was successful was because the *Globe* kept repeating it. The first story said "the current campaign is already ugly," implying that that was so because of the supporters of the Amendment.

January 9, 2002. "Accusations swirl on petition tactics."

Immediately after the signatures on the petitions were authenticated and the Amendment was certified to the legislature for its vote, the same reporter wrote a second story about the horse hoax. This appeared on the front page of the City & Region section, although there was nothing new to report.

March 26, 2002. <u>**"Horse lovers say they were duped."**</u>

Two weeks before the Legislature held its hearing on the Amendment (and twelve days before the story by the *Times*), the *Globe* published another story about the horse hoax by the same reporter.

Although the horse people themselves were careful never to *directly* implicate the plaintiffs, reasonable readers would assume that the *Globe* had checked the facts and kept running these bogus charges because the plaintiffs were guilty of fraud.

The horse people also kept up the hoax that they had been cheated. After six months of publicity, they were able to report the names of only 13 people (although they loudly and falsely claimed with the help of the defendant, to know hundreds, even thousands, out of over 130,000 who had signed the marriage petition) who said they had been tricked into signing. The horse people sent letters to 6,000 signers of the Marriage Amendment on February 21, to 2,438 more signers on March 15 and a final 19,613 on March 23. The letters were intended to discourage the signers of the Amendment and to impact the hearings in the legislature. The horse people began a suit against the Commonwealth, but that was dismissed in Suffolk Superior Court at the end of April (a fact which has never been reported by the *Globe*).

April 7, 2002. <u>**"Drive to Ban Gay Marriage Is Accused of Duping Signers."**</u>

The *New York Times* ran its "fraud" and "horses" story on April 7.

April 25, 2002. <u>**"Same Sex Marriage Ban Dealt a Setback."**</u>

When the legislative committee voted against the Amendment 15-0 (two abstained because they favored the Amendment, but that was not reported), the *Globe* repeated the horse hoax with these three closing paragraphs:

"The ballot question has attracted considerable controversy recently: Workers trying to gather the 57,100 signatures required to get it on the ballot have been accused of misleading some voters, telling them they were signing a petition to protect horses from slaughter instead. Members of the Save Our Horses campaign have sued the state because their signatures had been diverted to the marriage question, keeping their own initiative off the ballot.

"At the end of its written decision, the committee said members were concerned about the manner in which the signatures had been gathered, and that the process 'calls into question the fairness and legitimacy of the process itself.'

"Pawlick wrote that that claim was yet another 'unfounded' charge, and that only a handful of people thought they were signing a petition against horse slaughter."

Two more stories were only possibly libelous.

March 22, 2002 **"Romney kin signed petition to ban same-sex marriage."**

They continued the hoax that only "bad people" supported the Amendment with this story which put gubernatorial candidate Mitt Romney on the defensive.

April 11, 2002. **"Three priests oppose ban on gay marriage."**

The day after the hearing before the Legislature, the lead paragraph in the *Globe* was that three priests (out of about 1000 in the Archdiocese) opposed the Amendment.

Second Group of Stories Began on May 2

The next group of stories were mostly published during the summer of 2002 to falsely assure us that the President of the Senate had the lawful power to kill the Amendment by not allowing a vote in the joint session of the legislature.

May 2, 2002. **"Birmingham pressured to block same-sex marriage."**

The day after the Amendment was first considered by the full Legislature, the *Globe* wrote that gays were pressuring the Senator to kill the Amendment. The story indicated that Birmingham could just kill the measure — without any indication this would violate the state Constitution. "Because the Senate president presides over the full House and Senate when the bodies sit together as a constitutional convention, Birmingham will have full control over the agenda. Some gay leaders want Birmingham to use that power to ensure that the Amendment never reaches the voters, where they fear it could pass. ... As Senate president, Birmingham could choose to not schedule a proposed Amendment for a vote, which would scuttle the measure. Or he could use more subtle means of squashing it, rallying allies behind the scenes and then putting it up for a vote when he knows it wouldn't get the support it needs to pass."

Although the "more subtle means of squashing it" might be unfair and undemocratic, it would be legal, whereas not scheduling it for a vote would be a violation of the law. Birmingham indicated to the *Globe* that he preferred to follow the law.

June 14, 2002. "SJC ruling upholds marriage ballot measure."

The *Globe* reported that the SJC unanimously upheld the Atty. General's decision that this measure was proper for the ballot. This was reported accurately by the *Globe*. We included it in the documents we gave Judge Saris in order that she would have a complete picture.

June 20, 2002. "Birmingham blocks a vote on marriage."

The *Globe* reported the Constitutional Convention of the entire legislature, on June 19, where MCM had 200 spectators in the gallery who erupted in disbelief when Birmingham adjourned to July 17. The *Globe* wrote: "But the process can be strictly controlled by the Senate President ... If the vote isn't taken by the end of the current session on July 31, the Amendment will be dead."

July 16, 2002. "An ugly amendment"

On the day before the Constitutional Convention of July 17 (where 500 pro-Amendment spectators appeared in favor of the Amendment and witnessed the legislature violate the Constitution), an editorial was headlined "An ugly amendment." It first "covered itself" by saying that the Legislature should obey the Constitution and have a vote (which, of course, did not happen). Then it wrote, "However, legislators must focus on the merits — or, in this case, the ugly demerits — of the proposal. They cannot vote simply to pass the decision along to the electorate. The Constitution, by giving them veto power over constitu-

Birmingham looking to block gay marriage ban

By Chris Tangney
GLOBE CORRESPONDENT

Despite charges that he is thwarting democracy, Senate President Thomas F. Birmingham yesterday refused to rule out once again preventing a vote on a ballot question that would ban gay marriage.

On the eve of tomorrow's constitutional convention, Birmingham said he is seeking ways to defeat the measure, which he called "hateful" and "mean-spirited." Birmingham, who controls the agenda at constitutional conventions, last month refused to allow a vote on the measure, which outraged supporters of the ballot question.

Birmingham said he is strategizing with other opponents on ways to block the question from advancing tomorrow, but he would not detail their plans. The measure needs support from 25 percent of legislators in two successive sessions

to be placed on the ballot.

"I'm going to do what I can to defeat it," he said. "Our options are open."

Birmingham and gay rights groups appear to lack the votes to defeat the measure, so they are seeking other ways to impede it. Birmingham's maneuvers irk backers of the gay marriage ban, who accuse him of denying the public's right to vote on the question. Supporters of the marriage proposal collected approximately 130,000 signatures to place the question before voters in the 2004 election. Without a vote by the end of this year, the measure would not make the ballot.

"Tom Birmingham is using the constitutional convention, manipulating it, and taking advantage of procedure," said James Lafferty, spokesman for Massachusetts Citizens for Marriage. "The voters deserve the ability to make a

GAY MARRIAGE, Page B8

The day before the July 17th Convention, the Globe incorrectly put in a front-page story that the Senate President, Tom Birmingham, could "delay a vote indefinitely." It was clear he could not do so unless he violated the law.

---

tional amendments, demands a vote of conscience, not a rubber stamp. Legislators should see this measure as the mean-spirited attack on a minority that it is and reject it."

July 16, 2002. **"Birmingham looking to block gay marriage ban."**

The day before the Constitutional Convention, the paper wrote, "Birmingham and gay rights groups appear to lack the votes to defeat the measure, so they are seeking other ways to impede it. *** but Birmingham can delay a vote indefinitely."

July 18, 2002. <u>"Gay Marriage Ban Thwarted."</u>

After the Convention, the *Globe* wrote in the lead story on page one under the headline, "Gay marriage ban thwarted. Legislators kill ballot question," that a "procedural maneuver" had been used to defeat the measure. It was not a "procedural maneuver" but a violation of the state Constitution. The legislators were required to vote on the measure, which they did not do.

December 3, 2002. <u>"Swift to seek ruling on gay marriage issue."</u>

On the day when I was in front of the full SJC arguing that they must order the Secretary of State to send the Amendment on to the next legislature because the 2002 session had forfeited its right to vote, Governor Jane Swift suddenly filed papers asking the SJC for an advisory opinion on her duties. This was exactly the same relief that I had been requesting for Sally and MCM since July and was finally arguing before the full court on that day. (Sen. Birmingham filed a similar request two days later.)

Reporter Yvonne Abraham again reported in her story about the Governor's request that the Amendment had been killed by a "procedural maneuver."

December 21, 2002. <u>"SJC Declines to weigh in on gay marriage ballot debate."</u>

The *Globe* wrote another story by Yvonne Abraham which was totally wrong. It effectively put MCM out of business. On the previous day, the SJC had released its Advisory Opinion to Gov. Swift. It stated that the legislature had violated the Constitution on July 17 when they did not vote, and the Governor had also violated it since that time by not calling the solons back into session for the required vote. The Advisory Opinion by the SJC said that the action by the legislature on July 17 had not been a "final action" as required by the Constitution and there must be a "final action" by December 31.

This was exactly what I had been seeking: a statement from the SJC that Sen. Birmingham and the legislature had violated the law on July 17. That was a huge victory for the plaintiffs, but the *Globe* "spun" it away.

Sen. Birmingham had submitted a 20-page brief to the SJC in which his counsel, David E. Sullivan, had argued only one point. He

Lowe stymies Devil Rays, as Red Sox coast to 6-1 victory — Sports, C1

VOLUME 262
NUMBER 18
50 cents

The Boston Globe

NEVER SAY DRY
TODAY: *Mix of sun and clouds, humid, storms possible*
TOMORROW: *Mostly cloudy, cooler, could be some showers*
HIGH TIDE: 6:27 a.m., 9:36 p.m.
FULL REPORT: Page B12

THURSDAY, JULY 18, 2002

2 suicide blasts kill 5 in Tel Aviv

By Charles A. Radin
GLOBE STAFF

TEL AVIV — Two Palestinian suicide bombers blew themselves up one after the other outside a convenience store in a low-income area of south Tel Aviv last night, killing two foreign workers, one Israeli, and themselves.

It was the first time in months that terrorists have attacked a target in Israel's largest city, and the first time in recent memory that the double-bomber assault — used to maximize casualties by setting off a second bomb among people fleeing the first explosion — has been employed here.

More than 40 people were wounded by the blasts, which occurred a few minutes after 10 p.m. on Tisha B'Av, a solemn day of mourning and fasting on which Jews mark the destruction of the great temples built by Solomon and Herod in Jerusalem.

It was unclear whether Tel Aviv's Neve Sha'anan neighborhood was targeted because the rest of the city was closed for the fast or because foreign workers have largely replaced Palestinians from the occupied territories who worked in Israel before the current, 22-month-long Palestinian uprising.

Tens of thousands of these Palestinians will never regain employment in Israel, Israeli analysts say, even if there is a settlement of Israeli-Palestinian disputes.

Al-Manar, the Hezbollah television station in Beirut, reported that Islamic Jihad claimed responsibility for the attack, which followed by a day an assault on a bus at the gates of the West Bank settlement of Emmanuel for which four Palestinian groups claimed responsibility.

Eight Israelis, all but one of them mothers and children, were killed in that attack, in the subsequent manhunt, Israeli soldiers killed one of the Palestinian suspects in a clash yesterday that left
MIDEAST, Page A26

In a matter of minutes, half a family is wiped out

By Dan Ephron
GLOBE CORRESPONDENT

EMMANUEL SETTLEMENT, West Bank — The blast knocked Ayelet Shilon, her mother, and three children out of their seats and onto the floor of bus No. 189, just a few yards from the entrance to this Israeli settlement in the West Bank.

With bullets penetrating soft sections of the armored vehicle, her first instinct was to stretch her small frame over her children to shield them — a move that probably saved the lives of two of them.

But Shilon's next decision to dial her cellphone and call her husband probably left her a widow.

Like other victims of Palestinian violence over the last 22 months, settlers aboard the afternoon bus to Emmanuel on Tuesday faced a sudden torrent of carnage during what should have been a routine event — a ride home.

Among those killed was the youngest victim yet of the current spate of Israeli-Palestinian violence — a nine-hour old baby, whose birth was induced because his mother was shot and wounded by the gunmen. The infant died because his mother lost too much blood.

The Shilons also paid a heavy price. Ayelet Shilon's mother and daughter were killed in the spasm of bullets and grenades aboard the vehicle. Her husband died trying to
SETTLEMENT, Page A26

Gay marriage ban thwarted

By Yvonne Abraham

A scuffle erupted as people on both sides of the gay marriage issue were waiting to get into the House gallery for yesterday's vote.
GLOBE STAFF PHOTO/DAVID L. RYAN

Legislators kill ballot question

By Yvonne Abraham
GLOBE STAFF

Legislators yesterday used a procedural maneuver to kill a ballot question that sought to amend the state constitution to ban gay marriage, brushing aside 130,000 signatures from voters supporting the measure and turning a deaf ear to the hollers of hundreds of

supporters.

The legislative opponents of the ballot question, led by Senate President Thomas F. Birmingham, lacked the votes necessary to defeat it outright. Instead they voted 137-53 to adjourn the constitutional convention indefinitely, effectively blocking the question from appearing on the election ballot.

"It was wrong-hearted and wrong-headed," said Birmingham, a Chelsea Democrat, of the ballot question.

The legislators' move was a victory for gay-rights activists but set off anger from the hundreds of supporters of the ballot question assembled at the State House yesterday. They had gathered twice to put the question on the 2004 election ballot. The question also needed approval from 25 percent of House and Senate members at a constitutional convention during this legislative session and next to be placed before voters.

The ballot question appeared

to have that support, and more, but no vote was taken on the question itself.

"We had the votes today," said James Lafferty, spokesman for Massachusetts Citizens for Marriage, which had backed the amendment. "Mr. Birmingham has once again blocked the people of Massachusetts out of the process."

In a written statement, C.J. Doyle of the Catholic Action League accused Birmingham of
AMENDMENT, Page A24

The day after the Convention, the Globe said that a "procedural maneuver" had been used to defeat the Amendment. It was not a "procedural maneuver" but a violation of the state Constitution. The legislators were required to vote on the measure, which they did not do. The Globe was encouraging them to break the law.

argued that the vote to adjourn was the "final action" required by the Constitution. This, of course, was totally rebuffed by the SJC in its opinion to the Governor. The *Globe* story was an enormous spin job (only four days before Christmas when everyone was preoccupied with many other things). It was accepted by everyone, including the staunch supporters of MCM in the legislature, as the truth. They didn't know any better. Everyone still believes the *Globe's* spin today.

The Governor had also inquired whether she could refuse to call the legislature back if she believed that such an order from her would be "futile." That was what the *Globe* jumped on to mislead its readers. Basically, the Court had told the Governor: "We're not going to do all your work for you. You decide whether it's futile."

We must remember that this Governor had done absolutely nothing to encourage the legislature to obey the Constitution. The SJC noted its displeasure with her for waiting over four months before submitting her request. (And Justice Greaney later asked me at oral argument why I thought she had waited so long.)

But the *Globe* reported the story with this headline: "SJC declines to weigh in on gay marriage ballot debate." The story began with this sentence:

> In a ruling released yesterday, the state Supreme Judicial Court declined to say whether Acting Governor Jane Swift must recall legislators to a special session to consider a ballot question that would ban gay marriage. The ruling by the state's highest court left state officials uncertain about what steps they should take next on the measure. Responding to a question posed by Swift, the court ruled that a procedural maneuver used by Senate President Thomas F. Birmingham to block the question from reaching the state ballot last summer was not the final action on the matter.

> But the court did not specifically address the question of whether Swift now has a duty to call legislators back to vote on the matter. That ambiguity left Swift and Birmingham pointing fingers at each other last night, with a spokesman for each suggesting the ball is now in the other's court.

> If neither takes action to reconvene legislators, the ballot question will die Dec. 31. As of late yesterday, neither Swift nor Birmingham appeared eager to act on the controversial measure.

Here, three parties were colluding on what the SJC had said. All three of them, Swift, Birmingham and the *Globe* wanted the Amendment to be defeated. They were working for a common cause.

Yvonne Abraham used the words, "procedural maneuver" twice in this story, even though she was holding in her hand the opinion from the SJC, which said that it was much more than that, it was a violation of the Constitution.

PART III

Decay of New York Times
and
Supreme Judicial Court

Section IV

Who's Standing Behind the Curtain?

When attempting to discover why The New York Times Company lied, cheated and violated the law in order to paint decent citizens as criminals and intimidate the Massachusetts state legislature in 2001-2003, we cannot ignore who owns the newspaper.

It's not a mysterious group of gods sitting on a mountain peak. It's just good old Punch and/or Pinch Sulzberger hiding behind the curtain, just like the "Grand Wizard" in the *Wizard of Oz.*

Many readers will quickly laugh and say that is <u>ridiculous</u>. They will retort that those who work at the *Times* and the *Globe* are "intelligent, competent people." <u>However, no one is denying that</u>. Of course they are capable people. But <u>all</u> of them were handpicked by Punch or Pinch, who could just as easily have chosen other "intelligent, competent people" with ***diverse and totally different worldviews***. Those types of people do exist. But the people at the *Times* have been screened very carefully to be sure that they <u>all</u> tell the world only what the Publisher, whether it be Punch or Pinch, believes.

We do know that Punch disagrees strongly with his son on many issues, but not enough to pick a Publisher who is not a family member.

There is no longer *anyone* with the viewpoint of the "loyal opposition" on the *Times* staff (except for a token columnist or two).

Punch told how it all works in an interview with Edwin Diamond: "I don't believe in telling editors or reporters what to do. But I do believe in long, philosophic conversations with my editors

THE PRIVATE AND POWERFUL FAMILY BEHIND

The New York Times

THE TRUST

Susan E. Tifft
and Alex S. Jones

This is an outstanding book about the family behind the curtain at the New York Times. Although it is out-of-print, used copies are available at Amazon and other Internet sites. The picture is of Adolph Ochs and his wife, with their daughter, Iphigene and her family. Her husband, Arthur Sulzberger, stands beside her. The children are Marian, Ruth, Punch and Judy. The New York Times Building is pictured on the left.

about where the paper, the city and the country are going. We had those discussions all the time."

Adolph Would Not Be Happy

If you still believe that the *New York Times* is an impartial "newspaper of record" that can be trusted implicitly, you had better rethink that feeling because what you see today is not what Adolph had in mind.

The story of the *Times* is the story of the typical entrepreneur, excited and bubbling as he builds a business — then bored and restless as he discovers that his job has become tedious and has changed to managing, and keeping happy, all his employees — *and his college-age daughter*, his only child. The knowledgeable entrepreneur will quickly sell his business when he reaches that point.

This was especially difficult for entrepreneur Adolph Ochs because he wanted to keep control of the business even after his death. That resulted in great frustration and unhappiness for him.

Adolph never became a real New Yorker. A simple man, he loved Chattanooga and always felt his roots to be there. He never gave up his newspaper in Tennessee. Even after forty years in New York, he still felt that Chattanooga was "home" and his final resting place, until he discovered that members of his son-in-law's aristocratic family were buried in a cemetery near his getaway home in Westchester County. That changed his mind on the subject. When it came time to pick his successor at the *Times*, he wanted to choose his nephew from Chattanooga, a Princeton graduate who had been a hero in World War I and was simple, straightforward and honest like Adolph. But he did not want to hurt his daughter. Her husband, a handsome ladies' man, who evaded the War while strutting around stateside in his uniform, changed the *Times* from Adolph's vision into something much different; a broadside of his and his wife's opinions.

Despite the genius of Adolph, many members of the Ochs/Sulzberger family have always been behind the scene, pushing their own agenda, whether it was daughter Iphigene, nephew John, son-in-law Arthur, granddaughter Marian, granddaughter-in-law Carol or Babs, grandson Punch or any of a myriad of clamoring voices from the hundreds of relatives. It was impossible to discern the many cliques and whether they really liked you, your power and your money, or whether they knew the answer to that themselves.

The news and the editorials at the *Times* have always been a synthesis of the views of the Ochs/Sulzberger family. But it got much worse after Adolph died. At that point, the paper consciously moved away from his attempt at an impartial, balanced publication into one where reporters were told to "interpret" the news when they wrote their articles. And, of course, the family was the final arbiter.

But, even after that change, there had been a balance, with a humility and belief in the basic traditions of our society.

Pinch has none of that humility. He rejects what his family, including his father and all the previous publishers, has believed for centuries.

You need not trust what I am telling you. If you wish to discover who is behind the curtain at the *Times*, a good start would be any of the following five books. When Joseph C. Goulden wrote his book on the *Times*, he first read eleven lineal feet of books about the newspaper. So there are plenty to choose from. The major problem is that most were written by newspaper people. Even if they are unbiased and critical, they all stand in awe of the *Times*, as though it is the icon of journalists everywhere. The book you are now holding is the first by an outside observer, a journalist who is not involved with the general-interest news business, and therefore, not concerned about ruffling feathers.

Another important caution is to remember that most of what is in the books was, by necessity, told to the authors by the people involved. We can be certain that very few of those individuals said anything that would put themselves in a bad light. The books listed below are out-of-print but are easily obtained at ridiculously low prices at Amazon.com.

The Trust, The Private and Powerful Family Behind The New York _Times_ by the husband/wife team of Susan E. Tifft and Alex S. Jones is extraordinary, all 870-pages. It covers the entire period from the purchase of the *Times* in 1896 by the present family until 1999, when this book was published. As a side benefit, the reader gets a fascinating history lesson of the United States as the story unfolds. As a negative, the sad lives of these people are extremely depressing. If anyone wishes to write a soap opera, this would be an unbelievable source of material.

The authors don't appear to withhold anything, including the most personal facts. They spent seven years researching the book and conducted 550 interviews, all of the people being listed in the back of the book. The only problem is that the liberal bias of the authors comes shining through at times. But a bias is inevitable, no matter who would write it.

Tifft was a press secretary for the 1980 Democratic National Convention and a speechwriter for the Carter/Mondale campaign. She was an associate editor at *Time* from 1982-1991. Jones covered the press for *The New York Times* from 1983 to 1992, winning a Pulitzer Prize. He is now associated with the Joan Shorenstein Center on the Press, Politics, and Public Policy at Harvard University. Both are currently at Duke University. Jones has long family ties in North Carolina, as apparently does his wife.

Their book was written "with the full cooperation" of the Sulzberger family and has much fascinating and revealing information about this American institution.

<u>*Behind the Times, Inside the New New York Times*</u> Comparatively short at 394-pages, this book by Edwin Diamond is a fast-read and presents a very helpful inside-look at the company as it changed into a moneymaking machine. It covers the period when Punch Sulzberger took charge in 1963 until the publication of the book in 1993. Diamond reported on all the media for five years for *New York* magazine, taped 24 interviews with *Times* people and conducted 72 untaped interviews. In addition, he had access to the paper's archives. He was critical but with obvious "respect." He characterized the paper as "too smug to love, yet too important to leave." Professor Diamond died in 1997. He was also formerly Senior Editor at *Newsweek*, professor at MIT and at New York University's Department of Journalism.

<u>*Fit to Print, A. M. Rosenthal and His Times*</u> This book was <u>*not*</u> authorized, but Joseph C. Goulden interviewed 317 people to find

his story which was published in 1988. It is about Abe Rosenthal who was editor from 1969-1986. The relentless Goulden finally got to spend 20 hours with Rosenthal and had a guarded interview with Punch. Besides his other countless sources, Goulden read 11-lineal-feet of books about the *Times*. Goulden had been a Washington bureau chief for the *Philadelphia Inquirer* and newspaperman for ten years, before becoming a fulltime author of more than a dozen well-known non-fiction books.

Without Fear or Favor, An Uncompromising Look at The New York Times This semi-authorized volume by former reporter and editor Harrison E. Salisbury came from The Company's own book publishing company. Released in 1980, it told the story "that has never been revealed before" about "the metamorphosis of *The Times* from a newspaper which recorded actions to one which has become, like it or not, a considerable part of the action."

The Kingdom and the Power This 557-page volume from 1969 is the "defining account of the paper's news operation," according to Tifft and Jones. It was written by a former *Times* reporter, Gay Talese, who had left the paper to write books.

15

Times Is Still A Family Business

The *New York Times* has always been a family business since it was purchased in 1896 by Adolph S. Ochs.

Adolph was a young Jewish man whose father had emigrated from Germany and settled in Tennessee at the urging of siblings who already lived there. In 1878, when just out of his teens, Adolph acquired a struggling daily in Chattanooga with $37.50 in borrowed cash. By 1896, he was prosperous enough to buy the reputable *New York Times* which was facing bankruptcy.

Only five publishers, all family members, have run the paper since it was purchased. They are:

1896-1935 . . . **Adolph S. Ochs**
1935-1961 . . . **Adolph's daughter's husband**, Arthur Hays Sulzberger
1961-1963 . . . **Adolph's granddaughter's husband**, Orvil Dryfoos
1963-1992 . . . **Adolph's grandson**, Arthur O. Sulzberger
           (known as Punch)
1992-now . . . **Adolph's great grandson**, Arthur O. Sulzberger, Jr.
           (known as Pinch)

All of the above except Adolph come from the line of Adolph's only child, his daughter Iphigene.

The present publisher, Pinch Sulzberger, is the grandson of Iphigene. He was chosen as publisher at age 41 in 1992, but he had to wait until 1997 before he became Chairman of the entire conglomerate, which is known as The New York Times Company. (He actually began running the operation, under the eye of his father, in 1988 when he became Assistant Publisher.)

Pinch still holds only a miniscule number of shares of voting stock in The Company. His elderly father and three aunts (Iphigene's four children) are joint trustees for virtually all the voting stock, although they obviously will not be around for long. Punch, at 77, is the youngest of the four siblings and has Parkinson's disease. There are thirteen members of the next generation of this line, including Pinch.

The public has been allowed to buy shares in The Company since it went public in 1967, but they do not have any voting rights and the plan is they never will.[1]

This is a view over the Times Square area on December 28, 1986.

(The names of the conglomerate and the newspaper cause confusion because they both use the phrase, "New York Times." In order to keep this clear to the reader, we will italicize the newspaper as the *"New York Times"* or the *"Times."* The conglomerate, which also owns the newspaper, will be known as "The New York Times Company," its full title, or a shortened version, "The Company.")

Pinch could be swept out of office tomorrow if the extended family becomes unhappy with his performance. There's little doubt he's being watched closely by other family members, particularly after the

---

[1] The New York Times Company now owns, besides *The New York Times* newspaper, *The International Herald Tribune*, *The Boston Globe*, 16 other newspapers, eight network-affiliated television stations and two New York radio stations. It has more than 40 Web sites, and interests in two paper mills. In 2002, The Company and Discovery Communications formed a joint venture to co-own a digital cable channel. It has also invested in New England Sports Ventures, which includes the Red Sox and the New England Sports Network, a cable channel that reaches 3.7 million homes in the Northeast.

Jayson Blair affair. After all, he is in charge of almost all the family assets. His cousin, Michael Golden, who is two years older, was picked to watch and learn every day as Vice Chairman of The Company and Senior Vice President. He is ready to take charge.

Unlike his father, Pinch considers himself a newspaperman, having worked at a daily in North Carolina, where he wrote mostly obituaries. He was hired because the owners were friendly with his family. He also worked at the Associated Press in Paris, where his father was also very active and at the Washington Bureau of the *Times*.

Stockholders Could Mount Serious Charges of Nepotism

An outside member of the Board of Directors, Louis V. Gerstner, who was Chairman and CEO of IBM, began to raise questions about eliminating nepotism and bringing in qualified, experienced executives to run The Company, now that it is publicly owned. Gerstner was apparently appointed to the Board because one of the original owners of IBM, Thomas J. Watson, Jr., was a friend of the family. But Punch grew to regret the day he appointed Gerstner.

Gerstner's concerns were not frivolous; they were a serious matter. The Sulzbergers were not being fair to their outside investors and they appeared to be ripe for a stockholders' suit. But Punch didn't want to hear about it. He wanted to continue running it from his hip pocket even though it was now publicly owned. As The Company grew, the non-voting stock owned by the public had increased in quantity so that the family now owned less than 18% of The Company stock. But they still had total control of The Company because they owned the majority of the voting stock, which was now less than one-half of 1% of the total stock outstanding. Tifft and Jones said they could run The Company any way they wanted as long as they were not "perceived to be reckless or abusively nepotistic." But no outside person would choose Pinch Sulzberger to run this huge corporation. If any member of the Board became serious about aggressively pushing this issue, it would mean the end of Sulzberger control.

Gerstner finally did resign in the spring of 1997 in protest over the policy of having only family members like Pinch in top positions. He realized that not doing so would have violated his responsibilities as a

Board member and also made him subject to a lawsuit.

Another family-owned company, the *Los Angeles Times* had just gone through a similar experience, according to Tifft and Jones. When an outside executive from General Mills was brought in, the stock of the Los Angeles paper quickly doubled in price.

Like a Family Shoe Store

The New York Times Company is still run like a family-owned shoe store. The Sulzbergers know everything that is happening in every department at the store. They are totally in charge. That is why they have been so successful.

Sure, they used to have nice getaways on weekends when they tired of their New York apartments, such as a 262-acre estate that Adolph owned in the posh New York suburbs near Stamford, Connecticut. But that's within easy commuting distance of the city. They were always "watching the store." That concept has been very successful for them although it has raised the stress level.

That is why it was so ludicrous for Judge Saris to say that The Company has no control over the *Boston Globe*, which she said is a "separate" corporation.

The judge was not allowed to forget, as she was ruling, that she was dealing with the very powerful New York Times Company. All the papers which were sent to her from The Company's lawyers noted at the bottom that a copy was going to: "Of counsel: George Freeman, The New York Times Company, 229 West 43rd Street, New York, N.Y. 10036-3959." Freeman is well known as the second in command at the legal department.

If Judge Saris has any aspirations of an elevation to the Federal Court of Appeals in Boston, she understands that she had better not have an unhappy Pinch watching her.

Everyone has seen how the President of Harvard University quickly capitulated in 2002 when Pinch's big guns were trained on him for only two weeks about affirmative action at Harvard. They've seen what happened to the Catholic Church in 2003. Look what happened to Sally Pawlick when the big bully went after her. These are only a few of Pinch's latest targets in his efforts to change the world. He is a power unto himself. Judge Saris has the message.

Pinch had The Company's lawyers tell Judge Saris: "The *Globe* is published by a corporation separate and distinct from the New York Times Company, the sole defendant herein. Plaintiffs present no basis for disregarding those corporate entities, nor could they."

However, just a few of the ways that The Company treats the *Globe* as an integral part of the family business were pointed out in Chapter 4. If we had been permitted to do discovery, we would have found many more.

Family Is In Charge

No one has ever denied that the Sulzbergers are in complete charge of _everything_ at The New York Times Company. They are into the minutiae.

(They even send anonymous letters to the editor. Punch used the pseudonym A. Sock, a play on his nickname "Punch," to sign his letters. One of his letters can be found in the October 3, 1989 paper.)

• When a feminist was chosen to write a book review, Punch was so frustrated with her work that he sent this memo to editor Abe Rosenthal: "Every once in a while I get absolutely fascinated at the incredible gobbledegook that finds its way into the pages of the *New York Times*. The attached review by Ellen Willis is a perfect example. I can only assume that the editor was awed by the selection of her words and felt stupid if he didn't know what on earth she was talking about." The words that Punch thought were gobbledegook (he was right) were: "The pornographic image, which objectifies and degrades the (usually female) body, represents a ritual in which the (usually male) pornographer or user, playing both killer and victim, reenacts the murder of his bodily self, since the murder can never be truly accomplished, it must be compulsively repeated."

• When a story was run about unwed mothers, Rosenthal received this memo from Punch: "So far this morning [11:30 a.m.] my office has received four calls on the ... story on the glorification of having illegitimate children. ... Can't we be a bit more discriminating about what we run on that page?"

• When a photo in the fashion section showed a model with her back to the camera so that it was possible to see a blurred suggestion of one of her nipples reflected in a mirror, a reader complained and Punch sent this memo: "You put this bosom in the paper, so I think you should reply to Mrs. Byron. Was this the only picture we had and did we have to go this far?" The last phrase was underlined twice in ink and a handwritten sentence added, "I don't like it in the *Times*."

This power was usually exercised discreetly by the Sulzbergers, according to author Edwin Diamond:

"With both Sulzbergers, influence was exercised discreetly. It was not the style of either father or son to address lower-ranking editors or reporters directly, unless sorely provoked." There were exceptions, such as when Punch picked up the phone shortly after the first edition arrived and ordered the editor on duty to remove the word "crappy" from a story.

"In practice," Diamond continued, "the publisher's real authority lay in the power to pick the editors to execute these tasks — the men (and one or two women) who carry forward the vision of the paper. The way this authority was exercised at the paper in the late 1980s and early 1990s made reading the *Times* a challenging task, and especially enjoyable if the reader knew what to look for. Punch Sulzberger continued to run the paper together with his top appointees, while his son was putting together his own team of editors and managers, Arthur loyalists, who comprised a government in waiting.

"The *Times* system of hiring people when they were young and then selecting only from within for advancement to the top helped assure that no unknown quantities were promoted to senior editorships. The soil was familiar and well tested; exotic flora could not grow too high or survive very long. 'I don't believe in telling editors or reporters what to do,' Sulzberger summed up. 'But I do believe in long, philosophic conversations with my editors about where the paper, the city, and the country are going. We had these discussions all the time."

Editor Abe Rosenthal didn't really learn this lesson until he was at retirement age and decided he was going to pick his successor. Everyone was impressed by his careful search except for Punch and Pinch.

"As the 'process' actually played out, the power of selection did not belong to Rosenthal," wrote Diamond. "The entire Rosenthal selection process was a sideshow. To the extent that any of the participants believed that it mattered, they were fooling themselves. If Rosenthal, deep down, hoped to emerge from the process as the choice to stay, he was deluding himself as well. The Sulzbergers had their candidate, [Max] Frankel, in hand all along. There was no contest, because only the Sulzbergers made the rules. From beginning to end, Rosenthal was excluded from the real decision-making, along with everyone else. Outsiders need not apply; Rosenthal's men, older and younger, were never in the running; neither was Rosenthal [allowed to continue past 65]. A publisher at a rival newspaper watched the succession with a mixture of interest and bemusement; he extracted a moral from the story. People in the newsroom think they 'run' the *Times*, but they are mistaken. It is the Sulzbergers' newspaper; the family does what it wants without staging popularity contests or collecting employee ballots."

Few Intellectual Giants Are Seen

There are few intellectual giants visible among the family members. A large number have dyslexia, including Punch, who dropped out of prep school in 1943 to join the Marines and to become independent of his family. He served in the South Pacific toward the end of the war as a radioman and driver in rear echelons at the headquarters of General MacArthur.

Punch says, "Before I entered the Marines, I was a lazy good-for-nothing. The Marines woke me up." When he returned, he graduated from Columbia University where his father was a trustee. He had started school as a youngster at a private school in the city where he was forced to write with his right hand even though he was left-handed. His parents were convinced that this caused his dyslexia. He is the classic example of the "C" student who runs the world with all the "A" students working for him. Although all the family worried about whether he could successfully manage the company, he turned out to be an excellent businessman.

Pinch graduated without distinction from Tufts in Boston.

One person might lay claim to the title of the intellectual giant of the family. He is John Oakes, a nephew of Adolph, the son of a brother. The brother had changed his name from Ochs to Oakes during World War I to remove its German roots.

This cousin of Punch (who was 13-years older than Punch) was Phi Beta Kappa at Princeton, voted "most likely to succeed" by his classmates in 1934 and a Rhodes Scholar. Punch's mother was said to have told Punch many times, "Why can't you be more like Johnny?" Johnny was appointed editor of the *Times*' editorial page in 1961, just before Punch took charge. He stayed until 1976 when Punch finally was powerful enough to remove him. Punch was ready to name his own man, Max Frankel, as editor of the editorial page. It just so happened that cousin Oakes, who was very liberal, wanted Bella Abzug as U.S. Senator, whereas Punch favored Daniel Patrick Moynihan, who was not popular with liberals.

Oakes went on vacation to Martha's Vineyard in the belief that the *Times* would not endorse anyone in the primary, but Punch had an editorial written endorsing Moynihan published on the Friday before election. The cousin heard about it while on the ferry returning from his vacation and quickly penned a 450-word rebuttal but it was reduced to a 40-word letter-to-the-editor that ran on Saturday. A black member of the *Times* editorial board, Roger Wilkins, also penned a piece but Punch instructed that it was not to run until the day after the election was over, which Moynihan won (by a slim margin) thanks to Punch.

Oakes was far over on the liberal side of the spectrum, but he was somewhere in the mainstream. Max Frankel, who was Sunday editor at the time, gave a socialist viewpoint in an internal memo to Punch in 1974 in answer to a question (which was also given to Abe Rosenthal) whether the *Times* was "too left" or "anti-capitalist."

Frankel replied: "Ownership is about to be redistributed in a major way." His prediction was that socialism would soon control the world. "Capitalist institutions around the world have been shown to be inadequate. Populations want to reinvest some of their excess capital in public services and facilities." Despite that extreme socialist view, Punch chose him to head the editorial page.

Editors Also Slant Their Stories

Even the editors put their opinions in the paper. A reporter was star-tled in November 1965 while standing in the newsroom one evening to see Rosenthal and his deputy, Arthur Gelb, dancing with the cam-paign manager of John Lindsay when Lindsay ran for mayor. They were shouting, "We won! We won!" But the truth was that Punch had been behind the curtain again, pulling the strings for Lindsay.

Cousin Oakes was in charge of the editorials when the *Times* sup-ported our intervention in South Vietnam, which ratified sending teenage draftees to that country to kill and be killed. His editorial in 1962 said that the protection of South Vietnam "is a struggle this country cannot shirk." It set the tone. In March 1963, he continued: "The cost [of saving Vietnam] is large, but the cost of South-East Asia coming under the domination of Russia and Communist China would be still larger." In May 1964, he urged: "If we demonstrate that we will make whatever military and political effort [denying victory to Communism requires], the Communists sooner or later will also rec-ognize reality."

He and the paper continued to support the war until public opin-ion went against them. Then they sent reporter Harrison Salisbury to Hanoi in 1966, while Lyndon Johnson was in the middle of his term, to report on what North Vietnam had called "barbaric attacks" and "indiscriminate bombing" that killed civilians and destroyed non-mil-itary targets.

The reports from Hanoi began in December 1966. Pinch was an impressionable 15-year-old when he read about "U.S. atrocities." Punch had been Publisher for three years.

Salisbury flatly accused the United States of bombing civilian tar-gets: "Contrary to the impression given by United States commu-niqués, on-the-spot inspection indicates that American bombing has inflicted considerable civilian casualties in Hanoi and its environs for some time past. ... It is fair to say that, based on evidence of their own eyes, Hanoi residents do not find much credibility in United States bombing communiqués... ."

Two days later, he wrote, "It is apparent, on personal inspection, that block after block of ordinary housing, particularly surrounding a textile plant, has been smashed to rubble by repeated attacks by

Seventh Fleet planes. ... Whatever the explanation, one can see that United States planes are dropping an enormous weight of explosives on purely civilian targets. Whatever else there may be or not have been in Namdinh [a suburb of Hanoi], it is civilians who have taken the punishment."

A flaw in the stories was immediately apparent to *all* the news staff at Times Square in New York. The paper, at the time, still had a fetish for attribution of any fact that was reported. The man who had been Salisbury's deputy as national news editor, told Joseph Goulden: "When I picked up the paper, I sucked in my breath. He [Salisbury] reported flatly Americans had bombed civilian areas. He accepted what the North Vietnamese said and reported it as his own. Someone should have edited the attribution into the articles." The former editor felt that Salisbury might have been "set-up" by his enemies at the *Times* for embarrassment. Any number of editors had a chance to insert an attribution but none did. Not until the end of his fifth article was this done.

It's difficult to believe that while American teenage draftees were dying in Vietnam because the *Times* had been complicit in sending them there, the staff at the *Times* was later allowed to manipulate our history in order to satisfy a grudge against a co-worker they didn't like.

Time magazine printed two pages showing holes in the stories, concluding that Salisbury was "getting little more than a guided — or misguided — tour."

Aviation Week pointed out that the damage that Salisbury saw could have been caused by the enemy's own fire. There were 100 anti-aircraft batteries around Namdinh, not to protect civilians but to protect a thermal power plant, a rail-marshaling yard and petroleum storage facilities. It was also the impact area for anti-aircraft rockets fired from Hanoi.

The *Times* military correspondent, Hanson Baldwin, wrote that Salisbury did not know what he was talking about.

Pinch, along with the rest of the world, had been taught at a very impressionable age that America is an evil place. This happened because Punch allowed Salisbury to go all by himself to North Vietnam and report everything he was told by those in charge who, according to what we had been told a few years earlier, were the enemy in a struggle which our drafted teenagers could not "shirk."

But Punch, the former Marine with a tie clasp he still wore every day, nominated Salisbury for a Pulitzer Prize, which he did not get.

16

Pinch's Life Is Built on "Family"

Pinch Sulzberger's position at this newspaper is so strongly predicated upon his being a member of the Sulzberger family that the business is ripe for a suit under the Civil Rights Act of 1964.

Under the law, Pinch may not hold _any_ position in The New York Times Company predicated upon his race or religion, much less be its Chairman.

Nevertheless, every lawyer understands it would be extremely difficult for a plaintiff to win a suit against this powerful family. But an Italian family, which was not as powerful, lost a similar case in 1982 and unsuccessfully appealed to the U.S. Supreme Court.

The Italians had been in the garbage business for 73 years in California, with over 100 members of the family involved as shareholders and employees. The family members were given preference in driver jobs and management. In that case, from the Ninth Circuit of the U.S. Court of Appeals, the Italian family was held to be violating the Civil Rights Act. Under that ruling, the Sulzberger family is breaking both the letter and the spirit of the Civil Rights Act, which they say they enthusiastically support.[1]

---

[1] I do not agree that Pinch's job at this family business should be against the law. My second book, _Freedom Will Conquer Racism and Sexism, The Civil Rights Act Is Damaging Everyone in America, Especially Blacks and Women_, tells how the Civil Rights Act is damaging our country in this regard. But the Sulzbergers violently disagree with me. They worked hard to accomplish the passage of the Act in 1964 and supported all the changes thereafter to make it stronger. One would expect that they would follow it without having to be sued.

They have already been successfully sued by women in one action and by blacks in another, but that was back in the 1970s when every major company in America was being attacked and they realized it was fruitless to complain. Those suits don't necessarily mean they were guilty in either case as was pointed out in my book.

My first exposure to the _Times_ as a newspaper-of-record occurred when I was writing my book about the Civil Rights Act. When I started searching the _Times_ as a source for the history of the Act, I was startled to dis-

The Company is riddled with an unknown number of family members. Pinch's entire life has been built on a rigid belief in "family," whether he has ever thought about that or realizes it.

The <u>only</u> reason he is Chairman of The Company today is because his ancestors have <u>*always*</u>, for over 4000 years, been staunch believers in "family."

Yet Pinch refuses to allow other families in the Commonwealth of Massachusetts, or anywhere, to follow the same belief. Those people also wish to continue "family" as the foundation of their society the same as he does. Instead, Pinch has his newspapers lie about them. He holds them up to ridicule and libels them. He says that those citizens up in Boston are bigots who are guilty of **fraud**.

Family Has Always Been Important

A rigid structure of family has also been at the heart of most societies, including Europe. Even England created Counts, Dukes and other Lords. Everyone else in that country was a "commoner" who could never join the power structure of their country unless elected. Their legislature still consists of two parts, the House of Lords and the

---

cover that the paper was not only worthless as a "record," it was terribly biased and actively promoting its own agenda. Punch Sulzberger had just become the boss when the Act was being debated. He was still green and did not really know what was happening. I immediately began using the Congressional Record as my only source.

When the Act was first proposed, it was intended to protect only black people. It was very disillusioning for me to learn that the *Times* did not report it when "sex" was added as a surprise ploy by a Southern congressman to kill the Act, during a two-hour session on the Saturday afternoon of February 8, 1964. All the "responsible" Representatives tried to gain control of the session but the Southerners were successful in their ploy. The *Times* reported only a paragraph or two about the session on back pages and did not report it again. When the Act was passed, no one across the country knew that women had been included. When Lyndon Johnson used 70 pens to sign the bill in the glare of television lights, he said that it would protect citizens from being discriminated against "because of the color of their skin." Even at that time, there was no recognition that women had been included, except among the strident feminists.

The subject of women had been discussed previous to that Saturday afternoon by many people, but not in Congress. A President's "Commission on the Status of Women," chaired by Eleanor Roosevelt, had recommended against including women. All the startled liberals spoke against it on that day, including John Lindsay of New York, Rep. Mathias of Maryland, Rep. Thompson from New York, Franklin Roosevelt's son from California and Edith Green, who had just shepherded the "Equal Pay Act for Women" through Congress the year before. But they were no match for the colorful Howard W. (Judge) Smith who had the entire chamber guffawing in hysterics as he livened up that dull Saturday with his stories.

Seven years earlier in 1957, Smith had delayed a Civil Rights bill that President Eisenhower was supporting because Smith said he had to go back to his farm in Virginia to inspect a barn that had just burned down. This caused House Speaker Sam Rayburn to quip, "I knew Howard Smith would do most anything to block a Civil Rights bill, but I never knew he would resort to arson."

All five women who spoke joined in the frivolity and favored the Amendment except for Representative Green. This has caused problems through the years as the black community, without knowing the history, has been disturbed that their law has been preempted by middle- and upper-class white women who utilize it much more than blacks do.

House of Commons. The commoners used to be told that all the land belonged to the Lords and their families. The role of the commoner was to bow-and-scrape.

It was, in large part, this structure that caused early American colonists to flee England and create a country where any person could rise to the utmost extent of his abilities without any regard whatsoever to his parents.

This does not mean that the colonists wanted to destroy the family, as Pinch appears to desire. On the contrary, the early settlers built their whole society around the family and made it the basic unit of their legal system. If there is no family, who will raise the children, love, instruct and nurture them? This country has always had strong families, but we have not been rigid about it. We do not believe that people should be born into a caste system where they will not be able to rise to the full extent of their abilities. This country rejected kings and queens, lords and ladies.

But Pinch's family has restored us to that rigid viewpoint, and this has benefited Pinch enormously. He appears to believe he attained his goals solely on his own merits.

Pinch has personally known some members of his family who have believed in the rigid model, such as his grandmother, Iphigene, who died in 1990 (at age 97) and his father and his aunts. If those people had not believed that strong families are the cornerstone of every civilized country, Pinch would have had no chance of getting his position.

Just take a look at the five publishers of the *Times*. They were all family members, including him. Does he believe that they all got their jobs exclusively on merit?

Fear of Anti-Semitism and Hatred of Jews

The Sulzberger family has accomplished their success in large part through the use of the fear of anti-Semitism. They have created the fiction that anyone who criticizes the paper for any reason does so because he is anti-Semitic.

Apparently, Pinch's grandfather, Arthur Hays Sulzberger, sincerely believed that. When he was at Columbia University, Arthur became greatly upset because he could not get into a fraternity. The rejection

Even the members of his own family have always wondered a little about Pinch Sulzberger, but his father, Punch, was so powerful by the time he retired that no one could stop him from imposing his son on The Company, and the nation.

"embittered him," say Tifft and Jones. "I'm not kept out because I'm not American. I'm not kept out because of my looks, or my manners or whatever else you may say. No — I'm a Jew, and that's all, and that's enough." But he didn't stop to think that the same exclusion would have been applied to Italians, Chinese or many other peoples. This was mainly an inclusion system, rather than an exclusion system. It was largely a system of including the English, a throwback from which the colonists had fled. Many good people don't get into fraternities for many reasons. A good starting point might be because they do not weigh 250 pounds and play on the football team. How important is it that you don't get into a fraternity or club?

The former Jewish mayor of New York, Ed Koch, recently condemned the America First Committee as anti-Semitic because it tried to keep America out of World War II. Most parents everywhere do not want their sons going to war. The Committee represented the vast majority of Americans, which was why President Roosevelt was unable to actively enter the War, as he desired, until after Pearl Harbor. Mayor Koch, himself, stayed in college until he was drafted in 1943. He did not appear anxious to go to war.

It was American teenage boys like Mayor Koch (who received two battle stars as a sergeant) who liberated the concentration camps where so many died. But of the twelve million who died there, six million were Jews. Many of the others were there because they were caught trying to save individual Jews. In Boston, we have a memorial on public land to the memory of the Holocaust, with six smokestacks rising above it, to remember *only* the Jews who died there.

There were holocausts in other countries during the same period. A million Armenians lost their lives in Turkey from 1915-1923, according to many. There's little doubt that seven million died of starvation under Stalin in 1932-1933 as he tried to collectivize the peasants of the Ukraine. When they resisted the change from being independent farmers to a return to serfdom, a large number were shot or starved. Many of those people were Jews.

The *New York Times* was deeply involved in the Ukraine holocaust. Was that because of Iphigene, who was Pinch's grandmother? We know that the family discussed issues like this all the time among themselves and determined *Times* policy in that manner. Iphigene says that Barnard College "turned me into an early socialist," and that, "I never quite lost my leftist leanings." Like many in America, she believed the revolution in Russia had helped the people, even after the evidence showed the opposite to be true.

The world was told by a *Times* reporter, Walter Duranty, that the reports about the holocaust in the Ukraine were not true. He wrote that the Communist world of Joseph Stalin was a wonderful achievement for the workers and he received a Pulitzer Prize for his work. (However, in the summer of 2003, a Pulitzer Prize committee was appointed to consider stripping Duranty's prize from the paper, which would be the first time that such a thing has ever happened.)

A sample of what Duranty and the *Times* reported to the American public, and the world, was:

• "There is no famine or actual starvation nor is there likely to be." November 15, 1931.

• "Any report of a famine in Russia is today an exaggeration or malignant propaganda." August 23, 1933.

A Matter of Wombs

Pinch's family has proudly traced their ancestors back through many, many centuries.

They haven't looked at "relationships" or "partnerships" in their definition of families. It has always come down to wombs. From whose womb did you come? Under Jewish religious law, the womb had to belong to a Jewish woman.

This may be a reason that Pinch is confused. His direct link to Judaism was broken when his father, Punch, married his Episcopalian mother, Barbara Grant, and then divorced her when Pinch was four.[2]

If Pinch joins an Orthodox temple, he will have to go through all the training that would be necessary for anyone to convert to Judaism. If he joins a Reform congregation, he will most likely be allowed membership without undergoing any training, but it would probably be up to each rabbi to decide.

Diamond wrote about Pinch's religious beliefs: "Whatever other burdens [Pinch] inherited when he took charge of the *Times*, one aspect of 'the Jewish paper' issue had at last been put to rest. The *Times*

---

[2] The separation occurred while the family was in Paris. There are conflicting details about the reason for the divorce. Joseph Goulden wrote in his 1988 book that, "Punch's eye began to roam, and Barbara returned to New York with the children." But the 1999 Tifft and Jones book, which was written with the "full cooperation of the Ochses and Sulzbergers," said exactly the opposite. They wrote that Barbara had an affair with a reporter from the *Herald Tribune*. All of them agree that a short period later, a paternity suit was filed by a *Times* reporter against Punch and he agreed to pay support for the next 16 years to settle the case, although he denied he was the father.

of the 1990s was being run by an Episcopalian."

But Diamond, himself, destroyed that concept only a few pages later, "At the age of fourteen, in an act of adult resolve, the boy decided to leave his mother's house and move in with his father. He left his religion as well as part of his past behind. In a conversation with ... the religion correspondent for the *Times*, [Pinch] explained his 'betwixt and between state', that is, a member of a Jewish family raised as an Episcopalian, who now, as an adult, observes *neither* religion. [Pinch] told Goldman, 'Ninety-nine percent out of one hundred people consider me Jewish. How could a Sulzberger not be Jewish?'" Pinch was talking exclusively about his race when he said that.

His race was important again in 1977 while on an Outward Bound course. Pinch tried to energize himself because he was behind a blond male instructor in an eight-mile race and found himself thinking, "I'm not going to let this Aryan bastard beat me." He says his visceral feeling shocked him.

But his forebears believed that they were Jews *only* because of their faith in the God of their ancestors, Abraham, Isaac and Jacob. They did not believe that being a Jew was simply a matter of being a member of a race. It was not just a matter of womb. You had to believe in God or you were not a Jew. If that were not true, they believed that would be racism.

Pinch has broken completely with his ancestors about the meaning and purpose of life. It was their religious beliefs that made them different and successful.

His grandfather, Arthur Hays Sulzberger, who was publisher for 26 years, rejected the idea that Jews were members of a "race," as did Adolph, according to Tifft and Jones.

Arthur was vehemently against collective phrases such as *the Jewish people*. He launched a campaign to eliminate such terms from the paper. He instructed editors to substitute expressions like *people of the Jewish faith* or simply *Jews*, which, he felt, subtly conveyed the notion that being Jewish was something one could freely choose, like being a Methodist or a Presbyterian.

Of course, believing in family, like anything else, can be carried too far. This problem occurred in the Ochs/Sulzberger family. The Hays family thought they were superior to the Sulzbergers, and they both thought they were superior to the Ochs. This discrimination was painful to Adolph. Then when *his* descendants got control, they didn't want anyone coming to their 100th Anniversary party who was not a <u>direct</u> descendant of Adolph.

One woman, who was a descendant of Adolph, was bitter, as we will see, that she was excluded because she was not a direct descendant of Adolph's daughter, Iphigene, and her husband, Arthur Hays Sulzberger.

If that makes your head swim, don't feel bad. It becomes a very difficult problem when people are judged solely by their ancestors. At least, that's what we have always believed in America.

This is a very difficult area for everyone. It is good to help the members of your family against intruders. But how far should you go? Is your family member always right?

Ochs Family Has Never Been Poor

Although Tifft and Jones talk about anti-Semitism in their book, the truth shouts differently. The facts *shout* that the Ochs/Sulzbergers prospered into what has been termed "the most powerful blood-related dynasty in twentieth-century America" because of the good will of the people they encountered here.

In 1996, when they celebrated the 100th anniversary of the purchase of the *Times*, a lavish party was held at the Metropolitan Museum of Art for some 500 members of the family and important guests.

"[They were] arguably the most powerful blood-related dynasty in twentieth-century America. The family not only had owned the *New York Times* but had actively run it for a century, nearly half of the nation's history. The position of publisher had always been a family preserve, an office tantamount to a permanent, inherited cabinet post that passed from generation to generation, as unquestioned a divine right as the crown resting on the head of a Tudor or a Windsor. Presidents might come and go, but the *Times* was a constant, and its voice in the affairs of the United States had always been ultimately that of an Ochs or a Sulzberger, whether by birth or by marriage," according to Tifft and Jones.

All was not happiness and light at this event, however, although all the important people in New York were there. A professional party planner had assembled the list of guests and assigned the seating. Therefore, Diane Sawyer sat next to Punch, who hardly knew her, while Barbara Walters, a close friend of the family seethed. Sawyer had been placed there to signify youth and vigor.

But at least Barbara Walters got to go. It was clear that those family members who were not **directly** descended from Adolph were excluded on purpose. A granddaughter of one of Adolph's sisters was angry and bitter. Her father, Julius Ochs Adler, had been at the paper for over forty years, was the son that Adolph never had and lost the publisher's position only because of Iphigene's husband. "It [the exclusion from the party] was deliberate. I can't tell you how angry and bitter I am," his daughter related.

Punch was there with his bride and third wife. His wife of 39 years, Carol Fuhrman, had died of cancer only seven months previously, and it was common knowledge that that marriage had soured in recent years.

Family Prospered under Adolph

The Ochs family has never been poor. Adolph easily traced his grandfather to Bavaria, where he was a prosperous diamond merchant and Talmudic scholar. Adolph's father, Julius, came to Kentucky because he had siblings there. The work in Bavaria was dull and there were oppressive laws which restricted work and marriage for Jews. No one forced him to come to the United States. He did so because his siblings wrote back that this was a good country.

Pictures of the family in America as far back as the 1860s are of prosperous, well-dressed, happy people.

As the oldest child born in 1858, Adolph Ochs was the breadwinner at an early age for his father, mother and two brothers and three sisters. His father was not an astute businessman and the burden fell to young Adolph. At age 11, he began walking four miles daily to deliver 50 morning papers in Knoxville from 5 a.m. to 7 a.m., when he would attend school. He was soon joined by his two younger brothers and his father, who would also help. Adolph tried other ways to make money but did his best at both city newspapers where he worked as office boy, printer's devil and then apprentice to the printer. When he was fourteen he left school to work fulltime. For the rest of his life, he revered people with a formal education.

His favorite quotation was from *Othello*, the same one quoted by the U.S. Supreme Court in *Milkovich v. Lorain Journal*, 497 U.S. 1 (1990). He copied it from memory while in his teens, thus:

> Who steals my purse steals trash;
> Twas mine, 'tis his, and has been slave to thousands;
> But he who filches from me my good name
> Robs me of that which not enriches him,
> and makes me poor indeed.

It is ironic that the newspaper of which Adolph was so proud is used today to destroy the good name of anyone who dares to disagree with his great grandson.

Adolph was well on his way to making himself the emotional and economic fulcrum of his family before he was twenty. Less than six months after acquiring the Chattanooga paper, he hired his father as bookkeeper and his brother, George, as a reporter. Another brother, Milton, helped out between stints at college and later joined the staff full-time. Soon Adolph acquired a rambling twelve-room Georgian-style redbrick house with a white-columned portico. There he installed his parents, siblings, and his deaf, maternal grandfather, Joseph.

This was Adolph's grand plan: to provide security and employment for every member of the extended Ochs clan, say Tifft and Jones.

Strong Feelings of Prejudice Came from Other Jews

Some of the feelings of prejudice that Adolph Ochs experienced came from other Jews who "out-ranked" him. The best example was Iphigene's husband, Arthur Hays Sulzberger.

Sulzberger got his last name from his father who was a German Jew. His middle name "Hays" was his mother's maiden name. She was a descendant of the Sephardim, i.e., Jews who consider themselves to be, as expressed in the book *Our Crowd*, "the most noble of all Jews because as a culture, they claim the longest unbroken history of unity and suffering." They fled the Inquisition in Spain and Portugal in

1492.

The Hays lived in Holland for 200 years. They came to America in the early 1700s where they fought in the Revolution and prospered. They included one of the founders of the New York Stock Exchange as well as a physician and president of the New York Medical Society in the early 1800s. Arthur's mother was an active member of the Daughters of the American Revolution.

The mother's family never let the father's family, the Sulzbergers, forget that their bloodline was anemic compared to that of the Hays. And both families thought that the Ochs were way behind them both.

After Iphigene Ochs married Arthur Sulzberger, she said that her mother-in-law, whose maiden name was Rachel Hays, told her that her father "could never master the [strange and low class] name Sulzberger."

Adolph felt inferior to both the Hays and the Sulzbergers. When he discovered that his son-in-law's family, the Sulzbergers, were interred at Temple Israel, which was only minutes from his Westchester estate, he hired the architects who had designed the Empire State Building to build a mausoleum for him. It would be larger and more grand than the Sulzberger graves. Tifft and Jones explain it this way:

"Adolph's mausoleum would be the final magisterial gesture of his life. He had never shied away from P.T. Barnum-like pomp and swagger, and in contemplation of death he was no different. ... The result was a stately stone sepulcher with an imposing bronze door, glass windows crisscrossed with iron bars to discourage vandals, and a foundation covered with two coats of tar to keep out moisture.

"Adolph had located his tomb within sight of the more modest Sulzberger graves and those of their Sephardic relatives ... As a German Jew, he was all too aware of the Jewish pecking order that placed his background a firm notch below that of the Sephardim ... To lie in splendor mere feet from these Jewish aristocrats was both a fitting culmination of Adolph's ambitions and a mild rebuke to the old-line Jewish establishment that he felt had never fully embraced him."

While considering prejudice and Adolph Ochs, it should be noted that the Civil War had ravaged Tennessee as brother fought brother in that war. Chattanooga was particularly affected and its population dropped to 3,500 by war's end. As a consequence, when Adolph went there in 1878, it welcomed all people and had regained a population of nearly 12,000, of whom only 773 were native-born. It was a frontier town with no sidewalks. Cattle and hogs roamed the streets and gun- and knife-carrying mountaineers, rivermen and loggers stumbled out of saloons.

It was not only Jews who had to protect themselves and their families. That is the human condition everywhere. Most still believe that this country is the best in the world. That's why the Ochs told their family members back home to come and join them. Perhaps the best example of others who had problems were the Mormons who were chased out of Ohio, Missouri and Illinois by mobs in the mid-1800s. Twenty, including some children, were killed in one episode and the founder, Joseph Smith and his brother, were dragged out of jail in Illinois and killed by a mob. After that, in 1847, the Mormons traveled to the dry plains of Utah. Adolph experienced no problems like that in America.

His Reform Judaism rejected the old rules on diet, purity and dress. Jews were "no longer a nation, but a religious community." It denied the resurrection, heaven and hell, dismissed a return to Zion, and presented the search for a Messiah as the struggle for truth, justice and righteousness in modern society, in which it would participate along-side other religions and people of goodwill generally.

The biggest problem they encountered was the pogroms in Russia and elsewhere that sent two million Jews into the world looking for new homes. The German Jews did not want them coming here. The immigrants had little in common with the 250,000 genteel, Reformist, well-heeled, American-minded and increasingly apprehensive estab-lished Jews who greeted them.

The immigrants were Yiddish-speaking, Orthodox or Hasidic, wild-eyed and frightened, superstitious and desperately poor. For the first time, American Jewry began to fear new arrivals, especially in such staggering numbers. They believed that an anti-Semitic reaction was inevitable.

But crowded as they were, with 510,000 cramped into one-and-a-half square miles of the Lower East Side and working in the garment industry in the city, the new arrivals began to prosper and soon owned Bloomingdale's, Altman's, Macy's, Gimbels and Abraham and Strauss. In 1920, with 1.6 million Jews, New York was easily the largest Jewish city in the world.

Iphigene Ochs Sulzberger May Have Avoided Pinch's Debacle

The problems with Pinch might have been avoided if Iphigene, who was mother/grandmother of Punch and Pinch, had been around to guide him more. She had been well-trained by her father, Adolph, in the tradition of "family" as an integral part of their Jewish faith. As a result, she dedicated her life to that mission, even covering up the numerous affairs of her husband, although she did not take her Jewish faith seriously. She lived to age 97 and was the respected matriarch of the family. She impressed upon all the extended family, particularly her three daughters and Punch, that they must all stick together. This cohesiveness was expressed by Punch to his wife, "Don't ever try to come between me and my sisters."

Iphigene merely tried to continue what she had been taught and had believed all of her life.

Although her married family did not attend temple except on high holy days, and even then only sometimes, they did try to familiarize their children with Judaism. Punch was not bar mitzvahed.

Adolph wanted it known that he believed Judaism was a religion, rather than a national identity. He told his city editor not to give "too much space" to the American Jewish Committee to aid European Jews caught in the war zone during World War I. He explained, "Work to preserve the characteristics and traditions of the Jew, making him a man apart from other men. I am interested in the Jewish religion; I want that preserved, but that's as far as I want to go."

In 1925, he said, "Religion is all I stand for as a Jew." Jewish groups criticized the paper for its policies on the immigration of Eastern European Jews into America. One academic said: "No paper was more anxious to exclude those 'undesirables.'" The rise of Hitler in the 1930s produced studies showing the paper's "inattention" to the problem, but the paper was no different than the other major dailies.

Adolph's Reform Judaism had long opposed Zionism and a Jewish state in Palestine. After his death, that policy was continued at the paper until the Six Day War of 1967 when Punch changed it.

Treated Well in America

Certainly, Adolph himself was treated well in America. On his departure from his family home in Knoxville at age 17, his fellow compositors threw a farewell banquet of steamed oysters and beer. His first paper in Chattanooga when he was 19, resulted from a partnership with non-Jews. His purchase of the *Chattanooga Times* was largely because of largesse from non-Jews. His newspaper flourished there although Ochs never hid that he was Jewish. But he did not flaunt it either. When he was in New York, he also flourished.

Adolph did start receiving hate mail when the paper intervened in a murder trial of a Jew in Atlanta in 1914. Adolph was confident that he could talk sensibly with fellow Southerners about the trial of Leo Frank, who had been found guilty of the sexual assault and murder of a thirteen-year-old worker in the factory he managed. Adolph had no knowledge whether the man was guilty, but in a remarkable change-of-face, he championed the man's cause after being lobbied by the American Jewish Committee. It was the first time he got emotionally involved in a story. Many in the newsroom privately worried that the paper had "slopped over about Frank." After the Governor commuted the sentence to life imprisonment, a mob broke into the jail and lynched Frank.

Tifft and Jones recount the efforts of Adolph to get the Georgia newspapers to reprint a *Times* editorial calling on justice-minded residents of the state to prove Frank's innocence posthumously, but the authors appear to forget that this crime, whoever perpetrated it, was against a 13-year-old girl. It was certain to ignite passions. They give no reason to believe that the jury was not fair in its deliberations. It is reminiscent of the Sacco-Vanzetti trial where two Italians were convicted of murder in 1921 in Dedham, Massachusetts. Their innocence is still championed by many.

In the 1930s, the trial of a German carpenter, Bruno Hauptman, for the kidnapping and death of the infant son of Charles Lindbergh captured the attention of the nation because the evidence was weak at best. The public was so enthralled that the radio had a 15-minute broadcast every night about what had happened that day at the trial. Hauptman was found guilty and executed in the electric chair in 1936. Whether he was guilty or the victim of anti-German prejudice is still argued today.

The reaction of Adolph to the Frank case would appear to indicate that Adolph had *not* suffered badly from anti-Semitism, other than not being invited to join clubs or fraternities. He truly expected that his messages to Georgia would be accepted as the words of a friend. He apparently failed to understand that he was accusing them of a terribly despicable act — one that would not endear you to anyone if the charge were true. There was nothing revealed that would indicate whether this man was guilty. The fact that a mob lynched him did not make him any more or less guilty of the murder.

Adolph failed to consider how he would respond if a group from Atlanta came to New York to offer to help them in running their criminal justice system.

In any event, this event caused Adolph great distress and he was not the same after it.

He also learned in 1914 that if he appeared to be taking the side of the British in the World War, he would receive hate letters from German sympathizers. Anonymous letters asked why he didn't change his name to John Bull and inquired of Iphigene how she liked living off British blood money. There was anger and hate on all sides.

It is difficult not to like Adolph despite his frailties. He does appear generous and kind, despite other stories to the contrary. But, like everyone, he did have his faults. For example, when he fired an 11-year veteran bookkeeper in 1898 during a downsizing, the former employee started telling advertisers the truth about the circulation of the paper. It was only 10,000, not 25,000 as advertised. For some reason, the whistleblower is labeled as an anti-Semite by Tifft and Jones, although there is nothing to indicate that he was not just an unhappy, former employee. The circulation manager hired a Pinkerton detective to discover who was distributing the anonymous handbills. The detective finally took a lawyer and threatened the bookkeeper with a suit (for what, I cannot divine), which only made him more belligerent. Finally

Adolph himself talked to the man who was enjoying himself immensely and wouldn't budge. If he were taken to court, he later wrote Adolph: "I will have the great pleasure of seeing your books placed before the public."

Then Adolph had his usual stroke of genius. He was going out of business if he didn't do something quickly. So he desperately dropped the price of the paper from 3c to 1c on October 11, 1898. Everyone quickly forgot about the discrepancy in the circulation as it soared from less than 10,000 to more than 60,000 by December and a year later was at nearly 91,000. It no longer mattered that he had falsely told advertisers that he had 25,000 subscribers when he only had 10,000. He had more than double that now.

Adolph appears to be a likable person who should have sold the company when it became successful. But he was determined to carry the whole thing with him to heaven, and it just didn't work.

President John Adams Believed in Real Diversity

The America that caused Adolph's father to enthusiastically come to America in 1845 was built upon real diversity, although there were some, as in every society, who did not believe in or welcome it.

The best example of someone who championed diversity was our second President, John Adams. Unlike the Southerners of the time who had great wealth, Adams knew what it was like to scrabble every day on a soil that was stony and shallow, without the help of slaves, although he did become a lawyer.

(It is ironic that Presidents Washington, Jefferson, Madison and Monroe were so valuable to the fledgling nation in its infancy because of the system of slavery which provided them the opportunity to be well-educated, without the day-to-day burdens of tilling the land. They were all from Virginia and were elected in 1788 through 1820, save for Adams in 1796. His son, John Quincy Adams, was also elected for one term in 1824. Somehow, John Adams managed to become our second President. It is fascinating to think who would have risen to early leadership if the slave traders had never landed in our country. The issue of slavery was a terrible divisive issue from the very beginning.)

Adams wrote a letter to Benjamin Rush in 1810, ten years after his

Presidency, "Ask me not, then, whether I am a Catholic or Protestant, Calvinist or Arminian.[3] As far as they are Christians, I wish to be a fellow-disciple with them all."

As for Jews, he wrote in a letter in 1809, "If I were an atheist, and believed in blind eternal fate, I should still believe that fate had ordained the Jews to be the most essential instrument for civilizing the nations. If I were an atheist of the other sect, who believe or pretend to believe that all is ordered by chance, I should believe that chance had ordered the Jews to preserve and propagate to all mankind the doctrine of a supreme, intelligent, wise, almighty sovereign of the universe, which I believe to be the great essential principle of all morality, and consequently all civilization."

But his tolerance did not mean he was not proud to be a Christian. There is much talk that John Adams was an atheist or a humanist, but that is far from true.

Adams wrote in 1798 to the Grand Jurors in Greenfield, Massachusetts, about what was unfolding in France at that time, where a belief in humanism was dominant. That revolution was a copy of ours except that they had removed God from their beliefs. Their revolution was bloody and cruel. It was to fail with Napoleon becoming dictator. With great foresight, Adams cautioned the citizens that we should not undertake the new theory of humanism which would make things much worse. He wrote:

"If a new order of things has commenced, it behooves us to be cautious, that it may not be for the worse. If the abuse of Christianity can be annihilated or diminished, and a more equitable enjoyment of the right of conscience introduced, it will be well, but this will not be accomplished by the abolition of Christianity and the introduction of Grecian mythology, or the worship of modern heroes or heroines, by erecting statues of idolatry to reason or virtue, to beauty or to taste. It is a serious problem to resolve, whether all the abuses of Christianity, even in the darkest ages, when the Pope deposed princes and laid nations under his interdict, were ever so bloody and cruel, ever bore

---

[3] James Arminius was a Dutch minister and professor (1560-1609) who quarreled with John Calvin over predestination. Calvin's beliefs were historically followed in the Congregational churches, among others, in New England and in Presbyterian churches elsewhere in the country. The beliefs of Arminius were found in Methodist churches.

down the independence of the human mind with such terror and intolerance, or taught doctrines which required such implicit credulity to believe, as the present reign of pretended philosophy in France."

Soon after he wrote those words, Adams' dream of tolerance for all would be shattered as his Unitarian friends began to embrace humanism as a religion and a flood of Irish Catholic Christians in the 1850s[4] and Jews in the late 1800s created a peaceful genocide of the America that John Adams and other American patriots envisioned. It returned America to the old rules and laws from which its settlers had fled.

The treatment of women by these new groups also brought a reaction from the women who had enjoyed a new status in the U.S. that had not been seen before in the world as we began to enter the industrial age. That reaction would become hate and anger as these women from the new groups began their complaints in earnest after they had gained suffrage.[5]

As the grandson of poor Catholics who came from Ireland and Germany, it would appear to me that a return to some of the beliefs of John Adams, which is what attracted our ancestors in the first place, would benefit all.

This is what Adolph S. Ochs was seeking his entire life.

---

[4] Some 80% of the legislators in Massachusetts today are nominal Catholics.
[5] Betty Friedan wrote the following in *The Feminine Mystique*. "Women of orthodox Catholic or Jewish origin do not easily break through the housewife image; it is enshrined in the canons of their religion, in the assumptions of their own and their husbands' childhoods, and in their church's dogmatic definitions of marriage and motherhood."

17

Why Is This Dysfunctional Family Leading the World?

The leaders of the *Times* had mental breakdowns and illnesses, including Adolph Ochs. They cheated multiple times on their spouses, both sexes, and ignored their children without apology.

Although they present a unified, glamorous front, the bitter infighting among the family members is tragic.

The business has a bad habit of destroying the lives of anyone who gets too close. The combination of "power" and "greed" is too much for any human.

Punch's sister Judy best understood that, although it wasn't apparently helpful in her own personal life. (Judy's middle name, Peixotto, was one of the many family names that are remembered from generation to generation. This one was from Arthur's mother, whose grandfather had been a president of the New York Medical Society. The grandmother also had Peixotto as her middle name.)

"Judy wanted to separate herself from the Sulzbergers, the Ochses, and make a name for herself," said Dick Cohen, her second husband. A major reason for becoming a medical doctor was for her to get as far away from newspapers as possible. When she married Dick Cohen, her father, Arthur, was eager to bring him in as an employee, but Judy would not allow it.

The family loomed large when Adolph became emotionally disturbed in 1915 because of family pressures at the paper over who would become his successor. The battle ensued for many years until he died in 1935. He appeared incapable of doing anything to relieve the pressure on the contestants or himself.

The apparent heir to the throne was his nephew, Julius Ochs Adler from Chattanooga, the son of Ada, one of Adolph's three sisters. The boy's father, Harry Adler, had worked for Adolph in Chattanooga since 1878, soon after Adolph acquired the paper there and after Harry had married Ada. Harry eventually became General Manager of the Chattanooga paper and worked for Adolph for the rest of his life.

Julius was born in 1892 and lived in the Ochs home in Chattanooga, along with the whole extended family of Adolph, until the New York paper was purchased. He and Adolph's daughter, Iphigene, who was also born in 1892, were close playmates. During a wedding of one of Adolph's sisters, Julius and Iphigene were dressed as bride and groom. They preceded the bride down the aisle.

Since Adolph did not have any sons, he and Harry Adler often thought of Julius as the prime candidate to succeed Adolph. They even thought of Julius marrying Iphigene, which was often done in Jewish families in Germany at the time. Julius was like a son to Adolph. The extended family, including Julius, stayed with the Ochs every summer at a rented home in Atlantic City after Adolph bought the *Times*. Julius and Iphigene were close playmates during those summers. Later, Julius graduated from Princeton and Iphigene from the women's college at Columbia, just as World War I was starting. Julius immediately started working at the *Times*.

After the passenger ship Lusitania was sunk by a submarine in 1915, Julius immediately joined a weekend training camp during the summer for future Army officers at Plattsburgh, New York. During that period, he brought friends back to the Ochs home for visits.

One guest of Julius in the summer of 1916 was Arthur Hays Sulzberger who quickly became a suitor for Iphigene. She turned him down but rethought his proposal after she suffered through two broken engagements and he obtained a commission as a second lieutenant in 1917. The couple married in November 1917 while he was stationed in South Carolina. At that point, Arthur became a second contestant to succeed Adolph. He was the Sephardic Jew who made Adolph feel inferior.

Julius was shipped to Europe and returned as a major with the Distinguished Service Cross, the Silver Star with Oakleaf Cluster and the Purple Heart. He appears in pictures to be a confident, happy person. He was gassed during combat and spent several weeks in the hospital. Arthur never left the states and told everyone he was angry and frustrated that he never went overseas. He stayed at the rank of second lieutenant.

Julius was not demobilized until the spring of 1919. The family lore is that he returned to the *Times* to find Sulzberger at his desk. "Get the hell out of my office! I won't stand for this," he told Sulzberger.

Family Stress Puts Adolph in Depression

Adolph was distressed by the ensuing conflict but seemed incapable of dealing with it. Even before Julius returned, Adolph was so nervous that he went to Atlantic City to get away from it all. In May, he was going into a full depression. The family hoped he would recover but he finally entered a sanitarium in November and spent his time between there, New York City and his home on Lake George. By the spring of 1920 the danger to him seemed to have passed.

But Adolph hadn't solved his problem of who to put in charge of the newspaper. The problem was still very evident in 1932, the last year that Adolph worked at the paper as both candidates suffered breakdowns. Arthur had a coronary occlusion at age 41, caused by worry, fatigue and stress. It left him with a left hand permanently incapable of bearing any weight. A year later, Julius had a nervous breakdown that was officially attributed to long hours and overwork. He entered the Austen Riggs Center in Stockbridge, Massachusetts, where he stayed for six weeks.

Ochs never did make a decision as far as anyone was aware, but when his Will was read, it stated that three trustees of the Ochs Trust would decide who would succeed him. The trustees were the two contestants and Iphigene. Of course, the daughter chose her husband and he became the publisher. Julius was devastated but remained on for twenty years as a loyal employee.

One could conjecture that Adolph was assuming that something would happen to Arthur, and Julius would become publisher without

Adolph having to do anything. It almost did happen that way with Arthur's coronary in 1932. Or his daughter would tire of her husband playing with other women and send him packing, but that did not happen. Whatever the reasoning, this controversy did no one any good.

In 1922, Julius met and married a young flapper from Stanford, Babs Stettheimer, who was eleven years younger than he. They were invited to stay with the Ochs after the marriage, but the new couple quickly left after the second time that Adolph "chased her through the house in her nightie," according to Babs' daughter.

That story from Babs does not sound credible. All would agree that Adolph was not stupid. He would have to be addled if he chased Julius' new bride around where both Julius and his wife could see. I know of nothing else to indicate he would be that stupid.

It quickly became clear to the new bride that her husband was in a battle for the coveted role of successor. Arthur and Iphigene had been trying for years to present a baby boy to Adolph but had been unsuccessful.

The terrible rift between the Sulzbergers and the Ochs was still in evidence at the 100th Anniversary party in 1996. The woman who was so upset because she was not invited to the party was Barbara Katzander, the daughter of Julius. It was no accident. The Sulzbergers were never nice to anyone who could be a rival for power.

Adolph had been generous to Harry Adler and all his family, and they appeared most appreciative. However, according to Tifft and Jones, the generosity did not come without strings. Years later, a descendant who admired Adolph would criticize his "imperial domination" of the family. An executive at the paper was less kindly, "He treated his family as though he were an emperor in a castle with everybody else on a little plot of ground below."

Iphigene, Poor Little Rich Girl

Iphigene was "a poor little rich girl, spoiled and indulged yet slightly neglected," says Tifft and Jones.

But it was no wonder she was spoiled and neglected. Her mother, Effie, was the daughter of a prominent Cincinnati rabbi who was considered the founder of Reform Judaism in America with the goal of modernizing Jewish tradition. Another goal apparently was to have as many children as possible. He had ten by his wife who was also entertaining the many distinguished visitors who arrived almost daily. After she died, the rabbi had four more children by his second wife. As a result, said a granddaughter, Effie and her siblings "grew up wild, [they] used to torture their tutors ... and were not very disciplined." Having a stepmother did not help, and Effie was ready to leave home when Adolph came along when she was twenty-three.

The wedding of Adolph and Effie in 1883 was a lavish affair with a honeymoon in Washington where Adolph took his new bride to have tea with President Chester A. Arthur. But when they returned to Chattanooga, Effie quickly learned that Adolph's mother was in charge at Adolph's home. So the bride became a pampered recluse, rising at noon and saying little when the Ochs would argue about everything from the meaning of a certain phrase in Longfellow's "The Song of Hiawatha" to the Civil War. Her life was not helped by her numerous problems in having children.

When Iphigene was finally born in Chattanooga in 1892, four years before the purchase of the New York paper, Adolph was thrilled and overcome with joy. He was in New York at a meeting of the Associated Press at the time and unable to leave immediately. The family moved to New York in 1896. Adolph was too busy to worry about Iphigene's formal education, and it was almost non-existent. They were unaware that, like many family members, she had dyslexia. When they finally took her to a school, it was discovered she was unable to read or do simple arithmetic. She was pulled from the school by Effie but was allowed to reenter until the headmaster believed she had laughed during one of his lectures and told her to come to his office after school. When she remained sullen during his lecture to her, he asked her what she was thinking about. "I think you have no business talking to me the way you are," she responded. She was expelled on-the-spot, but later allowed to finish the year.

"I don't think my parents ever followed what I was doing in school," she said years later. "My father thought I was brilliant, and my mother thought that whatever I did was all right. She just assumed you can learn anywhere."

Growing up as an only child in a rich home, Iphigene was always lonely, said a friend years later, "lonely from the beginning." Effie's lack of discipline made her more of a fellow child to her daughter than a nurturing mother.

Adolph did spend a lot of time with her on weekends and other occasions, taking long walks and visiting museums and other interesting places. He took her to homes for the aged to learn that she would also be old one day and should treat them with respect. They went to factories to show her the life of working people. Unlike Iphigene and his other descendants, he knew that life very well.

When she was twelve, a well-traveled, intelligent Irish Catholic governess in her fifties arrived, became good friends with Iphigene and changed her life. For starters, she taught her how to read and then introduced her to good books. This transformed the girl's life.

She even attempted to inculcate her with Judaism. But at fifteen, after reading *Age of Reason* by Thomas Paine, Iphigene decided she was a Deist and believed that God made the world and then assumed no control over his creation. At this, Adolph became concerned and sent her to a rabbi for two years, which caused her to return to the fold, but she was not particularly an observant or devoted Jew.

Of Julius at that age, Iphigene said, "His parents were fantastically ambitious for him and not altogether bright in that respect, because they sort of counted me out. They nearly handed Julius to my father on a silver platter as his heir." But Adolph did not consider at that point that his daughter might have a role in the paper through a husband and he was complicit in the plans for Julius.

It was the support of her Irish governess that helped her break away from her domineering father. "It was [her] support that helped me gain my independence from my father. That was a struggle because my father didn't want me to grow up, I was his little girl."

Iphigene went to Barnard, the women's division of Columbia, where her father was a trustee. She had to enroll in a special non-degree program but after two years of intensive tutoring finally gained admittance to the regular school.

It was here that she learned that not everyone agreed with her father's conservative views. A history professor would wave the *Times* in class saying, "I am now going to show you a perfect example of the workings of the medieval mind."

She embraced the beliefs of Margaret Sanger, the founder of Planned Parenthood and those of an economics professor whose ideas "turned me into an early socialist. I never quite lost my leftist leanings." Adolph sympathized with her leanings but was troubled by her dogmatic views. "One of his gifts," according to Tifft and Jones, "was the ability to see an issue from all sides, to disassociate himself from the passion surrounding a subject and, instead, examine it as though it were a specimen under a microscope."

When President Wilson appointed Louis Brandeis to the Supreme Court, Adolph strongly opposed the appointment. He described him as a "professional Jew" and rejected his advocacy of Zionism, his liberal views on labor and his negative attitude toward big business. But Iphigene didn't agree: "I disagreed with my father on this appointment. I thought Brandeis's radicalism was great."

Was Arthur Hays Sulzberger Just Looking for a Job?

Arthur Hays Sulzberger was bored at his father's cotton-goods trade business, particularly with having to serve as an apprentice under his older brother. So one has to wonder whether it was Iphigene or the thrill of working at the *New York Times* that brought him into the Ochs family. There is no question that he was a handsome bachelor who spent a large part of his marriage romancing women other than his wife.

His most glamorous affair was with actress Madeleine Carroll who first visited in 1938. This started a 25-year correspondence with Arthur and frequent visits to their country home. No one disputed that Arthur had a number of extramarital trysts during his life. By the time Punch was born in 1926, they had separate bedrooms. "He had lady friends," said Punch. "I don't know whether he necessarily slept with all of them."

Some said that the problem was that he was not his own man. "When you work for your wife's father, there's an enormous desire to assert yourself in some way," said a family friend.

Iphigene had been well trained to put her family first and she did.

She was the glue that kept the family working together despite the tremendous pressures. For the most part, she buried the pain. "She concealed [the affairs] from herself," said Harrison Salisbury. "It was a conscious strategy." Her daughter Judy said, "I don't think she really ever saw her relationship with Daddy as clearly as anybody else saw it. [Even after he died] she said he never did anything that humiliated or hurt her. Ever."

But others disagreed. Dr. George Cardin, Jr., who treated both Arthur and Iphigene admired her loyalty and her desire to help Arthur "for the sake of the paper," but didn't think she loved him by then. Judy's husband, Dick Cohen, assumed from the first that theirs was a marriage of convenience. Her grandchildren noticed that her stories about him were never about their early romance and courtship. A close friend said: "I could tell by her attitude that there was an anger underneath."

When in his seventies and confined to the estate in suburban Connecticut, his wife discovered that he was paying a nurse for sex.

Free Love Conveyed to Children

Arthur's view of sex was conveyed to his children. His oldest daughter, Marian, the wife of Orvil Dryfoos, had serious marital problems and advised her daughters not to divorce. She had a modern solution. "Just get [your own] lover and keep your marriage going. It's European."

Marian did very well in that regard. The allure of the *Times* cannot be overstated. After Marian's husband, Orvil, died, she married the publisher of *Time* magazine, Andrew Heiskell. In order for him to marry her, Heiskell had to end his fourteen-year marriage to Madeleine Carroll, who had been Arthur's mistress (and from whom Heiskell had been separated for several years). When Arthur heard that in order for Heiskell to marry his daughter, he first had to divorce Arthur's old lover, Madeleine, he thought it was the most hilarious thing he had ever heard.

It was hilarious to everyone except Marian's children. "[Mother] just wasn't that interested in us," said her oldest daughter, Jackie. Marian later told her daughter that she had been the oldest of Arthur and

Iphigene's family and was tired of taking care of children. "I was tired of being a mother by the time I had children," she said.

Orvil was the opposite. He was warm, loving and kind, but he did not have a lot of time to see them. There were nurses and nannies to care for the children and a chauffeur carried them to school. Orvil would often stop at his brother Hugh's apartment on the way home from work. Tifft and Jones explained it this way: "He liked the cozy informality of the cluttered kitchen and [the wife's] hands-on mothering, both of which contrasted sharply with the nannies, starched napkins, and uniformed servants of his own household. He envied the easy laughter and love that was apparent between his brother and sister-in-law. 'Hugh and I were mad about each other, and it showed,' said [the wife]. 'I think in many ways Orvil was an unhappy man.'" When Orvil's son, Bobby, visited the uncle to get away from his family as a teenager, he said, "They were very, very warm. They treated me like their eldest son."

Not as smart as her mother, Marian relied upon charm to open doors that would take her away from the cares of raising children. When she discovered that she was good at raising money for charity, she became "wildly successful" at it. She served on several environmental projects for Mayor Robert Wagner. Then the Secretary of Interior, Stewart Udall, appointed her to an Advisory Board on National Parks to replace her cousin, John Oakes. Although she was the only non-professional on the Board, she didn't think that her closeness to the *Times* had anything to do with it. "I think [Udall] liked me," she said.

But it was not a fun lifestyle for her children. Orvil had been the glue that kept the family together. When he died, they all went in different directions.

The oldest, Jackie, liked Heiskell but always got into a shouting match with her mother when he was around. The mother was always putting Jackie down, said a former in-law, who continued: "The way she looked, the way she conducted herself, Marian was a tough mother." Bobby told his mother calmly, "I don't care what you do, if you marry him or you don't, but that man will never be my father and I will always call him 'Mr. Heiskell.'" The youngest and the only child living at home, Susan, wrote to Heiskell after the marriage, "I hope you understand why I hate you. ... I want my father back and you're not him."

In less than a year, the newly married Heiskells moved to the new United Nations Plaza residential complex and a new life far from the *Times*.

Jackie and Bobby both married the year after their father's death. "It was very clear that I couldn't go home and live with [my mother]," Jackie said. "We'd kill each other. Therefore, I had to get married." Within weeks, Punch had offered her husband, a 27-year-old graduate of Columbia Business School, Stuart Greenspon, a job and a good chance at being the next publisher. "We would look upon you as the leader of the next generation," he said. But after he started work there, Greenspon found Punch very remote. Jackie said, "There was a vagueness there that reminded me of my mother. It wasn't that either [of them] pushed you away, but you couldn't quite get what you needed." But fourteen years later, after Greenspon's divorce from Jackie, he finally realized he would never become publisher and left to start his own business, which made him a rich man. What may have made Punch concerned was an article in *New York* magazine in 1972 suggesting that Punch was not a good publisher and recommending Greenspon as his replacement.

Bobby was also having problems. Although he had been admitted at Dartmouth, Orvil thought he should mature for another year, so he called up the President of IBM, Thomas J. Watson, Jr., and got Bobby a job doing research at IBM. Bobby entered Dartmouth as expected three months after his father's death, where he quickly met Katie Thomas at Colby Junior College. He soon proposed to her but never told her about the *Times* connection. She thought he was poor until he invited her to a weekend in New York. At the end of the year, Katie discovered she was pregnant. In August 1964, there was what Punch described as a "shotgun wedding." Bobby dropped out of college the following year and the young family moved in with his mother and stepfather at their summer home in Connecticut. In September they moved to an apartment in White Plains where he resumed work at IBM. Marian asked President Watson whether Bobby got his job back as a personal favor. "That boy has gotten his job back because he's good at it!" Watson told her, clearly annoyed. "Never think that I would hire anybody as a favor."

Young Susan felt isolated and alone. A bright spot was meeting the daughter of Heiskell and Madeleine Carroll in Paris in 1965. Susan was 18 and Anne was 4 years younger. However, she was a beauty who looked much older. When she graduated from boarding school, she moved to New York and lived with her father but lasted only a year before Marian kicked her out, because she was running with a tough, drug-loving crowd. A decade later, she was no longer beautiful and dead of an overdose. Susan gave the eulogy. She recounted how the two had confessed their dreams and hopes for the future. "Somewhere, these dreams fell short," she said. "Somewhere her life got tangled in a demanding adult world. ... And we, her parents and friends, couldn't help her. I can't make sense out of why that had to happen to her."

Of course, it didn't *have* to "happen to her." Her tragic death result-ed from the failure of many of the 1960s adults to mature. They neg-lected their children in order to find their own fulfillment. But no mat-ter how long they searched or how many drugs they took, they never found the "happiness" they sought.

Iphigene Never Lost Her Radical Views

The reign of Arthur and Iphigene at the paper was much more to the left than Adolph had been. Both were firmly in the camp of tradi-tional liberals, although Arthur would bend a little and support a lib-eral Republican.

More important, they abandoned Adolph's practice of attempting to report only the news — <u>both</u> sides of the news. Now the news was interpreted by the reporters.

One must put a large share of the blame on Adolph. He knew that Julius was much more conservative and would follow Adolph's beliefs much more than Arthur would. But Julius returned from fighting for his country to discover his rival firmly in control at the paper because he had managed to stay safe in the United States until the Armistice on November 11. In addition, Arthur had the uniform of a second lieu-tenant to demonstrate his patriotism. He even wore it, including boots and spurs, on his first days back from South Carolina where he had been in charge of the discharge list for his unit. He put his name first and arrived home quickly, and after settling in, was already at the office on December 7, less than a month after the Armistice. Iphigene said, "He never got over his disappointment of not being a hero in the First World War."

Before the crucial vote in which Iphigene voted for her husband to be publisher, she took Julius to lunch and told him her plans. Julius was made physically ill by her disclosure. Iphigene believed that Julius was not the right man. She later said she believed: "He was too righteous ... and very conservative." Julius worried about the effect on the paper of Arthur's liberal thinking.

We will never know how Julius would have done as publisher. He made a terrible choice for his "flapper" wife when he was 30 and she was 19. But he was limited to a comparatively small pool of women if he was going to consider only Jewish women. Babs was unhappy from the beginning, as one would expect. The lure of the *Times* was undoubtedly strong in her mind inasmuch as her husband was expected to be the next Publisher. But when she arrived in New York after her honeymoon in Europe, she discovered that he faced a battle with Arthur, and it would help if she had a male child.

She later said she had never wanted *any* children, but she could see the necessity for a male child. She produced Julius Jr. (who received his first two names, "Julius Ochs" in memory of Adolph's father) in 1924, two years before Iphigene finally produced her baby boy, Arthur Ochs Sulzberger (also known as Punch). When Julius was dying in 1955, she was determined to make sure that she obtained the stock in The Company that Julius owned and she made it clear she would challenge any Will that was not to her liking. A Will was drawn which left her almost everything except the stock in The Company, which was left to the children. Julius summoned his children and told them, "I want you to understand why I've written my Will the way I have. I never want your mummy to have any voting rights in the paper, and I never want her to challenge the Will. So I've left her everything except the *Times* voting stock." And he added, "I've left your stock in trust because I'm afraid your little sister Nancy might leave her share to a dog-and-cat hospital."

To the very end, Babs tried to change his mind. When she heard that Julius had left instructions ordering her to share any leftover cash with the children, 31, 27 and 25, she stripped the money from the bank account just three days before his death. To add further insult, Babs attended his lavish funeral as a General (he had reached that rank in the Reserves) and war-hero at Arlington National Cemetery with her wartime lover. On the returning train to New York, Julius Jr. said good night to his mother and did not talk to her again for three years. The relations among the three children fared no better. They squabbled over their ownership of the stock and eventually stopped speaking altogether. Julius Jr. stayed at the paper for four more years. But it obviously wouldn't work for anyone and Arthur fired him in 1959.

During the 100th anniversary of the paper in 1951, Arthur commissioned an updated history of the paper by a revered *Times* reporter, who included an account of the tension between Julius and Arthur over the succession. But Arthur cut that from the book, along with other critical details of his publishership.

Iphigene was the most radical member of the family, following in the tradition of her father's mother, Bertha Levy, who had to flee Germany because as a fifteen-year-old student in 1848, she had dipped her handkerchief in the blood of an executed comrade. Bertha's family came to America as a result, following her and settling in Nashville. She changed her allegiance and became a big Southern sympathizer during the Civil War, although Adolph's father was an on-and-off officer in the Union army. She still insisted that she be buried with a Confederate flag. She was even discovered smuggling quinine across the border to the Confederates and would have been in serious trouble if her husband did not have such impeccable credentials.

Iphigene also felt an urge as a child to fan the radical causes of the day. "She didn't want to do any damage to her husband's ego," said the wife of the editor, "but deep down, she knew it was her paper." Her daughter, Ruth, said, "She was more of a radical than my father." During the Spanish Civil War, she sided with the Republicans while her husband was skeptical, and the paper was blandly neutral.

Tifft and Jones say, "Iphigene had no qualms about contacting top editors with her views, and for the most part, her interests never interfered with the objectivity of the *Times*."

When her husband died in 1968, she became like a new woman. She was suddenly emancipated from ten years of caring for him. "There was an extraordinary change in Iphigene's whole attitude, which had nothing to do with whether she loved Arthur or not, [because] she did," said John Oakes. "After his death, Iphigene blossomed. She became much less depressed, much warmer. She no longer had to be the wife, she could be the matriarch."

It was her leadership in the family that put Punch in charge at Orvil's death in 1963.

She had long been the most committed liberal in the family, but she had usually kept her opinions to herself in public. Now she was finally able to speak her mind. On a trip to Israel, she told the *Jerusalem Post* that the *New York Times* was "definitely for the survival of Israel and she was sure that Punch "would very much like to visit here."

Iphigene and Arthur Encouraged Huge Left-Turn in 1950

The country made a huge, left-turn in 1950 and there's no question that the *Times* was deeply involved. I am sorry to say that even Tifft and Jones still do not understand what happened then. They were also taken in by Arthur, Iphigene and their *Times*.

The issue was whether Communism was damaging or beneficial to the United States (and the world). But instead of having that be the focal point of the debate, the extreme liberals made the messenger, Sen. Joseph McCarthy (R-Wisconsin), the only issue.

No one disputed that many important posts under Roosevelt were occupied by those who were sympathetic with both Russia and the U.S. Communist Party. Largely because of the influence of Iphigene, the *Times* had given, through the dispatches of reporter Duranty, a rosy, false picture of Stalin's Russia.

After this became readily apparent to everyone after World War II, the *Times* helped to attack the messenger, Sen. Joseph McCarthy. They reported that the messenger drank too much, was crude, and would not be welcome at Sardi's restaurant in New York. They refused to discuss the true issues about Russia and Communism and continued the spotlight on the Senator.

Almost everyone knows the commentator William F. Buckley, Jr. Although they may not agree with him on the issues, most people will agree that he is an intelligent, capable person. He wrote a book defending the Senator and his views in 1954, *McCarthy & His Enemies*. The *Times* wrote about it, "This is the most extraordinary book yet to come forth in the harsh bibliography, pro and con, of 'McCarthyism.' Measured as a literary and polemical effort it is the most striking... ."

Yet I can guarantee that neither of Arthur, Punch, Iphigene or anyone else in power at the *Times* ever read it or wanted to. The book was reprinted in 1995, but no student in college today would ever be assigned to read it. Yet they all shudder at the dangers of "McCarthyism."

This became a very important issue in the 1952 Presidential election. And it became an even more important issue at the *Times*. Arthur was doing something he had not done before, and about which Adolph would definitely not have approved. He was entering directly into politics and *secretly* working for Dwight Eisenhower for President. The General was a moderate/liberal as opposed to Senator Robert Taft, who was leading the conservative wing of the Republican Party. Arthur had joined IBM President Thomas J. Watson Jr. and other Columbia trustees to bring Eisenhower to head the University. In the fall of 1951, the General was back in Europe, on leave from Columbia, in order to get European military commitment to NATO.

Eisenhower met with Truman over NATO matters in November 1951, and Truman invited him to run on the Democratic ticket, but Ike replied that he had been a lifelong Republican. The meeting was leaked to the *Times* by someone (Justice William O. Douglas took credit in his autobiography) which put it on their front page.

After that, Arthur wrote to the General that he had no qualms about using the *Times* to help "bridge the gap between your present post to that of a candidate." He then asked his two political reporters, Arthur Krock and Scotty Reston, for a memo about Ike's chances, which he sent to the General without their knowledge. Krock believed that the draft-Ike movement would never get off the ground without a statement from Ike. Reston admired the General's refusal to jeopardize his NATO work and said if he waited until May when the job was over, he would strengthen his appeal.

On January 6, Sen. Henry Cabot Lodge made the General livid when he announced he was entering him in the New Hampshire primary and forming an Eisenhower for President campaign. The ploy forced Eisenhower to announce the next day that he would accept the nomination if offered, and the *Times* announced on the same day that it would support Eisenhower "enthusiastically." Never before had the paper endorsed a candidate before the convention, much less seven months before and without even knowing who the Democrats would nominate. In the spring, they published a series of columns called, "Taft Can't Win."

But Arthur's enthusiasm about Ike began to wane as the question of Communism and Senator McCarthy began to surface. However, this was an important and divisive subject to those who had teenage sons who were being drafted and sent to Korea, which was most of the blue-collar folk.

President Truman had bungled us into war against the Communists from North Korea. This is the same North Korean government that is still there today and threatening us with nuclear weapons while being unbearably cruel to its own people.

Truman's Secretary of State, Dean Acheson, had made a speech on January 12, 1950, to the National Press Club in which he practically invited the Communists to invade Korea. Then he was surprised when they did so on June 25. Truman had to send troops to Korea that were not equipped. In his speech, Acheson had excluded from our defense perimeter not only Taiwan and Vietnam, but also Korea from which both Russian and U.S. troops had been withdrawn.

With the draft consisting mostly of blue-collar boys who could not afford college or marriage, the subject totally bypassed the leaders at the *Times*. The blacks were also not concerned. Although the segregation polices which were in effect in the service during World War II had been changed, there were not yet enough blacks in the services to make it a "white man's war" as would be claimed in Vietnam.

This was clearly an invasion. Ten years later, the Communists in North Vietnam were smarter and made their invasion appear to be a popular uprising. My best friend and roommate at Williams College enlisted as a second lieutenant upon his graduation and died a hero's death in Korea. I had just entered the University of New Hampshire for a degree in agriculture, which I would receive in 1952, the year Eisenhower was elected President, before being inaugurated in January 1953.

But Arthur and Iphigene had not really lost their belief in socialism or Communism although Arthur had been somewhat disillusioned. He had favored the Russian Revolution as a young man, but after seeing the country firsthand in 1929, he was no longer as fervent as before. His eyes were opened more in the 1930s when the New York Newspaper Guild, which he considered to be full of Communists and fellow travelers, tried to organize his newsroom.

"For Arthur," say Tifft and Jones, "the pivotal factor was Senator Joseph McCarthy, who for the past two years had exploited the public's fear of communism with his savage accusations of treason in high places. Fearful of damaging his chances with pro-McCarthy voters, Eisenhower proved unwilling to speak out against the deceit and demagoguery."

But that is an inaccurate statement about Eisenhower. In their next sentence, Tifft and Jones, themselves, show how inaccurate it is. They said in the very next sentence that Eisenhower told Arthur, in private and not before a waving crowd what he really believed. He thought that McCarthy deserved credit "for having awakened the country to some of its security problems." Note that Eisenhower had much more knowledge of our security problems than Arthur could ever have. The General made that statement in private to a supporter, with the obvious knowledge that it could seriously damage him. But Tifft and Jones have been so inculcated with the fear of "McCarthyism" that they do not think clearly on the issue.

Nevertheless, Arthur was "in despair" when the General agreed to be with the Republican Senator in Wisconsin. Therefore, Ike agreed to say something nice about General George Marshall at the same time. Based upon that, Arthur wrote an editorial for the morning after the appearance but the General had excised that part of his speech. "Do I need to tell you I am sick at heart?" Arthur cabled Sherman Adams,

Ike's personal aide. Arthur added that he was "close to physical ill." John Oakes also withdrew his support for Ike. Most of the staff was for Adlai Stevenson, including Iphigene, but Arthur kept a lukewarm support. He could not see that it was his failure to keep the *Times* a newspaper-of-record and not his own, personal journal, that had caused his embarrassment over the editorial.

His loyalties conflicted in the 1950s. His decisions on advertising do not appear to make sense. One would think that almost any ad which was a matter of opinion would be accepted. But he incorrectly refused to run an ad, in my opinion, for the commutation of the death penalty for Julius and Ethel Rosenberg, who had been convicted of giving atomic secrets to the Russians. He did correctly run an ad for a book by Howard Fast who had refused to tell the Un-American Activities Committee whether he was a Communist.

In January 1953, the month when President Eisenhower was inaugurated, columnist Walter Winchell reported that an undercover government agent, Harvey M. Matusow, had told Congress there were 500 dues-paying Communists working in newspapers, of which 100 were at the *Times*. Arthur tried to get the details through J. Edgar Hoover twice and then managed to contact Matusow directly, who finally gave a reporter in Los Angeles a two-day interview and signed an affidavit attesting to its truth. Matusow repeated the charge against the *Times* but said he knew only six there. McCarthy was aware that Matusow had made up most of his allegations, he claimed.

Arthur was timid about running the story and sent it to Hoover, who was outraged and quickly returned it, saying, "I could never, under any circumstances, attempt to influence any columnist or writer."

By the end of 1954, the Democrats had regained control of Congress, and McCarthy was censured in the Senate by a vote of 65-22. All the Southerners, who were mostly Democrats at the time, voted to censure McCarthy. That was the end of his investigating career.[1]

---

[1] This book certainly did not intend to include a discussion of Senator Joseph McCarthy, but it obviously has become necessary to do so because the *Times* was deeply involved in the issue. I recommend two Internet sites, which I discovered through Google, which provide the competing viewpoints.

One is from the U.S. State Department which is apparently now writing our history books for us. Its article on the McCarthy issue shows someone attempting the appearance of being fair, despite the use of language

Senator James O. Eastland (D-Mississippi) of the Internal Security Subcommittee then took charge. According to Tifft and Jones, he did so mainly because he was angry at *Times* editorials demanding that Mississippi immediately desegregate its schools in obedience to Brown v. Board of Education, the 1954 U.S. Supreme Court case which ended the separate-but-equal ruling, which had been imposed by a previous case in 1896.[2]

The two authors say that "the assault on the *Times* began in earnest" when Walter Winchell alleged that the *Times* reporter, Clayton Knowles, who was covering Senator McCarthy for the paper, was a former member of the Communist Party for six years while he was a reporter at the *Long Island Daily Press* but had quit when he joined the *Times* in 1943. It turned out that Winchell was correct. One of the persons who was reporting about McCarthy had been a Communist member, who now said he no longer belonged to the Party. His true nature at this point was difficult to divine, but it was obvious to anyone that he could not continue to cover the Senator. Was he merely a misguided idealist who had hidden his past when he started at the *Times* in 1943? Arthur removed him from the Washington bureau and

---

like, "even Dwight Eisenhower, who detested McCarthy, was afraid to stand up to him" and "Americans regained their senses, and the Red Scare finally began to wane." The article recommends for further reading the three most strident books against McCarthy. It can be read on the State Department's Internet site at: http://usinfo.state.gov/usa/infousa/facts/democrac/60.htm.

On the other side is an inclusive 30-page article from *The New American*, which can be found at: http://www.geocities.com/CapitolHill/Senate/1777/mccarthy.htm. Books listed on Amazon as being favorable to the Senator are: *Joseph McCarthy: Reexamining the Life and Legacy of America's Most Hated Senator* by Arthur Herman; *Venona: Decoding Soviet Espionage in America* by John Earl Haynes; *Treason: Liberal Treachery from the Cold War to the War on Terrorism* by Ann H. Coulter; *Useful Idiots: How Liberals Got It Wrong in the Cold War and Still Blame America First* by Mona Charen; *Witness* by Whittaker Chambers; and *Life and Times of Joe McCarthy a Biography* by Thomas C Reeves.

[2] Nobody at the *Times* was intelligent enough, unless they were a Constitutional lawyer, to realize that the *Brown* case was a threat to everyone's freedom. In 1896, a different set of judges had held that a state could *require* a white man and his black friend to segregate themselves while riding on a train. In *Brown*, it, in essence, ruled that a group of black people must mingle with all the white people on the train. If the Chinese in Boston had chosen to live together, they could no longer have a neighborhood school. That may be a desirable result in many people's opinion, but most would not believe that nine lawyers, who happened to be on a court and owned some black robes, should have the complete authority to decide that without any input from the Chinese citizens. But Arthur, Punch, Iphigene, John Oakes and many others cheered the decision, which should merely have reversed the 1896 decision where nine other lawyers (in black robes) revealed their bigotry. The sophisticated observers could see we were headed toward a quota system in 1954. The Court had skipped right over *freedom* in which everyone would sit where they desired and with whomever they desired. The Jews were violating the law by clustering in certain parts of New York City but nobody at the *Times* was smart enough to know that-or wanted to know it.

As far as the Constitution was concerned, we had skipped right over a color-blind society where a citizen could do what he or she chose to do.

Ed Pawlick (right), a 25-year-old rifleman in the Infantry with a shipping tag on his shoulder, prepares to board a ship for Korea in 1953 to fight the Chinese Army. Meanwhile, life for most in the U.S. went on as usual with only the poor being drafted. It was not as evident back then that it was a poor man's war because the Army was still mostly white, and poor boys were not as evident as when they had black faces.

brought him back to New York where he labored in low jobs for the rest of his career, pitied by some and scorned by others for not only confessing but also naming others who had been in the Party.

When a copy editor at the *Times* took the Fifth Amendment before Senator Eastland's committee, admitting only that he had not been a Communist since 1942, Arthur fired him, saying his lack of cooperation had caused the paper to "lose confidence" in him.

In early December, Eastland's committee held four days of closed hearings in New York City to probe the Communist influence in newspapers. Thirty of the subpoenaed witnesses were currently or formerly employees of the *Times*. After that, Eastland announced he would be holding open hearings in Washington in the first week of 1955. When their employees began receiving subpoenas, "a new air of defiance made itself apparent at the paper," say Tifft and Jones, as McCarthyism continued even though the Senator himself had been silenced.

Gay Talese reported that Managing Editor Turner Catledge had regarded Senator Eastland's father as a sort of hero when he was a young man in Mississippi but a meeting with the Senator proved unproductive. Talese actually wrote: "Catledge did not really know what to think after concluding his talk with Eastland, except to remind himself that the Eastlands were planter types from the Delta, and in Mississippi it was said by some Mississippians that Delta people were a most peculiar breed; they were property people, shifty as the seasonal cycles they lived by, social people who did not want to be caught treading on anyone's toes, oblique people who talked one way, acted another, and were hard to know-or so it was said." Talese apparently had no idea how bigoted those remarks were about an entire class of people.

On the first day of the hearings, Arthur succumbed to the belief of his staff that the *Times* had been singled-out. He agreed to run an editorial which had been written in case it was needed. Tifft and Jones say: "Painstakingly, the editorial made its case and slowly gathered speed and power, like a preacher warming to his sermon. By the end it became a clarion call, and in the final sentences Merz [the author] soared."

Those final sentences were:

> [I]f further evidence reveals that the real purpose of the present inquiry is to demonstrate that a free newspaper's policies can be swayed by Congressional pressure, then we say to Mr. Eastland and his counsel that they are wasting their time. This newspaper will continue to determine its policies. It will continue to condemn discrimination, whether in the South or in the North.
>
> It will continue to defend civil liberties. It will continue to challenge the unbridled power of governmental authority. It will continue to enlist goodwill against prejudice and confidence against fear.
>
> We cannot speak unequivocally for the long future. But we can have faith.
>
> And our faith is strong that long after Senator Eastland and his present subcommittee are forgotten, long after segregation has lost its final battle in the South, long after all that was known as McCarthyism is a dim, unwelcome memory, long after the last Congressional committee has learned that it cannot tamper successfully with a free press, *The New York Times* will still be speaking for the men who make it, and only for the men who make it, and speaking, without fear or favor, the truth as it sees it.

But the 35,000 American families who had just seen their sons drafted from their homes and killed by the Communist armies of

China and North Korea were left wondering what the elite at the *Times*, whose children were married or perpetually in college, knew about it. Those families would continue to worry whether those in Washington were helping or hurting the boys who were forced to do the fighting.

Punch was safely back home after playing Marine in his new Lieutenant's uniform just as his father had done at the end of World War I.

As for Eisenhower, it appeared that the relationship did not work for either of them. He is reported to have told John Foster Dulles that the *Times* was "the most untrustworthy newspaper in the United States."

18

Punch Was Suddenly in Charge of Vietnam and Containing Communism

The reign of Punch Sulzberger as Publisher of the *New York Times* newspaper demonstrates that nobody was in charge there, particularly at the beginning when Punch was only thirty-seven. It was a headless monster with everyone in the news department fighting for power. Who would pick a person with dyslexia, who is unable to read well and doesn't even look at newspapers, to head a newspaper? Certainly, it is not necessary that the head be a writer/editor (and it is probably better if he isn't), but he does need to be able to evaluate the paper on his own and command respect that he knows what he is doing. Happily, Punch did have the common sense to delegate those responsibilities to others.

Author Edwin Diamond, who was being paid to observe the *Times*, said in his book: "[Punch] Sulzberger was not pleased with the kind of news the *Times* had made: the Washington bureau revolt against New York in the late 1960s; the ouster of John B. Oakes and his editorial board in the mid-1970s; the reporters' cabal and Kosinski and Severo episodes, the list went on and on. Sulzberger kept asking his executives to 'calm down the place,' but to little avail."

It appears that Punch did an excellent job in running the business and making money. But is that the main purpose for which Adolph Ochs created the *Times*? To make money?

Before we evaluate Punch's reign and the two serious mistakes that occurred on his watch that damaged our nation irrevocably, let's look at his early life.

Punch Sulzberger (on right) is greeted by the Mayor of Paris and the President of the Washington Post, Katherine Graham, while attending an Associated Press meeting. Although many women complain that they have no power, Punch's mother, Iphigene, had more power than most men would dream of as the wife and matriarch of the Sulzberger family until she died at 97. Mrs. Graham had the power and the titles. These two women were among the most influential people on the East Coast and across the country.

Punch Led a Very Sheltered Childhood

Punch led a very sheltered childhood, just as his mother Iphigene had, but for him it was worse. Imagine a boy living with three sisters who were older than he (three, five and eight years older, to be exact) right in the center of New York City, complete with fulltime, watchful nannies. Sister Judy was closest in age and they played together so much, they were called "Punch and Judy." (Punch likes his nickname, whereas Pinch considers his to be childish.)

Punch's grandmother, Effie, the wife of Adolph, did not "produce" a boy to head the business, and then her only child, Iphigene, produced three girls in a row. Imagine the joy in 1926 when Punch arrived on the scene, just like a new king being born in England. Like many rich children, his was a lonely life. The family had ten servants in an enormous five-story town house on East Eightieth Street, just off Fifth Avenue. The children seldom ate with their parents. After breakfast, they went to say goodbye to Iphigene and Arthur who were served in their bedroom. At night, they also ate separately, although Iphigene would often read Greek mythology to them. With an eight-year-old sister when he was born, it was like having another mother for Punch (and as we have seen, his sister, Marian, didn't like it either).

The Jewish Sabbath was celebrated on Friday nights at the home of Arthur's parents in a somber atmosphere. On Sunday the atmosphere changed as the family walked to Adolph's house for a long afternoon of good food, storytelling and cards, in an atmosphere where Adolph excelled. If there was anything to celebrate, he would lead with party horns, whistles, cowbells and anything that made a good noise. Grandmother Effie was said to resemble an amusing and approachable Queen Victoria. "Granny was just ebullient," said Punch. "You ran and jumped in her arms whenever you saw her."

Adolph made up for the boring times in the city by inviting everyone in the extended family to their house on Lake George during the summer. Punch played with the rest at swimming, rowing, tennis and similar games. They would even go with Adolph to the Saratoga racetrack. There were seldom fewer than twenty at the big oak table, with Buffalo Bill, John Philip Sousa, Franklin Roosevelt and other famous guests being commonplace.

For a while Adolph would drop by every afternoon in New York with a present for each grandchild. This made Arthur's homecoming a bit tepid. When his protests were ignored, he started bringing home his own presents until Iphigene finally made Adolph stop the practice. "That was a glorious period of time," said sister Ruth, like a perpetual Christmas.

A picture of a happy five-year-old standing close to his seated grandfather in a family portrait, although obviously posed in a studio, portrays Punch with his hand draped over the patriarch's knee in apparent affection.

Arthur was not happy with Punch beginning at an early age. Although the father related well to his three daughters, he was not close to Punch. He told his parents when the boy was three: "I am afraid that my son and heir has not the heart of a lion. He prefers to pat the dog's tail rather than its head, and walks away whenever the dog looks at him." When the boy was five, his father insisted that he stop mimicking his sisters who played with dolls. When his mother was gathering toys for charity, Punch arrived with his two favorites, Sunshine and Marian, and placed them in the box. "Boys don't play with dolls," he said.

Punch did not do well in any of the private schools he attended. He had dyslexia as did his mother and so many others in the family. He was left-handed, and the teacher at his first school would bring him before the class and whack his hand. When he tried to write with his right, the results were almost indecipherable, but he ended up using his right hand for writing. His sister, Ruth, said later: "Nearly every school in the vicinity of New York was graced with Punch's presence at one time or another. They were all delighted to have him but wanted something other than a spectator."

He was not a "man's boy." Quiet, polite and fastidious in dress, he was happy in pursuing solitary hobbies, such as collecting seashells and hotel soap, hunting for turtles at the estate in Connecticut and tinkering with gadgets, which was always his true love. When he attended a political convention at age 10, he was fascinated by the news-ticker.

Although his mother clearly loved her son, she was not thrilled either. She said later, "There was no worship on either side [of this mother/son relationship]." His father, who enjoyed sports like soccer, was disappointed. "He just never really gave Punch the time of day," said Judy. The father, who was always composing rhymes for his children, wrote on Punch's thirteenth birthday:

> Of all the sons I've ever had
> You are the best one for your Dad,
> But don't forget that rating first
> May also mean you are the worst!

As Punch approached adolescence, Iphigene worried about his lack of male role-models and she hired male tutors or companions.

In 1940 at age 14, Punch entered Loomis, a boarding school in Connecticut. His parents had been considering Culver Military Academy, which made Loomis look good to Punch by comparison. "In comparison to Culver I would have taken anything," he said later.

He did not do well and had to repeat his freshman year. In 1942, after completing his freshman year for the second time, he decided he was going to quit school and join the Marines. He left school the following January, in 1943, at the age of 16 and never returned, turning 17 shortly thereafter. But it was a year later, in January 1944, before he was finally called for duty.

An Example of History Being Written

Punch's career in the Marines is an example of the way that history is written. Look how the different authors report his experiences in World War II.

Edwin Diamond: "The war provided a way to escape both family and school; in 1943, at age seventeen, he left the Loomis School in Connecticut to join the Marines, with his father's written permission. He did well enough, serving in the South Pacific toward the end of the war as a radioman and driver in rear echelons. 'Before I entered the Marines, I was a lazy good-for-nothing. The Marines woke me up,' Punch would later say."

Gay Talese: "[The drill instructor at Parris Island] achieved in a few weeks what a generation of educators and the *Times* family had failed to do in twelve years. ... During the war, Sulzberger was sent to the Philippines, serving through the campaigns at Leyte and Luzon, and later he was transferred to Japan. He acted as a naval interceptor operator and also as a jeep driver at MacArthur's headquarters. He was promoted to corporal, and then in the spring of 1946, which he thought was a very appropriate date, he was released from the service and was returned to New York."

Tifft and Jones: These two authors tell us that Punch's father was orchestrating the entire saga of his military career. Arthur couldn't stop Punch from enlisting, but he certainly could see that he didn't do anything dangerous. Even after the boy enlisted, Punch languished at home for almost a year before the threat of his being drafted into the Infantry finally made Arthur act.

Tifft and Jones say: "In December 1943, two months before Punch was eligible to be drafted, a family friend and captain in the Marine Corps intervened and saw to it that his application was acted upon." Obviously, the only reason that Punch languished during that year was because his father had talked with the captain many times previously.

But even these two authors colored the story slightly by telling the reader that Punch reported to Parris Island on January 22, 1944, "a desolate patch of South Carolina lowland" for a "brutal" training period, which was exactly the same training that millions of other teenage American boys have experienced.

With his three-month basic finished in April, Punch was still stateside in the fall when his father wrote a relative that Punch is "off to the Pacific taking his chances with a lot of others." The authors describe the letter as "disingenuous," which is a softer word than a "lie." It showed that Arthur was not a man of candor.

Punch could have been in the Pacific fighting the Japanese from island to island any time after 1943. He could have gotten combat experience for two years, if he was lucky enough to survive that long without becoming a casualty.

When Punch finally did leave the states, Arthur had already been talking personally to General MacArthur about his son. The father had visited the General in the Pacific a few weeks previously. It was arranged that Punch was going to be assigned to MacArthur's headquarters where he would be safe, working in the basement of his house. He was first assigned as a radio operator in which he had been trained by his father during his year in New York, but he was not fast enough in Japanese code (undoubtedly because of his dyslexia). He was then made a driver and gofer.

Then strangely, the authors (who obviously have no love for MacArthur) attempted to protect Arthur, who was ostensibly in the Pacific because of his involvement with the Red Cross. But Tifft and Jones wrote that Arthur did not go see the General in order to protect Punch but because the General wanted to ingratiate himself with the Publisher of the *Times* in case he ran for President. But the *Times* had earlier offered MacArthur $250,000 to write a book after the War. MacArthur never accepted the offer and apparently didn't even acknowledge it. That was not a man who was trying to ingratiate himself.

This is the way Tifft and Jones tell what happened next:

"A man of unbridled ego and ambition, MacArthur had been men-

tioned only months earlier in connection with the Republican nomination for president, giving him ample reason, as he looked ahead, to
want to court Arthur. On the day Arthur and Turner [**Turner Catledge,
Assistant Managing Editor of the *Times*]** arrived at headquarters,
MacArthur arranged a lunch for them in his mess, with Arthur carefully positioned on MacArthur's right. [**It's difficult to understand the
significance of "carefully."**] Afterward the two fell into conversation.
MacArthur asked whether Arthur had any relatives in the service, and
Arthur replied that he had a son in the marines. 'I hate the marines,'
said MacArthur. 'They sacrifice their men. They have no sense of the
value of life. Why don't you let me request him for headquarters?' [**Is it
credible that MacArthur really made that statement about the
marines to anyone, much less a newspaperman?**] Arthur explained
that Punch had chosen the marines himself. 'I can't interfere with him,'
he told the General. 'All right, but I think you're making a big mistake,'
replied MacArthur."

We don't know who could have given that story to the authors
except Arthur, the same man who wrote to his relatives a few weeks
later that Punch would be "taking his chances with a lot of others." We
must not forget that Arthur was very "upset" because he, himself, languished stateside during World War I while his cousin, Julius, was decorated and wounded. How does anyone know if the real reason he
stayed stateside was simply because he requested it at that time also?

At any rate, the story is that Arthur considered the matter for a few
days. "Finally, after much soul-searching, Arthur went to MacArthur
and said obliquely, 'I cannot say yes or no. I have to leave it to you.'"
What was that supposed to mean? Of course, Punch was then assigned
to the care of General MacArthur.

Their dislike of MacArthur is one of the very few failings of Tifft
and Jones. Even the index has the following entry for MacArthur,
"seeks Presidency." But when you turn to the indicated page, you find
only the story told above. MacArthur never sought the Presidency, to
my knowledge.

Arthur was said to brood over his decision. "[Arthur] had never gotten over his own lack of combat service during World War I. [**Who
would know that except Arthur?**] Indeed, when prior to seeing

MacArthur he and Turner had unexpectedly found themselves in the midst of Japanese sniper fire on the tiny island of Peleliu, the situation had privately given Arthur great pleasure. [**Who would get "great pleasure" at someone firing a rifle at him?**] He understood Punch's desire to prove himself on the battlefield, as generations of men had done before him."

This whole episode also makes one wonder about Punch. There was no way that he could not know that his father outranked him even when he was in the marines. He said later that after he learned of his assignment, "It became quite obvious when I discovered where I was that some sort of miracle had happened." Some ten years later, he is said to have confronted his father with anger. "I never really forgave him. But I understood what he had done, and we moved on in our relationship."

One of his friends said: "For the first time, Punch was one of the guys, he belonged to a group. For the first time, he'd really *done* it. And this action [by his father] singled him out totally as the son of the publisher of *The New York Times*. His father didn't understand how lonely that boy was, how isolated he'd been."

Punch spent most of his time in Japan with General MacArthur after the war ended, in the hospital with dysentery and skin eruptions and was sent back to the states in October.

All through his life, Punch always wore a tie clasp with the marine insignia on it.

Enrolls at Columbia

After his discharge from the service on April 1, 1946, Punch was admitted to Columbia where his father was a trustee. As usual, Arthur helped him with a letter to the school: "He's a good kid and an able one even though he has been slow in maturing." The school, nevertheless, judged him too unprepared but agreed that if he enrolled in an extension program and maintained a B average, he could enter the following year. Arthur was so impressed with his son's first year in college that he took him to Europe in the summer of 1947 as his secretary. But the stress got to Punch and he ended in a Berlin hospital, The Hospital for Tropical Diseases, which brought back memories of his stay in Tokyo.

His father wrote that his own schedule had been reduced to tatters because he had to "visit the brat morning and afternoon."

But none of this bothered Punch because he was in love, with Barbara Grant, a pretty blond cheerleader, who lived a mile from the family summer home, called Hillandale. They married in July 1948 and moved to an apartment one block from Columbia, to which she transferred.

After the Korean War began in June 1950, Punch's marine reserve was immediately called to active duty, but he got a student deferment. In February 1951, he applied for a commission. In June he and Barbara both graduated from Columbia. In July he reported to Quantico as a second lieutenant for twenty weeks of training and in September Pinch was born. In December, Punch returned home to New York for an eight-week course at the Armed Services Information School. By April he had received enough training and was sent to headquarters in Korea for three months before being sent back in August to Hillandale where his second child, Karen, was born in November. He was assigned to Washington and worked for an assistant to the Commandant of the Corps. It became obvious at this point that Punch no longer discouraged any help in staying far away from combat, if he ever had done so.

Punch watched as his father came up with a five-year plan for him: one year on the *Milwaukee Journal,* a year each on the business and editorial sides of the *Times* and two years in a foreign bureau. Punch arrived in Milwaukee with his wife and two children in February 1953, two months after his release from active duty. Several months later, Barbara had a serious miscarriage which almost took her life. She blamed Punch for not taking charge. "He acted like a boy instead of a man," she said, and his marriage began to unravel. Upon their return to New York in January 1954, after an unspectacular year as a newsman, Punch's mother sensed there was trouble with the marriage and had them sent to the Paris bureau of the *Times.* They arrived that summer even though Barbara had told Iphigene she didn't believe she was up to the change in living conditions. After Barbara went to the hospital in Paris, Iphigene took a hasty trip to see her but was convinced that everything was all right.

One day in the spring of 1955, Punch came home to find Barbara's lover in his apartment. She tried to get him to attend marriage coun-seling, but he refused and she moved to a small town on the Riviera with the children. The marriage was over.

Returns to New York

Julius had died only a few weeks earlier when Punch returned to New York. Orvil offered Punch a position as assistant to the publisher which he began in January 1956, but as usual they didn't expect much from him. The following month he was introduced by a brother of Orvil's to a beautiful Jewish divorcee, Carol Fox Fuhrman, whose father had made millions in the garment industry and then retired, shuttling his family between the best hotels in New York and France. "I don't think I ever had a meal in my house without a finger bowl," said Carol. "It was a very rarified kind of life. My sister and I were lit-tle American princesses."

Punch had also dallied with an employee at the *Times,* and she sued for support of the child. Punch said the woman was also playing around with others at the paper, but, of course, he didn't know if it was his child. So he paid support for many years, and the woman kept working at the *Times.* When the boy was older, he would sometimes be seen in the newsroom pointing at Punch and saying, "That's my father." When older, he himself filed a suit seeking his share, as an heir, of the Ochs Trust, and Punch had to buy him off.

But Carol understood and forgave. By August they were engaged, but first Punch had to settle with Barbara who said she did not want any Sulzberger money. She settled only for an apartment for the chil-dren and herself, furniture, the children's education and psychiatric care for herself. The day after the settlement Punch was off to Reno for six weeks to get a divorce. His mother came for a while to keep him company and sister Judy also came, to get the first of her three divorces. When he got back, Punch had to deal with the paternity suit.

Although Iphigene tried to stop Carol and Punch from marrying hastily because it would appear as though they had to do so, they were married with only five days' notice on December 18, 1956.

Punch had to borrow money from his parents to make all these deals. But, he said, "I got no lectures from anybody." He was continually strapped for money. By their tenth anniversary, he and Carol owed his parents $132,000 plus smaller amounts to various banks. Usually, Punch was too embarrassed to ask his mother, so his secretary would call Arthur's personal lawyer, who would call the mother. Part of the problem was that Carol expected to live like the wife of the Prince and have fine things around her as she did when she lived with her family. "She has shopped every day since the day she married him," said Punch's secretary. "It's her avocation."

Many thought, however, that Iphigene liked having her children come to her for money because it gave her power.

Not Interested in Newspapers

Although all the previous publishers had a great interest in the content and look of the paper, Punch's dyslexia totally prevented him from being a reader or a writer. But, as we will see, he did have the common sense to delegate all those responsibilities to someone who did have the necessary abilities. No one realized at the time that Punch had the ability to delegate; not even Punch understood that.

This was a difficult time for Punch. He had been at the paper for ten years and had spent a large part of that time just trying to straighten out his personal life. Harrison Salisbury said, "I think Punch had given up on the *Times*. He didn't think he was going anywhere on the paper. He was a wandering spirit."

But there was one person who took an interest in him. The managing editor, Turner Catledge, who adopted many strays, gave him guidance and a warm shoulder. Catledge thought it was degrading to give him housekeeping chores. "He felt I was being totally wasted in what I was doing," said Punch.

Of course, Catledge had suffered when Orvil took over as Publisher because he was not as close to Orvil as he had been to Arthur. So Catledge had an informal cocktail party every afternoon in his office after the conference about that day's paper. It was known as the Club, and Punch became a welcome member. "It was like a little seminar that anybody could participate in. Punch got his education from this group," said Clifton Daniel, an assistant managing editor. It undoubtedly did not hurt Catledge to have a member of the family and the possible publisher attending his daily meetings.

A strike of the typographers in December 1962 hit Orvil, the *Times* and the other New York papers. The papers were shut down for 114 days. The stress killed Orvil. The newspapers were totally unable to reach any settlement and they later realized that the president of the union was merely trying to increase his own power because he believed that a long strike would crack the power of the Newspaper Guild as against his International Typographical Union.

The day after the strike ended in April 1963, Orvil went to Puerto Rico for a rest. But he immediately had a stroke while there and was brought home, where he lingered until May 25.

The question of the day became who should be the next publisher? Under Adolph's Will, the three trustees of the Ochs Trust again would make the decision, but Orvil had been one of the trustees, so this meant that Punch's parents, Arthur and Iphigene, would do the deciding.

Many had doubts about Punch because he had never exhibited any ability at all. His father, Arthur, who was among the skeptics, floated the names of many people who could assist Punch if he were made Publisher, particularly that of Amory Bradford, a brilliant Yale lawyer who had been in a top Wall Street firm in 1947 and now was General Manager of The New York Times Company, having worked there for sixteen years.[1] Arthur feared Bradford might quit if he were not made the President with power over everything except the newsroom. If he quit, that would mean they had lost both Orvil and Bradford.

But Iphigene went to talk with her son, and we are told that Punch then strode into his father's office and told him that he would take the job without conditions or he wouldn't take it at all. We don't know who the witnesses were to those conversations where Punch stood up to his parents. Harrison Salisbury confirms my suspicions when he says that the history of that event came from Punch himself.

Scotty Reston, who expected to be considered, professed astonishment at the fact that the Sulzbergers had consulted no one about their decision. "I do not know how it all happened," he said. "Nobody on the paper outside the family was asked for an opinion. This at least was

---

[1] Although the authors of all the four books that I was using reported that Bradford was General Manager of the *newspaper*, all indications are that he was Manager of The Company.

true in my case."

Arthur wrote in a letter: "To say that I am relieved is to put it very mildly indeed. Just getting the whole thing over and being able to lie down and not think about it will be ... a tremendous relief."

Punch's Damage to Our Country Is Irrevocable

1966 — Vietnam

Punch's inability to rein in his cousin, John Oakes, who was considered by most as vastly superior to Punch, who was regarded as a miserable "failure," was tragic for the country. The story about Oakes (thirteen years older, a Phi Beta Kappa at Princeton[2] and a Rhodes Scholar) ignoring his young cousin has already been told. But Oakes' failure in regard to Vietnam and Punch's inability to control the staff, even though he apparently knew better, is still haunting our country as an entire generation became cynical, disenchanted and turned to drugs and sex for their attempt at happiness.[3]

Although Oakes and the *Times* were complicit, from the very beginning, in Kennedy's and Johnson's plans to escalate the war in Vietnam, Oakes had begun to have second thoughts after American troops were there in full force. He was able to sit in a peaceful New York office and decree what should now be done; it wasn't as easy for the thousands of servicemen and their leaders in Vietnam to suddenly decide that John Oakes had been wrong and it was time to go home.[4]

---

[2] It was apparent to me at Yale Law School, where the vast majority of students had been Phi Beta Kappa at the top schools of the country, that what those students had done in college was to memorize vast quantities of information and regurgitate it back to the professors. In law school, however, they had to memorize the important rules of law and then quickly apply them in examinations to very complicated factual patterns. Many of them were bewildered at this. Similarly, John Oakes may have been brilliant, but he may also have been unable to tie his shoes. We just don't know, but we can't give him a "pass" at solving the problems of the world just because he did well at Princeton.

[3] Although this book is not a history of Vietnam, some readers will be interested in a short section about our involvement there. Therefore, I have included in the Appendix, comments from English historian Paul Johnson in his *Modern Times* and from Stanley Karnow whose book, *Vietnam, A History*, was turned into a PBS series. I do not agree with either on all their points, but both are very helpful in gaining an understanding of what really happened there.

[4] When I was a private and a rifleman in Korea in 1953 and Harry Truman's bumbling war with China in Korea had just been ended by President Eisenhower within a few months after taking office, it was rumored we would be sent to Vietnam. The French were losing that country to the Communists. I was grateful that Ike was too experienced to send me and other draftees to another land war in Asia.

I couldn't believe my ears twelve years later in 1965 to learn that Lyndon Johnson and the Democratic Congress were sending draftees to fight in Vietnam. (Our soldiers would average 19-years-of-age in that war.)

The Democrats had taken charge in 1960 when John Kennedy became President. They were soon look-

If we had made a mistake in sending American teenagers to Asia, which we had done, why didn't Oakes and the *Times* point that out? All the American people would have agreed wholeheartedly. But how could the *Times* attack the teenage draftees they had forced to go there, and falsely report that they were killing innocent people?

As we reported in Chapter 15, it was the trip to Hanoi by Harrison Salisbury that damaged the country permanently. It ruined a whole generation, who believed implicitly what they read on December 27, 1966 in the *New York Times* — on Punch Sulzberger's watch.

Even the liberal *Washington Post* charged in an editorial that Salisbury's casualty figures about the damage to civilians from our airplanes were identical to those given in Communist propaganda pamphlets. To this, the embarrassed Managing Editor, Clifton Daniel[5], replied in a sarcastic Press Release: "It was apparent in Mr. Salisbury's first dispatch, and he so stated in a subsequent dispatch, that the casualty figures came from North Vietnamese officials. Where else would he get such figures in Hanoi?"

That statement which went only to the press was very cute, but it was also a lie, wasn't it? We know that it was not "apparent" in Salisbury's first several dispatches to anyone but those who worked at the *Times*. The truth was told by Daniel in an internal memo that went only to his boss, Turner Catledge, who was traveling, in order to answer questions that were being asked by an unhappy Punch.

> The Publisher [Punch] is perturbed about Harrison Salisbury's pieces. He will undoubtedly want to talk to you about them very soon after you get back. I will be glad to give you fill-in detail. Meanwhile, my summary conclusions are as

---

ing for a way for Kennedy to save face after the disaster at the Bay of Pigs in Cuba. He was advised by a member of the National Security Council: "It is very important that the government have a major anti-Communist victory to its credit ... the odds are still in our favor [in Vietnam]." A few months later, JFK told a reporter, "Now we have a problem in making our power credible and Vietnam looks like the place."

In November 1961, Kennedy sent 7000 troops to Vietnam as guards (the first American soldiers sent there other than a few hundred advisors). When he became frustrated with the lack of progress, he ordered the CIA in 1963 to stage a coup against the head of South Vietnam, our ally. This led to the murder of Ngo Dinh Diem. It was "the worst mistake we ever made," according to Lyndon Johnson. Then Kennedy himself was murdered three weeks later.

Bobby Kennedy had always been a hawk on Vietnam. He had assured the public in 1962 after a trip to Vietnam, "We are going to win." He was a hawk until he decided to run for president in March 1968 when he changed sides and began to attack the teenage draftees that he and his brother had sent to Vietnam.

[5] He was married to Harry Truman's daughter.

follows:

Getting into Hanoi was a journalistic coup. Harrison, as might be expected, very promptly dug up some interesting facts that weren't known before. He disclosed that there was considerably more damage to civilian areas than Washington had ever intimated. Washington was quick to acknowledge that this was so.

At the same time, he obviously gave comfort to North Vietnam by affording an outlet for its propaganda and point of view, and comfort to those who are opposed to the bombing and opposed to the war. Our mail to date shows more letters in favor of Harrison than against him.

While Washington has fought to counteract the more damaging allegations in Harrison's report, there has been, as far as a I know, no general denunciation of him or of the *Times* from high quarters or any attempt to bring pressure on the paper. ...

As you know, Harrison has complicated matters by failing in his first dispatches [*note that Daniel used the plural, "dispatches"*] to attribute casualty statistics and other controversial information to those from whom he received it. I asked him in a telegram to do this, and he has complied.

The desk was instructed not to print anything without attribution, or, if the attribution was obvious, as it was in most cases, they should simply put it in. For example, "147 were *said* to have been killed," or "This correspondent was told ..."

There have also been some expressions in the stories that readers might interpret to be editorial or emotional. I asked from the beginning that these be eliminated by the desk. Most of them were, but now and then one crept through. Consequently, I have now been reading all the copy myself.

Harrison, in general, betrayed the tendency of so many correspondents — of seeming to identify himself with the place from which he was writing and the sources from which he was deriving his information. ...

Joseph Goulden wrote that the last paragraph was "damning." He wrote: "Daniel's concluding paragraph was the most damning that can be written by a reporter. Prompted either by emotion or politics, Salisbury had allowed himself to be caught up in a news story to the extent that — by the judgment of his own editor, Daniel — he had lost objectivity. Such is a cardinal sin by a reporter of any rank. Although *Times* editors and executives defended Salisbury in public statements, what appeared in the paper was more resounding than their words."

Even John Oakes wrote an editorial that was close to disowning Salisbury: "... [W]e reject the sweeping deductions and false conclusions many Americans seem to have drawn from the statistics of civilian deaths and the pictures of destruction reported from Hanoi last week by this newspaper's correspondent, Harrison Salisbury."

But even more important, the paper knew that after he returned from reporting from Moscow during the Cold War, Salisbury had been under such stress that he spent weeks in the Payne-Whitney Hospital psychiatric unit. This was obviously not the man to send alone to Hanoi.

But someone decided that Salisbury had gone too far. It was probably Punch beginning to take charge. On the day that Salisbury returned to New York, it was announced that Abe Rosenthal was promoted to assistant managing editor for news and Salisbury would be working on "special projects."

Rosenthal detested Salisbury, both professionally and personally, according to Goulden. "He seemed to personify the worst feature of the *Times* foreign service, the inclination of certain correspondents to adopt revolutionary political causes as their very own, and push suspect characters without question. To Rosenthal, Salisbury stood as the inheritor of the soiled reportorial cape of Herbert L. Matthews, who had covered the Spanish Civil War from the Communist side [a side that Iphigene championed], and then wrote extensively about Fidel Castro's revolutions in Cuba without paying undue attention to evidence of its Communist underpinnings."

Abe Rosenthal had really come up the hard way. His father came from a portion of Russia adjacent to Poland, which had a long and bloody history of Jewish-killing pogroms with state sanction. Just before World War I, Abe's father saved enough to get to London, where an uncle gave him money to travel to Canada. A big strong man, he went to Canada and worked on a communal farm, as a trapper and fur trader. One by one, he brought over seven brothers and his sweetheart. They had five girls and then Abe in 1922. He quit Canada in a squabble with a brother over money and moved to the Bronx, where he worked as a housepainter. He hated the peasants of Russia who had treated him so badly. Deaths and tragedies were a large part of Abe's life. His sister Bess died of pneumonia when Abe was eleven. Next, his father fell from a scaffold and lived for three years in agony before dying. His oldest sister, to whom he was closest, died, leaving two small children. Sister Ruth died of an infection incurred as a result of childbirth. Her husband had been absent while fighting in the Spanish Civil War, which gave Abe another reason to hate Communism. All the deaths occurred during the period when he was eleven to eighteen. In addition, his legs began to hurt and he was in great pain with an acute infection of the bone marrow. It is said that some interns (residents?) attempted to help, did an operation but botched it and he was encased in a cast from his feet to his neck. His sister persuaded a charity to give him a ticket to the Mayo Clinic where they did eighteen hours of nonstop surgery. Abe was never quite right but he was no longer crippled.

Abe had won a Pulitzer Prize while in Poland. He had seen the Russian secret police in action and he did not like it. Meanwhile, Salisbury had, while in Russia in 1953, scoffed at the notion that secret police terrorized the Russian people. "Most people think of the NKVD [predecessor to the KGB] as a sinister secret police which carts off Russians in the dead of the night and sends them packing to Siberia. Well, there is something in that impression, of course. The NKVD does things like that, occasionally. ..." Abe wondered, says Goulden, "How the hell Salisbury could live in a police state and be so oblivious to reality is beyond me." He was troubled by the fact that young reporters idolized Salisbury.

Author Gay Talese thought that Salisbury had done a wonderful job in reporting from Hanoi. He quoted columnist Walter Lippman approvingly:

> Mr. Salisbury's offense, we are being told, is that in reporting the war as seen from Hanoi, he has made himself a tool of enemy propaganda. We must remember that in time of war

what is said on the enemy's side of the front is always propaganda, and what is said on our side of the front is truth and righteousness, the cause of humanity and a crusade for peace. Is it necessary for us at the height of our power to stoop to such self-deceiving nonsense?

Those, of course, are very nice platitudes, but very simplistic. There is not much depth in that thinking. The problems of the world are not that easily solved. One must wonder, for example, if Lippman would have approved a trip to Berlin in 1943 to discover Joseph Goebbels' views. I have a friend who was an 11-year-old girl in Germany at that time. She says that British aircraft strafed her group of civilian refugees. Would Lippman have sent a reporter to interview Joseph Goebbels and determine the accuracy of such reports?

Tifft and Jones have no mention at all of Salisbury's reporting from Hanoi. Salisbury, himself, had only one sentence, which was about the denial of his Pulitzer Prize by a one-vote margin. "Later," he wrote, "Catledge was to call the CIA and Hanoi stories the landmark journalistic achievements of his term as managing editor of *The Times.*"

1971 — Pentagon Papers

The Pentagon Papers represent a weird experience in American history. The *Times* had always favored American men being sent to battle in World War I, Korea and Vietnam, while many others, including me, opposed our getting involved in any of those wars, including Vietnam.[6]

We knew that the government — and the *Times* — had lied to us in all those wars, beginning with Woodrow Wilson, who had Julius Ochs volunteer for a war that was going to "end all wars." It was difficult to understand how the *Times* was allowed to publish stolen, classified information from the Pentagon. How could they possibly know whether any of this information would help the enemy? If they had reason to believe that this information was classified as "secret" merely

---

6 Although World War II was probably inevitable after our intervention in the First World War, many believe we should not have agreed to the demands for unconditional surrender. That certainly meant that many more Jews and others needlessly died in the concentration camps while the war dragged on. Meanwhile, people like the minister, Dietrich Bonhoffer, who left the safety of America after the War started and sought, at great risk to his own life, to craft a plan to kill Hitler, was rebuffed by the British. Were the British interests always in accord with ours? During the meetings with Churchill and Stalin, Roosevelt was a very sick man. Bonhoffer was ultimately executed by the Nazis one month before the end of the War.

because it would be embarrassing to those in charge, should they not have to follow some procedure, such as go to a judge and have him decide in secret whether the information was properly classified? Of course, their concern really was that they didn't consider the Communist governments to be "enemy."

It would appear obvious to most that a newspaper should not be allowed to publish every secret document it has stolen.

Even if you believe that the *Times* should be allowed to publish the Pentagon Papers, the *Times* had not done anything particularly difficult.

It had not accomplished any great reporting. It only printed the document which had fallen into their lap from Daniel Ellsburg (an "intellectual," according to Edwin Diamond) who had been a hawk but had soured on the war.

This became a "great victory" for the *Times* even though the document showed how stupid the paper had been in promoting our entry into the war. It proved how prescient others had been in shuddering over their stupidity about escalating the war in Vietnam. It was obvious all along that Presidents Kennedy and Johnson had lied to them, or the *Times* had lied to us, or a combination of the above. But who had the power to explain that to the American people?

In effect, the Pentagon Papers were an exposé of the *Times* itself.

They would not have made much of a splash if President Nixon had not given them so much publicity. " [Nixon should have] welcomed publicity, making one thing perfectly clear. The Vietnam morass had not begun on his watch but on his predecessors', the Democrats Kennedy and Johnson," according to Edwin Diamond.

The lawsuits that followed went through a series of courts as both the *Times* and the *Washington Post* brought suits. The case went before the Supreme Court which held 6-3 in favor of the newspapers, but only three judges said that they would never restrain a newspaper from printing such documents. The other three looked at the papers in this particular case and determined these particular papers posed no real threat to the government. This meant that six of the nine judges would not allow a newspaper to unilaterally publish such documents in the future without court approval.

Harrison Salisbury believed the issue had clearly indicated that the *Times* had become the fourth branch of government. He thought it so important that it prompted him to write his book, *Without Fear or Favor*. In the foreword, he said:

In the past quarter of a century the American Establishment has been shaken to its foundations by what amounts to a new American Revolution. Power has flowed into different and not always steady hands. The country has been passing through (there is no sign that the process is yet complete) an epoch of change which begins to rival those surrealist dramas, Russia in 1917 and China in 1949.

The totality of this metamorphosis lies beyond the scope of this book, but what I try here to document is the role of *The New York Times*, how it has participated in these new currents, affecting them and being, in turn, profoundly changed itself.

We think of a newspaper, even a great newspaper like *The Times*, as holding up a looking glass to history. For many years *The Times* described itself as "a newspaper of record." It is my thesis, to paraphrase McLuhan, that, in a sense, the mirror has become the message; that in showing us what we are and what we are doing; in reflecting the bloat, the complexity, the con-tradictions of the post-World War II society, **The Times has come to fulfill a new function; it has quite literally become that Fourth Estate, that fourth coequal branch of government of which men like Thomas Carlyle spoke.** [Emphasis added]

I have centered my attention on a half-dozen events, mile-posts, if you will, of this process. The great confrontation over the Pentagon Papers takes a central place because it stands as a metaphor of the emergence of *The Times* into its new social role and, moreover, is in every respect an exciting, a cautionary and an until-now untold tale ...

My emphasis has been placed on the modern *Times* and *its times*, and particularly upon the American experience, the expe-rience of the last twenty or twenty-five years [1955 to 1980], the experience of change in the American Establishment and the American charter. ...

It is concerned with Vietnam at home not in Asia; the consequences of *Brown v. The Board of Education*; with the CIA as a metaphor of homegrown, secret and out-of-control bureaucracy. ...

Amid it *The Times* reaches out with its reporting skills, identifies the new thrusts, the new players, and tries, sometimes with clumsiness, to act as surrogate for the people, seeking to strengthen the First Amendment powers which enable it to examine, as the people no longer can, the BIGS, Big government, Big Bureaucracy, Big Spying, Big Interests, Big Labor, Big Business, all the multiplicands that have transformed our Jeffersonian society into something quite different, quite frightening at times, seldom understood, carrying on the task, as Mr. Ochs promised, "without fear or favor."

I agree that our major problem is all the BIGS. But Salisbury left out a very important one: BIG MEDIA, particularly the *New York Times*. What we now have is **not** what Adolph Ochs envisioned, a newspaper which presents all sides of an issue. That vision was violated a long time ago by Iphigene and Arthur. They started to put a little opinion into the news and present only the "correct" side — *their* side. It's gotten worse over the years since then and is now totally out of control with the new occupant of the throne, Pinch Sulzberger.

But what we are studying at the moment is Punch Sulzberger. What did he think of all this? It did not thrill him, but he could not move quickly. He had over 900 newsmen. That in itself is quite a "balance wheel" that would prevent anyone from making drastic changes. Punch was only thirty-seven with no experience and no newspaper ability when he was suddenly thrust into running this huge organization. It is amazing he did as well as he did.

Punch, at some level, was troubled by the Pentagon Papers. He realized that there were two sides to the issue, but he was under pressure from the news people and he agreed to the publication, even writing, "We are going to look back on these days as some of the most exhilarating in the history of the *Times* and ... in the history of American journalism."

Tifft and Jones approved. "The publication of the Pentagon Papers was his grand, defining moment, a moment in which he took bearings from his heritage and his own values and instincts, and steered the paper safely and surely toward the 'right' decision." There is no question that his decision greatly increased and solidified his prestige in the newsroom. A question arose during the process whether the *Times* would actually print the documents or merely quote or paraphrase them. The editors were firmly in favor of printing the documents. Abe Rosenthal felt so strongly that he had privately resolved to quit if Punch did not do so. On the Friday before the Sunday publication, Punch agreed.

When book companies came after the *Times* to make the story into a book, the government entreated Punch that this would be a serious mistake. It was one thing to print them in a newspaper which did not have a long shelf-life. Despite what he believed, they said, there was some information that could threaten the life of CIA agents and damage the country's security. Punch agreed not to publish a book.

The Pentagon Papers were about 7,000 pages in 47 volumes. The study was conceived by Robert McNamara, Secretary of Defense from 1961 through early 1968 who had been the prime architect of our policy in Vietnam under Presidents Kennedy and Johnson. He had made it grow from a few hundred advisors when he and Kennedy arrived to more than 500,000 American troops when he left. Before leaving, he ordered a small staff in the Department of Defense to do a secret study of America's decisions about Vietnam since the end of World War II. The study was completed in 1969. Only fifteen copies of the top-secret study were made, but two went to the Rand Corporation where Ellsburg read it. McNamara refused to talk about the war until he wrote a book in 1995 about the war he had created, in which he said the U.S. had been "wrong, terribly wrong." In a 1999 book, he estimated on the first page that 3.8 million Vietnamese were killed in the struggle.

Punch Had to Be Patient in Getting Control of Newsroom

"Punch was the most conservative member of the family," said Harrison Salisbury.

But his mother made up for it. Salisbury continued: "There was no other member of the Sulzberger family as liberal [as Iphigene]." She was constantly at Punch's side and could easily intimidate him with her knowledge of the paper, which went all the way back to 1896. She had been very upset with her father, Adolph, when he would not consider her as a possible Publisher and even dismissed her from a reporter's job she had obtained without his knowledge, after graduating from Columbia.

Despite the immense pressures, Punch managed to keep the paper mostly in the mainstream. However, it was a long struggle to finally get his own people in place.

Six years went by before Punch got his editor, Abe Rosenthal, in 1969.

It was undoubtedly beneficial that Punch was not a talented newsman. He would have been unable to handle the financial pressures if he were worrying about the details in the newsroom. Abe did a good job of keeping those pressures off him, although it meant that Abe became the lightning rod.

The Washington bureau became a regular target of Abe's complaints, says Edwin Diamond, because those reporters were editorializing (or as Arthur used to call it, "interpreting") in their news stories. They quoted congressional liberals more, and more favorably, than conservatives.

Abe singled out the edition of November 7, 1969, for comment. "On page 7 we have a story about the G.I. trial at Ft. Dix. On page 8 we have the MIT sit-in and on page 9 we have the moratorium. On page 14 we have the Army memorandum about the anti-war protest. On page 22, the Chicago trial, in between two stories about poverty and housing demonstrations. On page 27 a story about job discrimination. There are others, this was not a particularly outstanding day for that kind of thing. But I get the impression, after reading the *Times* that the image we give of America is largely of demonstrations, an important part of the American scene. But I think that because of our own liberal interest and our reporters' inclination, we overdo this. I am not suggesting eliminating any of these stories, I'm suggesting that reporters and editors look a bit more around them to see what is going on in other fields and to try to make an effort to represent other shades of opinion than those held by the new Left, the old Left, the middle aged Left and anti-war people."

However, the reporters in the New York newsroom did not agree that they should present all sides of a story; they were deeply embedded into "interpretations." They believed that the editors were imposing their conservatism on the news department. A group began informal meetings and mockingly called themselves, "the cabal." Rosenthal arranged a dinner meeting with them. He enjoyed a good argument but didn't plan to change his beliefs. He talked about how decision-making over the years had broadened, but newsrooms weren't democratic assemblies. "The news columns will not be made into a political broadsheet — period."

Abe also complained when he found that a roundup story was "editorialized in the extreme and terribly naive." He complained to his deputy: "the whole thrust of the first few paragraphs is to equate lack of political action and demonstrations on the campuses with sleepy-headedness, social indifference, and boredom. Who says so? Did it not occur to [reporter] McFadden that a great many people believe that the purpose of a campus is not political action at all, but study? I really couldn't believe my eyes when I read those first three paragraphs."

On a Saturday night, August 11, 1979, he called the news desk, to order some changes in the second edition of the Sunday paper in a feature about the tenth anniversary of Woodstock. He ordered them to remove the reporter's "vacuous politicalization." The reporter had termed Woodstock a symbol of a "national, cultural, and political awakening," and "the culmination of a decade-long youth crusade for a free style of life, peace and tolerance," and he said that in the decade of the 1970's, radical politics "reverted to more conventional politics and even apathy." On Monday morning, Rosenthal told his editors, that the story was implying that "there was a downward scale from radicalism to conventional politics." Abe's comment was, "Good God!"

One of Punch's top aides, who was asked to retire as assistant to the publisher and give up his seat on the Board of Directors when he approached 70, was so hurt by the way it was handled that he said this: "People are close to Punch, [but] Punch doesn't feel very close to anybody. He was smart enough at some point in life to realize that people foam around the publisher of the *New York Times*, and if you're not careful, they're biting at you or sucking at you or licking at you. It suited Punch's character and personality to remain this rigid person unto himself and never to let very much of himself out to anybody."

Punch did make an effort to control cousin John Oakes, who had just been named head of the Editorial Page in 1961. Punch told him early in 1964 that he did not like a proposed editorial to eliminate subsidies for a supersonic transport that was being considered. When John proposed a new editorial, which was not much better, he received a note from Punch. "If no one on your floor feels the way I do, I shall be glad to write the editorial myself or get someone to write it for me." But Punch's tough demeanor didn't last long when John filibustered. Punch quickly abandoned the idea of trying to control John until 1976 when, as we have seen, Punch finally removed him while he was on Nantucket.

Besides getting the newsroom under control, Punch had to worry about keeping the newspaper in business. We will talk about that in the next chapter.

Punch Seemed Determined to Help the Anti-Semites

For some reason, Punch seemed determined to help the anti-Semites, who had warned when Adolph started the paper, that this would be a strictly Jewish enterprise. Both Adolph and Arthur were careful that this did not happen. They attempted to keep a fair balance of people at the paper, even going too far in the opposite direction. They apparently believed that having a Jew at the top of the paper meant that they should be careful not to make it appear as though it was the organ of only one group of people.

But Punch, for some reason which is not apparent, broke that tradition and went to the opposite extreme, particularly in the newsroom. He hired many Jews and even gave the impression that he was doing so on purpose, although it appeared that he would also hire non-Jews if they were good men. One would hope that being in a city where Jews were a large part of the population, he merely took the best people he could find. But, on the other hand, he was still proving the point of the anti-Semites that this would be a Jewish newspaper. He should have been aware that he was creating that appearance.

This became particularly apparent when he installed his son as President and Publisher, as if he were part of a royal family, a King.

19

Punch Was Changing the Paper In Order to Survive; No Longer Just a Newspaper, but a Highly Profitable Business

During Punch's rule, there were bad recessions at times which hurt The Company. In addition, readership of newspapers across the country dropped sharply as television took over. These forced extensive changes in the *Times* in order to survive.

Punch never was talented on the news side of newspapers. Now, he had to be preoccupied with the money needed to keep it afloat.

On August 30, 1976, the cover of *Business Week* magazine showed a picture of him, looking grim. The headline read: "Behind the Profit Squeeze at the New York Times." The reading inside was grimmer still. The magazine reported that Company stock was down from $53 a share in 1968 (the year that public shares began to be traded on the American Stock Exchange) to $14.50 a share in the summer of 1976. The second paragraph of the story reported a complaint that was familiar to Punch: "Editorially and politically, the newspaper has also slid precipitously to the left and has become stridently antibusiness in tone, ignoring the fact that the Times itself is a business. ..."

In order to survive, Punch had to change the paper.

"As we will see," wrote Diamond in 1993, "over the past two decades, the *Times* redefined the meaning of news. Led by its editor, A.M. Rosenfeld, the *Times* in the 1970s broadened coverage of 'soft news' topics and introduced the daily feature sections revolving around upscale consumerism: the so-called sectional revolution. The 'new' *New*

York Times, the paper's promotional slogan boasted. Some critics viewed the changes as frivolous, a violation of the *Times'* traditional mission. But the new sections attracted younger readers and vastly improved the *Times'* advertising revenues at a time when both the New York economy and the Times Company were financially strapped. ***

"The soft-news sections were only the most visible sign of change at the *Times* during the three decades of Punch Sulzberger's tenure. The geography of the *Times* changed. The security analysts understood that Punch Sulzberger no longer operated a New York City business; he headed a national enterprise, with a chain of newspapers in the Sunbelt states as well as a magazine group and broadcast properties. Less obviously, though the *Times* newspaper still called itself the *New York Times*, it had ceased to be a New York paper. There were no longer enough of the kind of readers the *Times* wanted to attract within the city and near suburbs. The readers of Sheepshead Bay had been written off; the paper now looked beyond to the nation across the Hudson. Walter Mattson, Sulzberger's top business-side executive, put the situation most directly in a confidential memorandum in early 1976, when New York was still feeling the effects of the municipal fiscal crisis, the loss of manufacturing jobs, and 'white flight' out of the city."

Changing the Paper In Order to Survive

Punch engineered a great "rescue" of the paper in the 1970s and 1980s when the whole enterprise appeared to be sinking, along with the municipal fortunes of New York City, wrote Edwin Diamond:

"Between 1970 and 1975, for example, the *Times* suffered severe circulation and advertising losses. In one six-month period alone in 1971, daily circulation dropped by some 31,000 to 814,000. The *Times* had increased its newsstand price from 10 to 15 cents per copy, and the message seemed clear: Some people didn't think the *Times* was worth a nickel more. 'I used to have a nightmare when I was editor,' Abe Rosenthal recalled two decades later. 'It's a Wednesday morning and there's no *New York Times*.' In Rosenthal's recollection, 'If no one did anything, and if we kept losing money, then the *Times* could have gone out of business. I'm not saying that it would have happened, but that it could have.'

"By the mid-1980's, however, all the trend lines had been reversed. Not only did the *Times* regain the daily circulation it lost in the early 1970s; it added another 100,000 readers between 1976 and 1982, then another 50,000 by 1984, and then another 50,000 more, to go over the one million mark in 1986. The city had come back and so had its leading newspaper. The *Times* shift to special interest coverage, its sectional revolution, became a model of the industry, and the faltering paper of the 1970s metamorphosed into the money machine of the late 1980s, throwing off operating profits of $200 million a year.

"The architects of its success were, in the commonly accepted accounting of events: Abraham Michael Rosenthal from the news department, and his opposite on the business side, Walter Mattson. Overseeing their work, leading the two leaders, was the third member of this pantheon of achievement, Arthur Ochs Sulzberger. They were, to be sure, a disparate team: Abe Rosenthal, son of immigrants, abrasive, driven, emotional; Walt Mattson, plain-spoken, curt, direct, a production specialist from western Pennsylvania, never wholly comfortable in New York; Arthur Ochs Sulzberger, the scion of privilege who had been treated rather dismissively by his family and associates in his earlier years. But, together, the odd trio remade the *Times*. They turned it into a contemporary guide to good living while maintaining comprehensive news coverage; they insured its continued preeminence in the new media landscape."

After all that great praise, Diamond argued the other side: "The actual sequence of events was at once less dramatic and more ambiguous." The *Times* wasn't the only paper making changes and it never came close to shutting its doors. Newspapers such as the *Washington Post* and *Wall Street Journal* improved their papers and the *Times* lost some of its best people during all the shuffling. The *Times* was always a snobby paper that did not worry about the poor and dispossessed of the city. It was always interested in the "wider world of national and international news." The *Times* typically maintained more reporters in London or Paris than in the outer boroughs of New York City.

There were cash problems again in 1991 and 1992. *Times* advertising sales continued to drop off in the key categories of retail (the department stores), help-wanted and real estate. The paper's profits fell by a third. "The *Times* had hidden annual costs, computer-system upgrades, and replacement of delivery-truck fleets, among other recurring outlays," Diamond reports. "For a paper the size of the *Times*, these costs ran as high as $50 million a year. They had to be paid for out of earnings. ... Arthur did what executives of most large corporations try to do in tough times. He looked for ways to reduce fixed operating costs. To cut the size of the staff, the *Times* in the summer of 1991 offered buyouts to employees age fifty-five or older and with more than fifteen years' service at the paper. The buyouts were a civilized preview of the *Times'* bare-knuckle negotiations with its blue-collar unions the following year."

Affluent, Suburban Housewives Read It for the Fashions

Between 1976 and 1978, the *Times* introduced its daily, consumer-oriented C sections (Sports, Monday; Science, Tuesday; Living, Wednesday; Home, Thursday; Weekend, Friday). The Monday-through-Saturday Business Day, a stand-alone section offered expanded coverage of business and finance.

All of them became money-makers though none did quite as well financially as the special magazine section called "Fashions of the Times," or FOTs. The paper had become the darling of affluent, suburban housewives. The *Times* so dominated the upper end of the newspaper audience in the Northeast that space buyers could go only to *Vogue*, *GQ*, and the glossy magazines for alternative print options.

In the mid-1970s, when the *Times* was being considered to be a faltering enterprise, *Business Week* magazine had criticized the paper's "leftist" bent and Punch's apparent disdain for profits. In the magazine's issue of April 26, 1986, *Business Week* couldn't find enough compliments to pay Sulzberger and his *Times*. According to *Business Week*, the *Times* was "flush with record profits." The company had spent some $400 million on acquisitions in 1985, and was still a "hugely profitable engine for growth." With the "flagship paper throwing off cash," *Business Week* concluded, Sulzberger now presided over a company with "an embarrassment of riches."

Profits Used to Acquire Boston Globe

When The Company bought the *Boston Globe* for $1.1 billion in 1993, Punch traveled to Boston to announce the deal and talk with reporters at the Parker House and later at a hotel in New York.

When asked what he was going to do now, he turned to the former owner of the *Globe*, William O. Taylor, and smiled, "My first executive decision, Bill? Not to work. I'm giving myself the weekend off."

But some raised the problem of too much power in one person. "In terms of high-quality buyers, the *Globe* could not do much better than the Sulzbergers," said Ben H. Bagdikian, former dean of the Graduate School of Journalism at the University of California at Berkeley.

"But," he added, "there is a deep philosophical problem in leaving so few people in control of most of the printed news in this country. In the long run, even the best protect themselves in the news columns when central corporate interests are at stake."

Taylor said that his autonomy at the *Globe* had been assured, and Punch agreed he would not fix something "that wasn't broken." But a top executive at the *Times* added, "Of course, he'll [Punch] be very interested in what goes on at the paper. That's only natural."

The then-retired editor, Abe Rosenthal, who was then a columnist, said, "In all the years I've known him, he has never, ever used the *Times* for personal or political or social or financial gain. Ever."

Rosenthal also related how Punch had accepted an award at Columbia University. "After a whole bunch of pompous speeches, Punch went up there and they gave him this award and then he just said: 'Well, I believe in following in my father's footsteps. I just thank God that he wasn't a kosher butcher.'"

Section V

Is Pinch an Extremist?

This is where we discuss the significance of the Jayson Blair tragedy and the gay marriage scandal in Massachusetts that have been foisted on the gray lady (or perhaps we should say, "gray, gay lady") by Pinch Sulzberger.

20

Punch and Pinch Clash over Homosexuality; As the Two Extremists Battled, Nation Was Unaware

It happened on Thursday, October 16, 1997. After that day, some subjects would no longer be debated in our country. Pinch Sulzberger would keep us informed as to what was acceptable.

He had been granted complete and total power over the entire structure of the enormously powerful *New York Times*. He was now Publisher of the *Times* and Chairman of The Company.[1] He immediately began doing things *his* way, regardless of what his father or anyone else thought. Everyone within The Company who had challenged him had been banished, including his father. He alone would decide the issues.

His fascination with homosexuality, which began in his teen years, was puzzling. For whatever reason, his first priority was to attack homophobia, particularly that of his father and all his ancestors, which would not be a bad thing to do in itself. But Pinch had lurched into a phobia of his own, a dislike for straight, white males, known as heterophobia.

This change began to impact us in Massachusetts shortly thereafter. We didn't realize for a while what was happening. We couldn't connect

---

[1] When he chaired the Board for the first time, he wore the wristwatch his wife, Gail Gregg, had given him in celebration, with his initials on the back and an inscription from his favorite TV program, Star Trek: LIVE LONG AND PROSPER. He also wore the gold cufflinks Gail had given him when he became Publisher of the *Times* with that date inscribed: January 16, 1992. These talismans authenticated the power he had been granted by some unidentified force.

the dots because we didn't know that the dots existed. But it all came together beginning in 2001 and culminating in 2003 with Pinch's triumph of gay marriage through the Massachusetts Supreme Judicial Court. His plan isn't to implement that triumph only in one state. Therein lies our story.

Pinch's father didn't deserve this shoddy treatment and therein lies another story.

Punch Didn't Deserve Shoddy Treatment

Punch had labored long and hard for thirty-four years, from 1963 to 1997, dedicated to the vision his beloved grandfather had entrusted to him at an early age. He was tired and more than ready to retire. More important, he was in love. He deserved it. He and his new wife, Allison Cowles,[2] a 63-year-old widow, were like lovesick teenagers, holding hands and slipping their arms around each other at every chance. His daughter, Cathy, said, "I've never seen my dad like that." Punch told visitors he was having trouble concentrating. He wanted to run away from work.

The transformed, happy couple was married on March 9, 1996.[3] After that, Punch became anxious to do the more important things, like taking Allison on trips around the world. "Once things get decided and done, I'm the kind of person who puts it behind [me]," he said later. "There are other things to worry about. Like walking the dog." (Allison had a black-and-white collie which she brought to New York with her.)

Allison was someone whom Punch deserved: A Phi Beta Kappa from Wellesley College and editor of the college newspaper, she later became a Trustee of the college. She had married Bill Cowles, the owner of two dailies in Spokane, Washington, who came to know Punch well during thirty years of association at the American Newspaper Publishers Association. The two families had become very close, even sharing two-bedroom suites at Claridge's during stays in London. When Bill died of a heart attack while jogging in 1992, Punch

---

[2] Allison was two years ahead of my wife, Sally, at Wellesley College, 1955 and 1957.

[3] Despite the urgings of his sisters, Marian and Judy, Punch had apparently never gotten a lover as they had suggested. Therefore, he didn't have any complicated entanglements other than the family that everyone knew about. He could marry Allison quickly and shout his love to the world.

had flown to the funeral in Spokane. Allison had continued to be active in the Publishers Association and Associated Press.

Before getting to "the more important things," Punch had one more pressing chore: implementing his choice for successor, which he did the following year. Then he faded enthusiastically into the sunset to enjoy what remained before Parkinson's disease would take its toll.

However, Punch had hidden, even from himself, the tremendous conflict he had with his son over homosexuality. He had no idea that this unresolved conflict of two extreme views would quickly shake and transform our nation in a way that would have made his father, mother, grandfather and everyone in the family shudder.

Was Punch Really a Homophobe?

Punch didn't have much knowledge about homosexuality or any desire to learn, nor did his father and grandparents. There were other things that loomed much larger in their lives. As a result, Pinch immediately, and publicly, labeled them all as "homophobes." The *Times* suddenly jumped from the homophobia of Punch to the opposite extreme, Pinch's dislike, and possible fear, of heterosexuals, particularly male heterosexuals. This problem of Pinch and others was rapidly becoming known as heterophobia.

There is a common sense, middle ground, but the Sulzberger family was unable to find it. Their problem in coping with homosexuality had transformed a family disagreement into a serious problem for the entire nation.

We witnessed an abrupt and unexplainable change in the *Times*.

Abe Rosenthal Had Tried to Bridge the Gap

When Abe Rosenthal had returned from overseas to New York as Metropolitan Editor back in 1963, he had been struck by the new presence of the homosexual community and had an apparently balanced story written about the change with no problems from anyone.

But on Sunday, April 6, 1975 an entirely different kind of story appeared. The headline across the lead article in the travel section of the *Times* was **The All-Gay Cruise: Prejudices and Pride**. It told of a weeklong cruise, with intimate details, of 300 homosexuals on a French liner from Florida to the Yucatan. It had made homosexuality into a "fun event," one that anyone might want to try as their next cruise. This was in the "Travel" section.

The scene in Punch's office the next day, with the travel editor and Sunday editor Max Frankel, is described by Joe Goulden:

"Sulzberger was livid to the extent of his abilities. How dare the *Times* and its reputation be sullied by such an article! Since when are orgies news? And especially *orgies* by a bunch . . . a bunch of . . . he had to force the words through lips curled with disgust . . . *orgies by a bunch of faggots.* [Italics in original.]

"Even his mother, Sulzberger continued, had called in indignation. How am I as her son and as publisher of our newspaper, how am I supposed to explain such an article, much less defend it? You have caused me great embarrassment, you have offended my mother, you have put a stain on *The New York Times*. Iphigene Sulzberger was an understanding woman, Sulzberger went on, but she was also a lady, and ladies did not like reading such 'garbage' anywhere, and especially on Sunday morning in her very own newspaper."

There's little question that Punch was upset that details about this type of conduct were described and printed in his paper where his mother and children could read it.

Attitudes Were Changing Because of Psychiatrists

Because he had dyslexia and was not a good reader, Punch didn't realize that the nation's psychiatrists had changed everything two years earlier in 1973. Homosexuality suddenly became "normal." The *Times* could no longer deal with this matter by engaging in a shouting match.

The American Psychiatric Association voted in 1973 (while America was distracted by the war which the *Times* had urged upon us) that homosexuality would no longer be considered a "disorder." (The APA's change came as a response to violence at their annual meetings.) But Punch surely didn't know that. He didn't know that only one-third of the psychiatrists had participated in the vote in 1973. He didn't know it because it wasn't reported in the *Times*. He didn't know it four years later when 69% of the psychiatrists reported they disagreed with the vote. That also was not reported in his newspaper. He probably didn't know it in 1993 when the "gay gene" myth *was* reported to the world by his own newspaper. As a result, for six years the "sophisticated" would believe in the "gay gene." But Punch was too busy, and besides, he would rather ignore the whole matter, as would all of us. He also probably didn't read it when his paper reported in 1999 that researchers had been unable to find any truth in the theory of a "gay gene."

Extremism at *Times* Caused Problems When AIDS Came

The extremism of the Sulzberger family about homosexuality caused serious problems for them, their country and the world when AIDS arrived.

There was no serious voice of reason within the paper itself, only homophobes and heterophobes shouting on both sides, with apathy from most people who just tried to "stay out of it." The *Times* had become a serious detriment to the nation on this issue, just as it had in the 1960s when Punch's cousin, the editor of the editorial page, lurched from one extreme on Vietnam and then to the other.

Punch acted foolishly in 1975 at the time of the weeklong, homosexual cruise in the Caribbean. He got his point across, but he frightened the editors from ever discussing the issue with him again.

Also in 1975, *Chorus Line* opened on Broadway, next door to the *Times*, to rave notices. It continued to run until 1990. Didn't Punch know that? The psychiatrists had indeed, changed everything. The musical was a paean to dancers and to homosexuality. The show and the audience laughed at homophobes. It was a great example of art transforming a culture. No one realized while they were laughing that its creator was a homosexual who died in 1987 without ever revealing that he himself had AIDS.

As a consequence, when AIDS did come along, the *Times* was unable to treat it as just another one of the many venereal diseases which have troubled the world ever since its creation. This was different, we were told; it wasn't a venereal disease at all. This was the fault of homophobes like Punch, his mother, his father and grandfather and anyone else who didn't glorify the practice of homosexuality.

Certainly, Punch had valid qualms about the practice of homosexuality. Even most homosexuals do. It is not a lifestyle that most of them enjoy. That is why their culture is so heavily into drugs and alcohol. But the homosexuals earnestly believe they are stuck with it; they were "born that way." Instead of intelligent discussions about the many issues surrounding this lifestyle, Punch tried to ignore it and hope it would go away. He was obviously concerned because of the pressure from Iphigene. She had made him rigid.

Goulden's description of what happened at the paper was: "The *Times* treatment of gays, its ignoring of them, more accurately, is acutely illustrative of the paper's [family's] arrogance in dealing with issues with which it is not comfortable ..."

Trying to ignore the issue had been a total failure. It did not allow the *Times* to take the high ground when AIDS arrived. It would have been tough for the paper in any case, because the activists were well organized as the psychiatrists had discovered. Also, people had to feel sorry for those who suffered from AIDS just as they did those who suffered from a lifetime of smoking cigarettes. There were many stories about people who smoked like chimneys all their lives and lived to one hundred, just as there were stories of homosexuals who died late in life. But no one could reasonably question the terrible health risks of both practices.

Ignoring Homosexuality Had Been a Failure

Homosexuals did not want to hear that they held the keys to their own health. Even without AIDS, the practice of homosexuality does tremendous harm to the body. Many diseases such as tuberculosis, syphilis and damage to the rectum are serious problems. Drug use is high in that community. The whole idea of taking personal responsibility for one's actions had fled our nation after the Vietnam War, leaving only the "victim" mentality. There have always been consequences from unrestrained sex. Punch did not invent it.

The really tragic cases were those unfortunates, particularly children, who became infected and lost their lives because of tainted blood transfusions.

In 1981, the *Wall Street Journal* wrote the first AIDS article which appeared in a major newspaper. The reporter sensed a major tragedy in

the making but he was unable to convince his editors of the seriousness
of the disease. When asked by Goulden why that had been true, he
responded, "Because no one else was covering it. You know, 'How
come there's an epidemic going on in the *Times's* backyard, and they're
not writing about it?'" The simple answer, which the *Journal* didn't
know, was that Iphigene forbad it.

The *Times* did have small stories in 1982-1983, mainly on the science page. In April, 1983, the Gay Men's Health Crisis bought out
Madison Square Garden for a performance by Ringling Brothers
Barnum & Bailey Circus. Some 18,000 persons attended, probably
most of them were homosexuals. Mayor Edward Koch was opening
ringmaster and Leonard Bernstein directed the circus band in the
National Anthem. Stories about the fund-raiser appeared the next day
in the Chicago *Tribune*, the Philadelphia *Inquirer*, and the Washington
Post — but not in the *New York Times*.

That did it. The *Times* relented after the outcry, but, under the leadership of Punch, they continued to look stupid on this subject. They
slowly changed after being forced to meet with strident activists. But
they obviously didn't know where they were heading. They provided no
leadership. In June 1983, they ran two long stories on the impact of
AIDS on "ordinary people." But they were responding only to the
activist homosexuals, the extremists.

Pinch Embraced Homosexuality

Immediately upon arriving at the *Times* in the early 1980s, Pinch
repudiated his heritage with unbounded enthusiasm and became a
secret, under-the-table supporter of activist homosexuals at the *Times*.
That story is related by Tifft and Jones:

"[Editor] Abe Rosenthal's despotic quirks, coupled with his clear
squeamishness about gays, had conspired to create an atmosphere of
cowed silence among homosexual reporters. [I, obviously, have a problem with that description of Abe. He had gotten his marching orders
from Punch and the family.]

"To protect their careers, they remained resolutely in the closet.
[Pinch] found the climate disturbing and uncomfortable; like most
members of his generation, he accepted sexual orientation as a matter

of course. In reaction, he decided to send a signal that he didn't support this particular aspect of the Rosenthal regime.

"In the course of a week, [Pinch] individually took the reporters on the metropolitan desk whom he suspected were homosexual out to lunch. 'So,' he began with each one, leaning over the table, 'what is it like to be gay at the *New York Times*?' After his guest had recovered his composure, [Pinch] went on to say that he considered it 'crazy' to work together so closely and 'not have this behind us.' Denying one's sexual orientation, he said, is a 'silly way to live our lives.' As news of [Pinch's] 'outing' made its way through the newsroom, the reaction among gays was one of immense relief. ...

"It turned out to be a benchmark moment for [Pinch] as well. Soon word filtered back to him that his colleagues had viewed his behavior not merely as a warm personal act by an assignment editor who cared about his reporters but as a bellwether of the presumed future, a brave new world with [Pinch] as publisher. 'All of a sudden, I was being seen in a different light,' he said. 'That was the first time that had happened to me.'"

One has to wonder about the brazenness of an employer who would invade the personal life of an employee in that manner. Was he implying that homosexuals are easily identifiable? Do they stand out in a crowd? What if he made a mistake and asked a straight man? Did he include women in his survey or did he not care about them? How much time did he spend observing his employees with their sex life on his mind? How spooky would that make you feel if you were an employee? Did Pinch keep a list of homosexuals? What other lists did he keep?

You also must wonder about his loyalty to his father, his editors and everyone else at the paper. He was undermining their ability to run this business. He obviously thought he was in charge as a divine right.

Of course, the ultimate question must be asked: Was this a setup by Pinch in an attempt to improve the image of the unpopular son of the owner who had to get someone on his side?

An interesting anecdote from this period was when Pinch was caught reading Abe's telephone messages on his secretary's desk. One day, a secretary saw him with the messages he had lifted off a spike on her desk. "Who the hell do you think you are?" she demanded. "I'm a reporter, I've got all the instincts, I can't help it," he responded in his usual wiseass manner.

In 1989, one of the first things Pinch did, as the newly appointed Assistant Publisher of the newspaper, was to send a public message of support to a national association of gay and lesbian journalists, publicly aligning the new *Times* with its cause, thus going to the opposite extreme. As a consequence, Pinch had, by himself, put the prestige of the *Times* squarely behind the concept of granting homosexual reporters the power to send their message to unsuspecting readers without contradiction or attribution.

In 1994, Pinch went behind his father's back once again after he had become Publisher of the *New York Times* newspaper, but before he was made Chairman of the whole conglomerate.

Punch discovered to his surprise one day (while reading another newspaper) that the *Times* had just signed a new contract with the reporters' union, which included health benefits for "partners" of homosexuals. (This fulfilled the promise Pinch had made to the National Lesbian and Gay Journalists Association two years earlier.)

This discovery made Punch livid. Not only had his son approved the contract, he hid it from his father because he knew Punch would not approve.

However, Pinch showed little remorse. He really didn't care that he had angered and embarrassed his father. He called Punch to apologize but he didn't mean it. He said a few days later, "He had a right to be pissed at me. I finagled it; I did an end run." But after that mea culpa, he said with great certainty: "My father's position is wrong [on homosexual health benefits]."

Punch's feelings about his son wavered at that point. The most troubling aspect was the devious way that Pinch had done this. The general counsel of The Company pointed out: "Punch has to take into consideration the judgment of the person that he's appointing [as Chairman], and that was not great judgment not to tell his father." In other words, Pinch had shown himself to be a sneak, even to his own father. And Pinch never did understand that. He believed he had a "right" to control the *Times*, a right that no one could deny him.

The question that will never be answered is: What would have happened if the *Times* had been on top of this story from the beginning, as Abe had tried to do, and had reported it in a balanced way? The answer is that our nation would not have fostered the tremendously powerful homosexual activists we see today. Only 3% of the population is homosexual and the activists are probably .003% of the population. Iphigene and Punch unintentionally created the power of the extremists because of their dogged, unyielding position at the opposite pole.

21

Pinch's Lurch Was Felt Immediately In Massachusetts

We became aware of the change almost immediately here in Massachusetts.

It was in October 1998 that we first learned about "The Legend of Matthew Shepard," a myth perpetrated by Pinch Sulzberger.

Shepard's tragic story was that of a young man, a homosexual, who went to a bar in Laramie, Wyoming, left there with two psychopaths (or two men high on drugs) who robbed and murdered him, leaving him barely alive, tied to a fence. They returned to town and attacked two straight men, hitting one of them with a pistol and opening a wound in his head which required twenty-two stitches to close. They stopped only when one of the others hit back with a stick, giving one of the attackers a hairline skull fracture.

The killing occurred on October, 6, 1998, but it was not reported by the *Times* or the *Globe* until October 10. After all, it was only a local story of robbery/murder.

Between those two dates, People for the American Way (PAW), a liberal advocacy group, notified the papers that the crime resulted from "hate" by Christians. Of course, the two murderers had no connection whatsoever with any Christian. The headline on the PAW press release was **"Religious Right's 'Lying About Love' Campaign."**

The legend was that the crime occurred because Christians had promoted a "climate of hate." They had placed advertisements in major newspapers across the country saying that homosexuals can and do change their orientation. The headline of the Christians' advertisement was: **"We're standing for the truth that homosexuals can change; Thousands of former homosexuals can celebrate a new life because someone cared enough to share with them the truth of God's healing love."** That message was not new, but it certainly went against Pinch's vision for America.

The simple truth, however, is that many homosexuals _have_ changed their lives. The psychiatrist who led the change at the APA in 1973, Dr. Robert Spitzer, Chief of Biometric Research and Professor of Psychiatry at Columbia University, has done studies which show that homosexuals can and do change.[1]

"Like most psychiatrists," he says, "I thought that homosexual behavior could only be _resisted,_ and that no one could really change their sexual orientation. I now believe that to be false. Some people _can_ and _do_ change.

"Contrary to conventional wisdom, some highly motivated individuals, using a variety of change efforts, can make substantial change in multiple indicators of sexual orientation."

Dr. Spitzer has interviewed 200 men and women who have experienced a significant shift from homosexual to heterosexual attraction and have sustained this shift for at least five years. Many of the persons had sought change because of disillusionment with a promiscuous lifestyle and unstable, stormy relationships. Many reported a conflict with their religious values and others had desired to be (or to stay) heterosexually married. By the time of the study interview, three-quarters of the men and half of the women had become married.

One surprising discovery was that of the men who had _rarely_ or _never_ felt any opposite-sex attraction before the change effort, 67% now reported significant heterosexual attraction. Even those whose orientation did not change, but who gave up homosexual behavior, experienced a significant improvement in emotional health.

Dr. Spitzer cautioned against an "either/or" view of orientation change. A better way to conceptualize change "is to see it as a diminishing of unwanted homosexuality and an increase in heterosexual potential, recognizing that for some, change is possible along a multi-

---

[1] The study is published in "Archives of Sexual Behavior," Vol. 32, No. 5, October 2003, pp. 403-417.

dimensional continuum." While cautioning against any form of coercive treatment, he added, "I believe patients should have the right to explore their heterosexual potential."

Right now, psychiatrists and psychologists are frowned upon when they help patients change their orientation. Some say it is unethical.

According to the Sulzberger/Shepard legend, the Christian advertisement was said to be "hateful" speech. The "spin" was preposterous, but the *Times* and the *Globe* repeated it over and over and continue to do so until this day. To the best of my knowledge, they have not reported the Spitzer findings which are finally being discussed at the APA meetings.

Pinch Created the Legend

Ten days after the murder, the *Times* had a headline, **Men Held in Beating Lived on the Fringes**. The story informed us that the two criminals had had serious problems with the law and with mayhem long before Matthew Shepard came along. Their entanglement with him was nothing new in their disordered lives.

(There are many stories of innocent heterosexual boys who have been grotesquely murdered by homosexual men. We had a particularly gruesome case right here in Newton, Massachusetts, a few years back. Prosecutors say the killers were sexually obsessed with young Jeffrey. They lured him from his neighborhood with the promise of a new bike. When he resisted, they smothered him with a gasoline-soaked rag. The two men molested and murdered the boy before stuffing his body into a concrete-filled container and dumping it in a Maine river. The story of Matthew Shepard is very sad but why is it more tragic than what happened to little ten-year-old Jeffrey Curley? No one believes that *all* homosexuals were responsible for the young boy's murder. To make such a claim would be as absurd as saying that Christians were in any way responsible for the murder of Matthew Shepard.)

The PAW report started with this statement, "Anti-gay hatred is a staple of Religious Right organizations and figures." Then the President of PAW's foundation was quoted, "If this campaign is about truth or love, then George Orwell must be its honorary chairman."

As proof, it quoted a mayoral candidate in Springdale, Arkansas, who said, "Homosexuals are perverts....I will do everything I can do to keep them out of Springdale." Needless to say, he was not elected.

A "Christian" radio talk-show host in Costa Mesa, California, was also cited as proof. He is supposed to have said: "Lesbian love, sodomy are viewed by God as being detestable and abominable. Civil magistrates are to put people to death who practice these things." It would be enlightening to hear from *anyone* who thinks that *any* Christian could believe that statement.

It's no wonder that the people at PAW see hate everywhere when they are so obsessed with it themselves.

Anti-Christian Aspect Was Serious Concern

The Matthew Shepard legend became important to me personally when a column in the local New Bedford *Standard Times* jumped out a few weeks later with the headline: "The Long Sorry History of Christian Bigotry Continues Unabated."[2]

That aroused my curiosity. Was the *Standard Times* accurate in its denunciation of Christian leaders in America? I had no idea; perhaps it might be true. After only a few days of research, it was readily apparent that what the New Bedford paper wrote was a tissue of lies. What happened to Shepard was a grotesque tragedy, but grotesque tragedies happen to many people every day.

---

[2] I now understand why I never received a response to the following letter I sent to Pinch on May 16, 2002, although at the time it left me puzzled and concerned.

Arthur Sulzberger, Jr., The New York Times Company, 229 W. 43rd Street, New York, NY 10036
Via Federal Express
Dear Mr. Sulzberger:
Many in New England were saddened and hurt on May 9 when a columnist for the Boston Globe, Alex Beam, penned an offensive remark about Jesus Christ.
The columnist used both Jesus Christ and John the Baptist as comparisons to minivans. His exact words were, "With hindsight, we see that the very profitable minivan was the John the Baptist for Detroit's version of Jesus Christ — the criminally profitable SUV."
It is difficult to know what was going through Alex Beam's mind — or the mind of the Globe editors — when that language was approved. But it certainly appears to have been intentional. What are we readers to make of this?
The incident is particularly difficult to understand since you are Jewish and one would expect that you would be especially sensitive to the feelings of persons of other religions.
You would not be happy, nor would we, if Beam had written, "With hindsight, we see that the very profitable minivan was the Abraham for Detroit's version of Moses - the criminally profitable SUV."
You would not think that was funny and neither would we.
Would you please advise whether this was an aberration, or was it the true feeling of Globe management?
Sincerely,
Atty. J. Edward Pawlick, Publisher

The legend refuses to die because Pinch works very hard to keep it alive. For example, it reappeared in March 2002 as a huge splash on the front page of the Living Arts section of the *Globe*, taking almost the entire page to tell about this "folk hero" and "hate crime" victim.

However, in the next-to-last paragraph of the very long story, the author of an empathetic book about Shepard is quoted, "I still don't feel I understand what happened that night. I don't think anybody does. I don't think [the killers] can really explain to themselves what they did with any absolute certainty."

And in the last paragraph of the *Globe* story, a man who produced a play and a drama about Shepard for PBS was quoted: "[The author of the play and drama] agrees [with the above quote], but believes that appropriating and simplifying tragedy is a necessity. 'Anything that becomes devoured by the mass culture in which we live suffers from the process,' he said. 'At the same time, it encourages dialogue on a national level. And that is more important.'"

In other words, "Sure it's propaganda, and not truth. But the lie serves my purpose." And it also serves the purpose of Pinch Sulzberger.

Pinch Reaches Into Our Schools

I also discovered, while researching the New Bedford column in order to see if anything in it was true, that Governor Bill Weld, in appreciation for the efforts of activist homosexuals who helped him win a close election in 1990, had begun efforts in the schools to indoctrinate children in the homosexual lifestyle, beginning with preschool. In response, in January 1999, I published a 28-page piece and mailed it to 15,000 schools and religious groups around the state. I called for an "intelligent discussion" on the subject, but I understand now why that was very naive. There was to be no discussion about anything after Pinch Sulzberger had stretched his long arm into our state with his subsidiary, the *Boston Globe*.

The *Globe* did have to acknowledge my 28-page article because all the other media did. They had the following headline on January 22, 1999: "Gays Say Lawyer Sent 'Hate Mail.'" The lead sentence was: "Some 15,000 copies of a Web-based newspaper, including an article that gay community leaders have assailed as 'a piece of hate mail,' were sent to church and school leaders across the state ..."

Pinch's people at the *Globe* knew they couldn't describe my article as "hate mail" because it wasn't. So they called some of their friends and had them say it for them, and then they printed "hate mail" in the headline. It accomplished what they wanted. They are very clever that way.

But a short time later on Sunday, February 7, the *Globe* agreed that the "gay gene" was not proven. They also printed a large empathetic story the same day about two former homosexuals who said they had changed.[3]

I wrote at the time, "They [at the *Globe*] know about our article because they printed a story about it on January 22. They also know that they will not win by making personal attacks on me and that Massachusetts News is a reputable, intelligent endeavor. We hope that we can keep nudging them toward a fair and balanced coverage with all sides participating." (My original 28-page article can be found in the MassNews archives by searching for "An Intelligent Discussion," or by typing the following address: http://www.massnews.com/past_issues/2000/Politics/homo.htm)

In July of that year, the Taylor family would be suddenly ousted as publishers of the *Globe*. Did those two stories upset Pinch so much that Benjamin Taylor was fired without notice on July 12, 1999?

Globe Was Not Without Bias Even Then

I do not mean to give the impression that the *Globe* did not have a bias. However, they had agreed with my two fundamental points. I was hopeful we had started an "intelligent discussion."

Under the headline, **The Fading "Gay Gene,"** the lead article in the Focus section, the *Globe* said, "The [gay] gene still has not been found, and interest in-and enthusiasm for, the 'gay gene' research has waned among activists and scientists alike. And there is a growing consensus that sexual orientation is much more complicated than a matter of genes."

The *Globe* never reported, however, that the man, Dean Hamer, who "discovered" the gene in 1973, is a homosexual, even though it

---

[3] This was the beginning of a routine that the *Globe* still follows. They never admit they read our paper but they "answer" many of our stories a week or two later.

quoted him extensively in its article. He was referred to only as a "molecular biologist at the National Cancer Institute."

The other scientist who was quoted was Dr. Richard Pillard, a professor of psychiatry at Boston University School of Medicine, who had stated in a well-known paper that his goal was to "counter the prevalent belief that sexual orientation is largely the product of family interactions and the social environment." Those are not uninvolved, dispassionate scientists as we were led to believe in the article.

There's no question that the *Globe* agreed with us when it said in its concluding paragraphs: "It means there are no easy answers about where sexual orientation comes from, only questions about how we respond."

Then it totally distorted the image of Christians when it ended the story with the following: "We are left with the question of, 'Do we accept people who are sexually different?'"

The answer for any Christian is, "Of course we accept them." As an example, one of the most "virulent" groups in the minds of the *Globe* would be the American Family Association from Mississippi, which devoted ten pages of its 24-page magazine of January 1999 to homosexuality, which was summarized in the following:

"[O]ur sin is on a grander scale than that of the homosexual. ... Scripture never singles out homosexuality for special disapproval. It comes from the same heart that generates greed, envy, strife, disobedience to parents, and gossip." In other words, homosexuals are no worse than the rest of us.

The Catholic Church had an interesting document for parents of homosexual children in which it agreed that the child should always be loved but it cautioned, "It is not to be understood as an endorsement of what some call a 'homosexual lifestyle.'" The Catholic Church was clear, "God does not love someone any less simply because he or she is homosexual. God's love is always and everywhere offered to those who are open to receiving it." Its publication was "Always Our Children."

The article about "change" appeared on the same day. It was an empathetic story of two ex-homosexuals who were working in a Christian ministry. It was in the *Boston Globe Magazine*, under a headline, "Struggling to be straight."

Gov. Bill Weld was the person who brought homosexuality to Boston after he survived a very close race against John Silber, President of Boston University, in 1990. Weld felt so indebted to the homosexual activists for their support that he became an advocate for their causes, particularly in the schools.

The two men worked with a local chapter of Exodus International to help homosexuals in New England who wished to change.

The story, written by a freelancer, was a straightforward account of the change in lifestyle and the continued struggle of these two former lovers who still lived together but without intimacy.

However, although the story was well balanced about the two men, it still had the *Globe* bias in much of the other information. For example, it was very subtly critical in its treatment of NARTH, the organization of psychologists and psychiatrists who work with homosexuals. The story said NARTH "maintains that homosexuality is a disorder that *should* be changed." [Emphasis added] This reinforced the old canard that NARTH wants to go out and capture all of the homosexuals and put them in a detaining cell until they change. A correct statement would have been, "NARTH maintains that homosexuality is a disorder that can be changed, *but only if the person desires to do so.*"

The story also made a blanket attack on Christians when it said, "Publicly, Exodus eschews the harsh, homophobic rhetoric of many fundamentalist groups..." I have yet to see any "harsh" or "homophobic" rhetoric from *any* Christian group, although I am sure you can find some if you look under enough rocks. Certainly, there is none from the Catholic Church, American Family Association, Christian

Coalition, Focus on the Family, Family Research Council, Rev. D. James Kennedy or any of the other responsible Christian organizations which sponsored the advertisement.

Never Heard of Pinch

My problem was that I had never heard of Pinch. I knew nothing about him, or that he even existed, until the spring of 2003 when I began preparing the libel lawsuit against the *Times*. Like everyone, I assumed I was dealing with a "normal" big corporation.

I was trying to create an intelligent discussion in 1999 in the pamphlets I was mailing around the state, before we started our full-color, tabloid newspaper. I didn't realize yet that there would be no discussions at all because Pinch was in charge. You did it his way or suffered the consequences.

When I read in 1999 about a young man being treated at the Sexual Behaviors Consultation Unit in the winter edition of [*Johns*] *Hopkins Medical News*, I queried them immediately. It looked to me as though it might be possible to start a discussion. They wouldn't have a discussion with me about the issue, but they would answer my correspondence. There was no question that the *Times* could have initiated a real discussion with them, an impartial group with a dispassionate view of the subject.

The Hopkins story was about a 17-year-old boy who was brought to a meeting of a dozen professionals of the Unit because his parents had found pornographic, homosexual literature in his room, after which he announced he was homosexual. Some of the questions that were being asked by the parents were: "Is their son engaging in risky sexual interactions? Is his homosexual orientation set in stone? Or is this just a variation of an ordinary adolescent identity crisis?" Although we never hear what happened to the boy, it was clear that no one at Johns Hopkins took his decision lightly.

It was evident they believed this to be an important point in this young man's life and we should not blithely accept his statement that he is "homosexual." Later in the article, it referred to him as a "troubled" teenage boy. When I sent a copy of my comment to Johns Hopkins, they answered, to my surprise. They said my story was accurate.

Ever since a teenage "homosexual" boy told Sally and me in tears that he didn't want to be different, outside this Unitarian church where he had just outed himself during a church rally (which turned out to be a homosexual activist rally), I have been unable to stay silent when I see how the schools are treating these vulnerable children and encouraging them to practice homosexual sex.

But the Massachusetts schools did not stop their mantra that this was not a serious matter and homosexual teachers were all that such an adolescent needed. Nor did the *Globe* express any interest in the doctors at Hopkins.

A short time before that, my wife and I were talking with a reporter from a homosexual newspaper in Boston outside a Unitarian church after a rally had been held against the "hate" I was spreading in town. (The minister and others in attendance were surprised to see me and my wife walk in and sit in the front row.) Only about four or five church members had appeared plus the same number of residents, along with about 85 homosexual activists from around the state. The TV crews were not allowed inside the church because the minister didn't want them to discover who it really was in that large crowd.

One of the rally events was a teenage boy from our town who "outed" himself there. While we were talking afterwards outside, the teenager came up to me, started crying and saying, "I don't want to be different. I don't want to be different." It turned out that the high school's female principal was unable to cope with the older, large teenage boys. Instead of doing her job, she would call the police to do it for her whenever this boy complained. As a result, she was isolating this youth even more and exacerbating his problem about being different. I will never forget the anguish of that poor kid who just wanted someone to help him cope with the world. He seared my soul against what was being done to him and countless others. (The President of

Boston University, John Silber, later reported that he had had excellent results with some female principals of our local high schools who were able to control teenage boys.)

Are Three-Quarters of the *Times*' Front Page Editors Homosexual?

In 2000, it was stated by the National Political Correspondent of the *Times*, Richard Berke, that three-quarters of the people who decide what goes on the front page of the *Times* are "not so closeted homosexuals." Berke, who is homosexual, reported to the National Lesbian and Gay Journalists Association on April 12 in Washington, D.C.:

"This is at a newspaper where not so long ago — when I started there 15 years ago — the department heads were asking for lists of the gay reporters on different sections so they could be punished in different ways. So things have really changed at the newspaper. Since I've been there there's been a dramatic shift: I remember coming and wondering if there were any gay reporters there or whatever. Now it's like, there are times when you look at the front-page meeting and ... literally three-quarters of the people deciding what's on the front page are not-so-closeted homosexuals. ... [It is] a real far cry from what it was like not so long ago."

We do not know whether Berke is telling the truth, but there is no question that he made that statement.

How About the Globe?

There was persistent talk across the state during 2002 that three of the top news managers at the *Globe* are gay activists.

Not wanting to deal in rumors, but being aware of the fact that the *Globe* has been the main enemy of the Protection of Marriage Amendment, *Massachusetts News* decided to ask the managers themselves.

Five persons were listed in the paper as the top executives in the news department. Three of them were said to be gay activists. They were Richard H. Gilman, the Publisher who suddenly arrived from New York in 1999; Martin Baron, Editor; and Helen W. Donovan, Executive Editor.

Reporter Ed Oliver did the questioning. He tried Editor Martin

Baron first and got through to him directly after a couple of tries. He asked if the rumors were true that Baron is gay. "He sort of laughed and asked me why I want to know. I said because of the *Globe's* editorial positions. He said, 'I am not in charge of the editorials, but the news coverage.' Before I could get out another word, he quickly said, 'Anyway, it's a stupid question, go away, thanks.' Then he hung up."

Oliver talked next with Helen Donovan. "I asked Donovan in the interest of disclosure if she was gay. She said she was not going to discuss her personal life. I asked about other editorial personnel. She thought that was funny, but said there is no reason to discuss their personal lives. I asked if she didn't want to at least say no, she is not a lesbian. But she wouldn't say.

"I explained that it is a valid question because there is a National Gay and Lesbian Journalist Association which has an agenda. She said groups push them to do things or not do them all the time. I said that members of that organization also work from inside news media organizations to accomplish their agenda. She said she can see my point in asking, but nobody from their organization is doing that."

Oliver was unable to get through to Publisher Gilman. "They wouldn't put me through to the publisher, Richard Gilman, insisting I had to talk to PR people. I left several messages with them and talked to one, but they have not returned my calls."

People were concerned because of the tremendous hostility of the *Globe* toward the Protection of Marriage Amendment.

I Have Always Accepted Homosexuality "As a Matter of Course"

As an average person, the same age as Punch, I have always accepted homosexuality "as a matter of course." But I have never recommended the practice. In 1939, it turned out that my scoutmaster, a nice man we all liked, had been using his position as a way to find boys with whom he could have sex. My father was chairman of the troop committee. Nothing was done except to remove this man from the Boy Scouts. He probably should have been charged with molesting that 13-year-old boy, but he wasn't. Was the boy a "homosexual"? I don't know, but I doubt it.

It was at Williams College where I first met someone who was obviously homosexual. He was in my freshman dorm, was also interested in writing and very talented. He got into a good fraternity. But he died in his forties.

When I started my newspaper for lawyers in 1972, I hired several homosexuals because they were intelligent and industrious. I was not interested in their personal lives nor they in mine. That does not mean that I thought they were making good choices in life. However, I did not approve the discrimination law that Massachusetts later passed. It' said, in effect, that I had to hire any homosexual who applied for a job, and he or she could exact special treatment or keep me eternally in court with baseless lawsuits.

However, I would not accept homosexuality as a matter of course if I were in a battle unit in the Army again. When you're sharing a tiny pup tent, half of which you always carry with you, you do not want to have to worry about his sexuality, particularly if he is a corporal and you are a private. All the people who say we should allow homosexuals in combat units have never been an enlisted man. Nor do they understand that you are an indentured servant, just like a slave, in those units, except your slavery lasts only for a limited number of years.

Tifft and Jones Apparently Did Not Realize the Problem

Tifft and Jones ended their monumental book about the *Times* at the time when full power was passed to Pinch in October 1997. A short time later, in the beginning of 1998, they wrote this comment for the final page, including a quote from former editor Gay Talese:

"As the twentieth century neared its close, [the Sulzbergers'] stewardship and sense of noblesse oblige, and the paper's self-proclaimed quest for honesty and excellence, were all the more remarkable for the stark dearth of such qualities elsewhere in the culture.

"We don't have trust in government. The Wall Street world? Forget it," said Gay Talese. ... "Where can people [go] who have values and a sense of right and wrong, of standards? ... I think today the Sulzberger family and *The New York Times* [are] our only hope. And if they weren't there, I don't know where you would look."

In their epilogue, written in June 1999, Tifft and Jones wrote:

"[Pinch Sulzberger] is bolstered by a family that has willingly sacrificed wealth and personal ambition for the sake of the institution that is both their obligation and their glory. Now his task is to preserve the *Times*, and all it represents, and pass it on to yet another generation. It is the job, one might say, he was born for."

Certainly, Tifft and Jones were caught in a spirit of exuberance. They didn't really mean *everything* they wrote in those final sections. They had done a masterful job of pointing to the good and the bad in the family and in the *Times*. They knew that Pinch's role was yet to be proven. He had a lot of personal problems to deal with and would have to do so without his father's help. That became abundantly clear five years later with the Jayson Blair fiasco.

The main problem, however, would continue to be the unresolved, extremist views father and son held about homosexuality.

22

Who Is This Pinch?

Pinch has been the person in charge at the *Times* since 1988 when he became Assistant Publisher. He was named Publisher four years later in 1992. He's the one behind the curtain. After parting away all the layers of editors and reporters, one discovers that Pinch is the manager of the store.

He has good cause to be an angry, different kind of person. He was born in 1951 and catapulted into the 1960s generation when he was only five-years-old. He was living with his father and mother in Paris when they entered into the throes of divorce. As a consequence, Pinch had to leave his father. The divorce happened because Punch's "eye began to roam," according to the sources of Joseph Goulden.

That's not the way Tifft and Jones tell it. We don't know who the sources were for these authors. Someone was not telling the truth, which is not surprising when you have to ask those who were involved.

No matter which adult initiated the separation, it was the boy who was hurt. In any event, everyone agrees that Barbara, his mother, now had custody of Pinch. For eight years, Pinch played the part of the "modern" child, bouncing back and forth between mother and father. Punch had his two children, Pinch and his younger sister, Karen, every other weekend.

"The divorce was hard on the children, and on Barbara," wrote Tifft and Jones. "Barbara tried to be a better mother than she had been in Paris, but [Pinch] and Karen needed some convincing. When their French nurse, Georgette, returned to France and Barbara didn't hire a replacement, Karen asked in bewilderment, 'Who's going to take care of us now?' 'Well, I will,' said Barbara. Karen stared at her mother in disbelief. 'I remember thinking, "Well, she is this very nice, pretty lady, but she doesn't know what toys I like in my bath or how I like my food cut up or any of that kind of thing."'"

Pinch suggested one day to his mother that they have a tea party, "just the two of us." When she appeared in the dining room, she found the windows had been shuttered in order to see the candlelight he had provided. A vase of flowers had been borrowed from the living room, and Pinch's favorite song, "Old McDonald Had a Farm," was playing. After a few moments of tea and cookies, Pinch said, "Oh, Mother, isn't this fun? It's so cozy."

Punch tried but he didn't know much about roughhousing himself. So he took the kids to see the Statue of Liberty and other sights and worked with them in his workshop, making handicraft. "I remember making a thousand ashtrays," Karen recalled.

Barbara said, "[Pinch] wanted a male in his life. Anybody I would date, he would ask me whether I was going to marry [him]." Finally she did marry a good man in 1958 when Pinch was seven. "He was a big, fun, charged, energized father figure who played with us on the floor," recalled Pinch. "He was the kind who would throw the ball and walk you to school." But he and Barbara produced a boy and girl of their own. This made things pretty complicated for Pinch.

When Pinch was fourteen, he left Loomis in the middle of his first year there, never to return, like his father had done. That's when he went back to New York and told his mother he was moving in with Punch.

At that point, he had a sister, Karen, one-year younger. She was unhappy when she had to continue living with her mother. She began to "fall apart" in school, according to Punch. At his father's house, Pinch started living with a half-sister, Cynthia, who was thirteen years younger, and an adopted half-sister, Cathy, who was the daughter of his father's second wife's prior husband. She was two years older than Pinch and sixteen when he arrived. Her bedroom had to be divided when he arrived, but she was leaving for college the following year anyhow. In addition, Pinch's mother, Barbara, had had two children by her second husband which had made her home rather chaotic and she would soon get a divorce and move to Topeka. The tea parties had ended a long time ago.

"I was fourteen when I came to his [Punch's] house, so he had me for a year and a half before I became an asshole," he later remarked.

Pinch walked to his father's, when he moved in with him, second-wife Carol, and his two half-sisters. His stepmother, Carol, came to dislike him very much. She never changed that opinion until her dying day. That did not make for a happy family relationship.

Barbara's second marriage ended in 1971 when she married an administrator at the Menninger Foundation in Topeka. Pinch had just completed his first year at Tufts.

Why did Pinch decide to leave his mother and move in with Punch? Did he really know or like his father, or was he merely safeguarding a desire to run The New York Times Company? Or was he running from Barbara's house? Punch did not make things easy for him. Later, Punch told many that his sister's son, Steven Golden, should not be dismissed as a future publisher.

Pinch was small and slight. He had allergies. He was subdued and lacking in confidence, always the last chosen in pickup games of baseball. These experiences left him with a life-long distaste for team sports.

Powerful Yearning to Claim His Rightful Place

The separation from Punch produced a powerful yearning "to claim his rightful place in the extended Sulzberger clan," according to Tifft and Jones. His determination only increased after his father unexpectedly ascended to the publisher's job, with the sudden death in 1963 of Orvil when Pinch was twelve.

While at Tufts, Pinch was arrested twice at antiwar demonstrations. He had been fifteen when his father's *Times* reported Harrison Salisbury's inaccurate stories about American air raids on Hanoi. The air raid stories and the Pentagon Papers, which were published while Pinch was at college, obviously had a deleterious effect not only upon the nation, but upon Punch's son. After Pinch's second demonstration, Punch felt he had to fly to Boston to talk with his son. Pinch confronted his father by saying that were a single American soldier to come upon a single North Vietnamese soldier, he would prefer that it be the

American who was shot. "It's the closest he's ever come to hitting me," Pinch later recalled.

Pinch graduated from Tufts in 1974 and worked on the *Raleigh Times*, which was owned by friends of the Sulzberger family, and then with A.P. in London. In 1978, he joined the *Times* in their Washington bureau. There were 12 cousins of Pinch who also had to be considered as the next publisher. In 1990, his grandmother, Iphigene, died and Punch turned 65 the next year. In January 1992, Pinch was named Publisher of the *Times* newspaper, but only after The Company's directors first tabled his appointment because of his "seeming immaturity and lack of leadership."

A second attempt to dethrone him by non-family members of the Board of Directors, led by Louis Gerstner of IBM, was fought off in 1996. An in-house rival, The Company president, Lance Primis, was fired for the same reason.

When Pinch was finally named Chairman of The Company in October 1997, his aunts and cousins insisted that he not receive all three positions of power that Punch had held. As a result, Russell Lewis, a non-family member, was named CEO. In addition, a cousin, Michael Golden, was named Vice Chairman of the Company.

Plays Hardball, Fires His Cousin

Within 18-months of being made Chairman, Pinch fired one cousin and accepted the resignation of another. He showed that he and his father always play serious hardball.

One of those fired was Cousin Dan Cohen, who had been very close to Pinch, being one of his best friends during much of his adult life.

Dan was the son of Judy, Punch's sister. She was a medical doctor and the one member of the family who never wanted anything to do with the paper because she thought it destroyed people. Dan had been devastated when his father abandoned him after divorcing Judy. The second husband adopted Dan, only to unhappily leave when the third husband arrived, whom Judy also divorced. (When Punch was feeling lonely during the cancer illness of his wife, the two siblings who advised him to just find himself a lover were Judy and Marian.)

Much of the extended family gathered at Punch's summer home in 1971. They saw Dan and Pinch alienate everyone with their childish antics. "They loved each other, but they made everyone else ready to kill them," said Judy. They showed up at cousin Michael Golden's wedding with Pinch wearing his standard wire-rim glasses, a string tie and a headband, while Dan was in a choir robe with a thick gold chain around his neck and his hair in an Afro. The mother of the groom, Aunt Ruth, was not happy. Dan said, "She took ten years to recover." But the truth was that she and most of the people probably never did forget. "No one has ever forgotten that," said Dan himself. "People look at Arthur and me and have this visceral response: 'Oh God, here they go again.'"

Dan and Pinch went to Tufts together in 1970. Dan was unable to concentrate for long periods of time, even having to move around when attending a movie. But Tufts allowed him to design his own major, which included oceanography, theater and lighting design.

After graduating from Tufts, Dan did not go to work at the *Times* as Pinch did. He dropped in and out of jobs but we are told he finally did well as a TV news reporter in Orlando where he met his future wife, Leah Keith, a Phi Beta Kappa from the University of Georgia. She first met Pinch when he and his wife met the couple at the airport. Dan made sure they were at the end of the line when he and Leah debarked with Groucho glasses with bushy eyebrows and big noses. However, the nose was actually in the shape of a penis. Leah was impressed to see Dan and Pinch embracing and kissing.

Soon after his wedding, Dan called Punch and got a job at The Times Company in 1983. However, Pinch was way ahead of him in terms of his career. He would be in charge of the *Times* the next year as Assistant Publisher. They saw little of each other and Dan told friends they now had a love/hate relationship. When an oral historian for the American Jewish Committee asked him to describe his goals at the *Times*, Dan responded as being "able to rise to the top, being able to perhaps be the president [of The Company]."

When Pinch was made Assistant Publisher in 1988, Dan was angry that his cousin had been on a training program that would make him the publisher. So Dan decided to map his own training program and requested an assignment in advertising which was granted. Tifft and Jones called it a "critical career misstep."

When Pinch was named Publisher of the *Times* in 1992, Dan felt bitterness and asked his mother to give him her seat on the Board, but Punch convinced his sister that it was not a good idea. When Pinch became Chairman of The Company in 1997, he had just returned from a camping trip in Utah with Dan where he talked about his future advancement. "That's when all the air was cleared," said Judy hopefully.

In 1994 Dan told the president of the *Times* that he wanted to be considered to head the new electronic media group but received a frank answer. "You should be thinking about a *demotion*, not a promotion." It was the first time in his eleven years at the *Times* that anyone told him how he came across, that he was still the wise kid who had upset everyone in his family. Of course, Dan would be correct if he noted that Pinch was that way also. But he was Punch's son.

The Company found a management coach to help Dan with his abrasive personality. After enduring that for several months, he was promoted to Vice President of Advertising Sales, where he apparently did well, reaching over $1 billion in sales, an unheard amount of money.

But a year after Pinch become Chairman, he had the president of the *Times* fire Dan, who left in March 1998. Instead of praise for the $1 billion in sales, Dan said he was told "the same old stuff," that he appeared unfocused and people were afraid of him. After his termination, he and Pinch reported they were now closer than ever. Dan told his wife, Leah, who was bitter: "It was the right choice."

The questions must be raised: Why would anyone put such an idiot in charge of a $1 billion dollar sales operation? Or was he not an idiot, but a very talented individual who had become a serious threat to Pinch?

Another Cousin Left Two Months Later

Two months later, Cousin Steve Golden, 52, announced that he was leaving to pursue a law degree and a master's in American Indian studies at the University of Arizona.

Steve was a son of Ruth who had served with the Red Cross in Europe during World War II, after graduation from Smith. While there and stationed with a unit of the Army Air Force, she fell in love with an officer, Ben Golden, who was from Kentucky where his father was an automobile dealer. He had been a handsome football player and a good dancer. There was one other item: Ben was married, but had no children after ten years.

Despite the family's misgivings, Ruth married this hard-drinking man with few intellectual interests. Although his name sounded Jewish, Ben's family was from Ireland. He had been a manager at the Tennessee Valley Authority in Knoxville with a salary of $2800 a year. So the couple moved to Chattanooga where Ben went to work for the *Chattanooga Times*. It didn't work. Ben felt as though he had sold his soul. He became angry and resentful. He would tell people he was not Jewish. "Ruth is Jewish," he would say, pointing to his wife. "*She's* Jewish. *I'm* not Jewish."

But Ruth was determined to make a go of it. She had told a friend that her children would never be raised as she had been. "My children are not going to be raised by nannies. They're going to be raised by *me*." She stayed with Ben for nineteen years, but finally was unable to take any more abuse. She forced him out in 1965 and became publisher of the Chattanooga paper. A serious alcoholic, Ben died by himself in Florida in 1970.

The children from the Tennessee Sulzbergers, Steve, Michael, Lynn and Arthur, who were children of Ruth and Ben, were obviously raised differently from their New York cousins.

Steve was bookish and sensitive, with an interest in poetry, music, philosophy and acting. Michael, who was two years younger, was his father's favorite. "Dad could watch me play football and baseball. Stephen wasn't interested in that," he related.

Steve dropped out of college in Chattanooga in 1966, right after the divorce, after barely a semester in college. He proceeded to New York when only nineteen with the plan of working at the *Times* for a while before going on to the London bureau. Abe Rosenthal nicely told him the facts, befriended him and got him into Columbia. While there, Steve married a speech and linguistics teacher at Yeshiva University.

Although Abe was in Japan at the time, he flew in for the wedding and then back to Tokyo.

Steve dropped out of Columbia in May 1970, after the Kent State killings, in order to elect antiwar candidates.

The young man had become very close to Punch while he and his wife were living, during the summer of 1971, at Punch's country home with other family members. Some said it was too bad that Punch was not as close to his own son.

In the fall of 1973, he told Punch he wanted to come back to the paper where he had worked briefly when he first arrived. Punch sent him to the general manager, Walter Mattson, whose response was: "He's not qualified to work at The New York Times. Send him off to the bush leagues and let him get the edges rubbed off and learn more about the business, then bring him back."

So Punch sent Steve to their Gainesville paper to work on the business side. He was there for a year and then became assistant publisher for two more years. After that, Steve went to Punch again, who sent him to Mattson again, who took him to lunch and looked him straight in the eye. "I don't like nepotism," he said. "Me neither," responded Steve, "and your son better not ever ask me for a job here." The story is that they both laughed.

Steve went to work on the business side of the *Times*. Within two years after the birth of his son in 1978, he was divorced. His former wife never married again. He started dating the personnel director of the *Times* and married her in 1986.

In 1998, Steve resigned from the *Times*.

Only Michael Golden, Steve's younger brother, remained as a threat to Pinch in New York He is still down the hall in case Pinch fails or dies.

Another Threat in Boston

But another threat did remain in Boston. It was in the form of Benjamin Taylor, publisher of the *Globe* which Pinch and his father had bought in 1993. According to a story in the *Globe* at the time, the agreement "contained explicit clauses that leave decision-making and editorial control of the *Globe* in the hands of its management." When

Pinch finally had Taylor fired in 1999, the *Globe* publisher was 52-years-old, four years older than Pinch. He was well respected in the industry and his family had run the *Globe* since 1873, which was twenty-three years before Adolph bought the *Times*. Two events occurred early in 1999, before the firing.

In January the *Globe* agreed with me that there was no "gay gene." It also published a balanced story about two homosexuals who were changing their sexual orientation. Those stories were anathema to Pinch's plan to institute gay marriage in Massachusetts.

In April, an internal, private memo intended only for top management from Metro Editor Peter Canellos was posted by someone on the paper's bulletin board and consequently reported in the *Boston Herald* and the *Washington Post*. In it, Canellos complained about the "lack of talent" on his staff. The memo said, "The major obstacle, as with many priorities in Metro, is the lack of talent on the staff. Most of the Metro staff — perhaps three quarters — is not capable of writing a marquee Sunday piece. Most of the editors aren't capable of editing them ..."

Only three months later, Richard Gilman was dispatched to Boston as the new publisher. In retrospect, one must wonder if the unknown memo poster could have been one of Pinch's operatives creating an excuse for his taking charge. (There were many staffers at the *Times* who would have been happy to write a similar memo at their paper, according to what is reported by both Diamond and Goulden.)

The ouster of Taylor was spun as a business decision but it also eliminated another serious threat to Pinch if some Board member got serious about finding non-family executives to replace him as Louis Gerstner had done.

In the next four years, while the *Globe* was under Pinch's direct control, the Sunday circulation had dropped from 730,000 in 1999 to 705,000 in 2003, despite more liberal accounting rules. The weekday circulation dropped 6.3% to 449,000, the worst performance in that accounting period of any major American newspaper, as word spread in Boston about the growing incompetence of the *Globe*, thanks in part to my new newspaper, *Massachusetts News*. But I still had no idea about its new owners. I didn't learn about the Sulzbergers until I started my libel suit against the *Times* in April 2003.

Found His Wife in Topeka

Pinch found his wife, Gail Gregg, across the street from his mother's home in Topeka in late November 1973, when they were both twenty-two. She was the daughter of an insurance executive and was determined to get out of Topeka and lead her own life. Pinch sent her an airplane ticket upon his arriving back home. She landed in Boston on January 3, 1974, moved in with Pinch and never left.

Their relationship was well described in a ditty sung by Pinch's friends at a small celebratory party soon after he became Chairman: "He's got a wife with brains / Who's smart enough to refrain. / From letting on/that she's the one / who often takes the reins/ Can do / Can do / That Gail's got a high IQ." Another ditty at the party was about Pinch: "The monarch of all I see / The ruler of the whole company."

(One of the guests was Congressman Chuck Schumer, who would soon become a Senator and the bitter, attack dog for the Democrats against President Bush or anyone else who got in the way of the Democratic Party. The liberal/radical urgings of Gail and Pinch were apparent. About a year later, he appeared at a Park Avenue Halloween party dressed as "Senator Putzhead," an obvious and intentional dig at Republican Senator Alfonse d'Amato, who had been ridiculed in liberal circles for using that name to describe a political rival. His outfit included the Groucho hat with which he appeared to have become obsessed, the one with a big penis for a nose.)

At their initial meeting, Gail had appeared to Pinch to be forceful and assured, the very strengths he was seeking for himself. Tifft and Jones described her as "slim, dark-haired, and doe-eyed, with a huge arresting smile."

Gail had lived in Germany, France and Italy during the year after college before meeting Pinch, working and traveling. She spoke German and French. (Pinch was terrible in language skills.) The oldest of five children, she was raised with solid Midwestern values which she rejected. She wanted to leave the dullness of Kansas and get into journalism which had been her major at college.

When she first arrived in Boston, Pinch's friends thought themselves superior to this hick. Dan Cohen planned a party where they were greeted by a crowd of male guests garishly dressed in drag. But Gail did not allow them to bother her. The next day, Dan apologized. A friend of Gail's commented: "Gail never let the laugh be at her expense. She always laughed with them or at them."

She went to North Carolina with Pinch when his father sent him to the *Raleigh Times* with the admonition: "Do what I did, and get away from the family and go out where somebody didn't care whether he was Arthur Sulzberger [or not]." But it didn't work that way, of course. The managing editor when Pinch arrived said later, Pinch was "absolutely, totally green" compared with his colleagues. "We would not normally have hired someone like [Pinch] with zero experience. It was very much like dealing with a college intern."

The green newcomer tried not to look rich while they were there. But he tooled around in a Porsche, which would be difficult to hide. He later tried to downplay the expensive car: "It wasn't the fancy Porsche. It was the cheap Porsche, the one with the Volkswagen engine in the middle. It was the low end."

While there, Gail studied at the graduate school of journalism at the University of North Carolina.

Like most reporters, Pinch spent most of his two years in Raleigh writing obituaries, but he seemed to be spending more time doing that than the average newcomer. The city editor laughed one day, "Can you imagine someone who cannot spell 'hate?'" Pinch had spelled it several times: "Hait."

Nevertheless, two of the stories he did write were sent by Pinch, himself, to the Assistant Managing Editor in New York, with this note: "Perhaps, if the desire hits you, you might throw them up to the fourteenth floor and let the old man see them."

After Gail told her mother that she was living with Pinch, she received a note from her grandmother saying she did not know what was wrong with the mother. "Every time I mention your name to your mother, she bursts into tears."

They were married in the garden of the Gregg home in May 1975. Pinch came dressed in white: white pants, white belt, and a white tuxedo shirt, open at the neck with no tie or jacket. Gail was in a jade green, sleeveless dress. Author Edwin Diamond described the wedding as "a scene from a modern marriage; the groom's side of the family was represented by three fathers, two mothers, one stepsister, three sisters, (half, step-, and full), a half brother, and 'an assortment of long-haired cousins.'" Gail kept her maiden name.

As his next step, Punch arranged a reporting job for Pinch at AP in London and for Gail at UPI. The first draft of his letter for Gail told the head of UPI: "We think she is smarter than he is." But Punch's secretary told him he couldn't say that.

When Pinch started working for the *Times* in New York, he stopped seeing anyone socially from the paper and asked Gail to do the same. He also requested that she stop doing freelance work when it became painfully obvious that everyone knew she was married to a Sulzberger. She had hoped to be a distinguished reporter but acceded to his request. In any event, she soon had two children and a chance to pursue her ability in painting.

Tifft and Jones said of the marriage. "They [the family] considered her smart, focused, grounded, a woman with strong convictions and a healthy impatience with inflated egos. In short, they thought she was good for [Pinch]. 'Gail takes no shit from him ... and she keeps him honest,' said his cousin, Doug Adler [a grandson of Julius]. She didn't hesitate to call down her husband in public when his jokes bordered on the insulting. In private she demanded that he make time for their family and not spend every minute at the office. Their marriage was one of trust, friendship, respect, political sympathy, teamwork. Unlike Punch, who never discussed business with Carol, [Pinch] valued Gail's counsel and freely told other executives that he ran many decisions by her.

"Still, the relationship seemed emotionally cool. Gail's toughness and unswerving belief in her own vision made her something of an authority figure to [Pinch] and reinforced his propensity to be a loner. Like his father, he tended to retreat, hovering slightly out of reach. 'I like Gail, but she's not so mothering or nurturing,' said Cynthia Sulzberger [Punch's daughter and half-sister of Pinch]. 'I'm sure they love each other, but to me they have a different kind of relationship.' Unlike Punch, who had contentedly spent every weekend at the family compound at Hillandale, [Pinch] rented a house in New Palz, New York, far from the social demands of the Hamptons and other leisure-time venues of the moneyed and the media elite. There, he spent hours in the Shawangunk Mountains by himself or with his son, rock climbing, a sport he loved for its meditative aspect, tactical nature, and the element of fear it involved. 'I think he likes the loneliness,' observed Toni Goodale, wife of former *Times* executive vice president James Goodale." Gail was described as an "avowed atheist."

23

Credibility Lost in Attempt to Fire Jeff Jacoby over Homosexuality

In the year 2000, Pinch's new man in charge at the *Boston Globe*, Publisher Richard H. Gilman, attempted to get rid of Jeff Jacoby, the paper's popular, token conservative columnist.

This drastic attempt of extreme bias caused alarm bells to ring among the press across the entire country.[1] There was an uproar but no one connected the dots for us, if they even understood them themselves.

Jacoby had previously gotten into trouble in 1997. He had written about Christian students at Harvard Law School who announced a meeting with a young man who had stopped practicing homosexuality. The students had to watch as vandals destroyed their signs on campus. (Jacoby is a practicing Orthodox Jew.)

Jacoby was publicly chastised and warned by the paper's ombudsman, who revealed that *both* of Jacoby's editors, both "gay activists" according to the ombudsman, had been adamant that the column should not be printed.

The ombudsman opined that the editor was correct in running the column even though it was "offensive" and "a high price to pay for freedom of the press." Jacoby had written "homophobic" columns before, the ombudsman said. He warned that in the future, "Jacoby's articles about homosexuality will be judged case by case."

---

[1] This is another problem the country faces as the *Times* saturates the country with its alumni who did not make it in New York or couldn't stand it. They are mostly liberal or Punch wouldn't have given them a job in the first place. They are found in important posts everywhere across the country.

Jacoby said that the incident had a chilling effect upon him, but it wasn't chilling enough to make even him understand that Pinch had taken charge after the purchase of the *Globe* in 1993, and he was watching. Pinch wanted Jacoby out of there. The columnist should have been extremely careful.

The signs at the law school were replaced by the vandals with others such as, "For those struggling with Judaism, there is hope in the truth. You can walk away. (To the gas chambers.)"

Jacoby wrote: "There is no hate in [the young speaker's] story. He doesn't berate gays, or mock them, or demand that they renounce homosexuality. He knows that many gays are content and happy with their lives. ... How was inviting this man to speak at Harvard analogous to sending Jews to gas chambers? Isn't his experience also an element of human 'diversity?' What does it say about gay advocates, who so loudly champion tolerance and freedom of sexual choice, that they are so poisonously intolerant of people who make a choice different from theirs?"

I wrote at the time in *Massachusetts News*: "We have oppression and censorship occurring at our most important source of information, *The Boston Globe*." But I had no idea about the full extent of the oppression, nor did anyone else.[2]

Less than three years after the warning to Jacoby, the popular columnist was suspended by the paper for four months without pay in July 2000. Jacoby said he had been invited to resign. "I was put on notice that if I do choose to return in four months, there would have

---

[2] What was happening at the *Globe* was almost inevitable because of the Massachusetts Civil Rights Act. It is one reason why two homosexuals monitor Jacoby. Unlike the federal law, the Massachusetts statute includes homosexuals as one of its protected groups. Therefore, no newspaper in Massachusetts would dare to print what you are presently reading in this book. It would be sued immediately by the Massachusetts Commission Against Discrimination. That was what undoubtedly happened to talk show host Jeanine Graf. Homosexual employees complained to management about Graf. They became concerned at the station that fictitious charges of discrimination would be filed if they did not stop her from speaking.

Even if a company had large amounts of time and money to spend with their lawyers to fight such a suit and they won, they would still be branded as "homophobes" by the other media across the state, particularly the *Globe*. It is not worth the effort. And what chance would the paper have to win when the "court" where they would present their case would be composed of the members of the "Massachusetts Commission Against Discrimination?"

Any business with six or more employees is covered under the Massachusetts law. This means that *Massachusetts News* is limited in the number of employees to five or less, or it will lose the right of free speech and freedom of the press, which supposedly is assured under both the state and U.S. Constitutions. This is a severe restriction on freedom of speech.

Senator Edward Kennedy (D-Mass) is busily trying to impose these rules across the entire country.

to be a 'serious rethink' of the kind of column I write."

The column that Pinch and Publisher Gilman pounced upon to purge Jacoby was about the signers of the Declaration of Independence.

Jacoby explained on the Internet to his readers after the suspension: "Several readers of my recent column on the signers of the Declaration of Independence have pointed out that these stories have been written about before. A few have wondered about my sources for this material. Still others have written to assure me that everything in the column has long since been debunked. Worst of all, some readers charged me with plagiarizing the column from, variously, Rush Limbaugh, Paul Harvey, and even an anonymous e-mail that has been circulating on the Internet. ...

"In short, whatever-happened-to-the-signers is an old, old theme in American inspirational writing. It didn't start with Paul Harvey, Rush Limbaugh, or the author of that nameless e-mail. And it won't end with me. These stories have been repeated so often, and by so many people, that they have risen to the level of American legend. Which is why it didn't occur to me to take up valuable space in the column with footnotes or citations to earlier versions (many of which I didn't know about when I was writing)."

One of those who was most upset by the *Globe* was Nat Hentoff, the well-known liberal columnist and a fixture for years at the *Village Voice*, then at *Editor & Publisher* magazine.

Hentoff wrote the following under the headline, **Jeff Jacoby Will Survive, But Will the Globe's Reputation?**

"The internal gag order on Boston Globe columnist Jeff Jacoby has been the most widely reported journalism story across the country, including the pages of E&P, since columnists Mike Barnicle and Patricia Smith were forced to leave the same paper for alchemizing fiction into fact. But in suspending Jacoby for four months without pay, and indicating to him that he'd be

Columnist Jeff Jacoby was savagely attacked by the Globe Ombudsman on Nov. 3, 1997, who revealed that both of Jacoby's editors were "gay activists."

wise to look elsewhere, the Globe accused the columnist neither of plagiarism nor of making up stories. The charge is 'serious journalistic misconduct.' Worth examining is the 'journalistic misconduct' of Globe Publisher Richard Gilman, Editorial Page Editor Renee Loth, and Ombudsman Jack Thomas."

Everyone survived. Jacoby's columns returned to the paper on November 8, 2000. Needless to say, he is reluctant to talk about conditions at the paper since his return. That is left for your conjecture.

*****

This satirical piece about the suspension of Jeff Jacoby was written by Myron Robert Pauli.

Boston Globe Suspends Thomas Jefferson

July 7, 1776

The Boston Globe today announced the suspension of noted anti-tax, anti-gun-control columnist Thomas Jefferson for four months after the columnist published a controversial column entitled "Declaration of Independence" on July 4.

The Globe specifically cited Jefferson for "serious journalistic misconduct." According to Editorial Page Editor Thomas Hutchinson, "Jefferson's work clearly was not entirely original. In fact, similar ideas had been expressed by numerous natural law philosophers such as John Locke, David Hume, and Jean Jacques Rousseau." Hutchinson pointed out that the phrase "life, liberty, and the pursuit of happiness" is almost taken verbatim from a previous work of John Locke. "Our readers expect originality and not just recycled old material," stated Hutchinson.

Adding to the accusations was that, while Jefferson's column started off with "All men are created equal," Jefferson had circulated an earlier version to fifty-six of his friends (including Benjamin Franklin and John Adams) in which Jefferson himself admitted that the ideas in his column were "self-evident." Jefferson apologized for not stating that explicitly in the introduction to the column which he cut down for space. He offered to issue an admission that the ideas he had were not uniquely his but were self-evident and had been previously circulated by many other "natural law" philosophers.

Hutchinson, however, said that the Globe cannot be put in the position where columnists can recycle self-evident ideas over and over again. The fact that Jefferson had circulated the column to Adams, Franklin, and his other friends only seemed to anger Hutchinson more. The Editors felt that the Globe owed it to its readers to take a firm stand on the lapse, which some characterized as trivial. Others claimed that Jefferson, the only anti-monarchist on the newspaper, was being punished for his political views.

Globe publisher George "King" Hanover III, however, said that "our paper would never single out a columnist for his political views, however bizarre they are." Hanover continued to back the decision of Hutchinson to suspend Jefferson, citing the need to maintain high standards. He mentioned that Jefferson's anti-government views had been tolerated for years, in spite of the fact that most people employed at the paper dislike his ideas and that many in the newsroom have referred to the controversial columnist as a "self-righteous, disloyal, treasonous, anarchistic, atheistic, rebellious, tobacco-growing, slave-driving hypocrite." Hanover mentioned that Jefferson would be allowed to try to keep writing at the paper after the four-month suspension was over. "At that time, we will all be able to reassess how to continue the relationship."

The news of Jefferson's dismissal started a wave of protest. The Globe's ombudsman, Charles Lord Cornwallis, responded to these protests with further attacks on Jefferson and his supporters. "Our readers are entitled to information that is fair and balanced," said Cornwallis. "Jefferson goes on and on and on with repeated and scurrilous attacks on the King. Nowhere in this 'Declaration' of his does he offer equal time for the King to respond to this slander." Cornwallis added that the people protesting Jefferson's dismissal carried no weight with him or the other editors. Specifically, Cornwallis pointed out that he received letters from people such as the Marquis de Lafayette, Baron von Steuben, Casamir Pulaski, and Thaddeus Kosciuszko. "These are not our regular readers but just a bunch of 'freedom fighters' and ideological extremists. Why, Poland is not even within our home delivery area!"

The controversy is likely to last a long time. Little did Thomas Jefferson realize that, when imitating the style of Patrick Henry, he wrote about pledging "lives, fortunes, and sacred honor," it would apply to himself as well.

24

Not Disturbed When Homosexual "Fisting" Is Taught to Teenagers

Some of what is being taught in Massachusetts schools is vulgar and disgusting to heterosexual and homosexual alike. After much debate, it is repeated herein for your information. If Pinch continues to have his way, it will be coming to your state soon. Keep a sharp lookout for the Gay Lesbian and Straight Education Network (GLSEN).

During the 1990s, Massachusetts was the foremost supporter of homosexuality in the schools under its new Governor, William Weld. He was a moderate Republican on economic issues and a liberal on social issues. In 1990, he narrowly defeated the Democrat candidate, the President of Boston University, John Silber, a conservative on most issues.

Fistgate was downplayed by the Globe which editorialized that the resulting outrage was merely an "Attack on sex education."

Weld was indebted to the homosexual activists who had been helpful during his campaign. Therefore, he began supporting them and their causes, including the new concept of homosexual clubs in schools, which became known as gay/straight alliances.

It quickly became clear that a number of schools were giving explicit instruction in homosexual sex to some students. Someone had decided those students were "different." Many, if not most schools, encouraged those students to attend private homosexual organizations where older men (in their twenties) would show them how. This was unknown to their parents. No one in authority wanted to hear about this. (Lieutenant Governor Paul Cellucci, who shared Weld's views, had automatically replaced him when he quit the office in July 1997 so that Cellucci would succeed him.)

Therefore, in March 2000, a parent activist group, the Parents Rights Coalition under the direction of Brian Camenker, taped parts of a conference of the national organization GLSEN. About 400 teachers and students would assemble every year for the conference at Tufts University (where Pinch went to

Former Governor Cellucci never admitted that Fistgate even happened. He could not have survived that foolishness if the Globe was not here. He got a surprise in 2001 when he was almost not confirmed as Ambassador to Canada by the U.S. Senate as a result of the outrage from Massachusetts citizens. It took a phone call from President Bush and a pledge to Jesse Helms before he was finally approved.

school). Because Camenker is an Orthodox Jew, he could not attend the Saturday event. A young law student, Scott Whiteman, did the taping of a raunchy, explicit workshop.

The state Board of Education, which had been a sponsor of the event, traveled to the western edge of the state for their April meeting so they could avoid answering Camenker and Whiteman's questions. But Camenker rented a bus and thirty of his members followed the Board to their new meeting place. While there, the head of the state Department of Education, David Driscoll, told Whiteman this was not a "parents rights" issue.

"It was only then that we decided we had to go public with these tapes," Camenker told *Massachusetts News*. "We didn't want to report this vile stuff, but we have no other way to let the fathers and mothers know what is being taught to our children."

It wasn't until *Massachusetts News* (which had been in business a little over a year) wrote a story for its Internet site and mailed 250,000 copies of their May newspaper around the state, that outraged citizens finally learned about Fistgate and what was happening at the gay/straight alliances, which by this time numbered over 180 clubs. (It must have disturbed Pinch to discover the power of the press.)

Commissioner Driscoll immediately changed his mind and apologized for the explicit teaching. "There is no question," he said, "that the comments of the Department of Education staff and the other consultant in those workshops go beyond the boundaries of what our staff should have done."

The story was subsequently picked up across the country because of the *Massachusetts News* Internet site, which by this time was being read everywhere by over 10,000 persons a day. The largest Internet site in the country, *WorldNetDaily*, wrote a large article. Even the *Globe* was finally forced to acknowledge Fistgate in a story on May 2 but it didn't acknowledge the role of *Massachusetts News* until May 26.

When Pinch's staff at the *Globe* realized how big the story was, you can be sure they didn't plan a celebration for whistleblowers Camenker and Whiteman. These particular whistleblowers were on the wrong side of the issue.

Instead the *Globe* went the mode of "cover-up," which meant nasty, personal attacks upon what Pinch perceived as the enemy, anyone who opposed Pinch's worldview.

There were many ongoing, agonizing debates at *Massachusetts News* about whether to print the filth that occurred at Fistgate. But they all ended in stalemate. No one could devise any way to tell the citizens what was happening except to let them see exactly what their children were being exposed to in public schools.

Difficult to Hide this Story

The workshop which caused the most trouble for Pinch was titled: "What They Didn't Tell You About Queer Sex & Sexuality In Health

Class: A Workshop For Youth Only, Ages 14-21."

Three state-employed, homosexual teachers, acting in their professional capacities in the Department of Health or Education coaxed about 20 children into talking openly and graphically about homosexual sex.

The syllabus included: "What's it like to be young, queer and beginning to date? Are lesbians at risk for HIV? ... We will address the information you want about queer sexuality and some of the politics that prevent us from getting our needs met."

The instructors, who described themselves as homosexuals, were Margot E. Abels, Coordinator HIV/AIDS Program, Massachusetts Department of Education; Julie Netherland, who had the same title; and Michael Gaucher, Consultant, HIV/AIDS Program, Massachusetts Department of Public Health.

• **How do we know whether we've had sex?** The workshop opened with the three adults asking the children "how they knew, as gay people, whether or not they've had sex." Questions were thrown around the room about whether oral sex was "sex," to which the Department of Public Health employee stated, "If that's not sex, then the number of times I've had sex has dramatically decreased from a mountain to a valley, baby."

Eventually the answer presented itself, and it was determined that whenever an orifice was filled with genitalia, then sex had occurred. Michael Gaucher had the following exchange with one student, who appeared to be about 16-years-old:

> Gaucher: "What orifices are we talking about?"
> Student: [hesitation]
> Gaucher: "Don't be shy, honey; you can do it."
> Student: "Your mouth."
> Gaucher: "Okay."
> Student: "Your ass."
> Gaucher: "There you go."
> Student: "Your pussy. That kind of place."

But since sex occurred "when an orifice was filled," the next question was how lesbians could "have sex." Margot Abels discussed

The whistleblowing, law school student, Scott Whiteman, who did the taping of the Fistgate Conference and exposed the criminal abuse of minors by the state, got no help from Margaret Marshall's courts, which went after him instead of the abusers. Whiteman is still defending against a case brought by GLAD, the organization of Attorney Mary Bonauto, the friend of Marshall. None of the state money, given to Marshall to help such people, will ever go to Whiteman.

whether a dildo had to be involved, when one was too big or too small, and what homosexual resources students could consult to get similar questions answered.

• **Carpet munching**

Then the children were asked to role-play. One student was to act the part of "a young lesbian who's really enraptured with another woman, and it's really coming down to the wire and you're thinking about having sex." The other student played the "hip GSA (Gay, Straight Alliance) lesbian advisor, who you feel you can talk to." The "counseling" included discussions of lesbian sex, oral-vaginal contact or "carpet munching," as one student put it. The student asked whether it would smell like fish. At that point the session turned to another subject.

• **A lesson in fisting?**

There was a five-minute pause so that the teenagers could write down questions for the homosexual presenters. The first question was read by Julie Netherland, "What's fisting?"

A student answered this question by informing the class that "fisting" is when you put your "whole hand into the ass or pussy" of another. When a few of the students winced, Gaucher offered: "A little known fact about fisting, you don't make a fist, like this. It's like this," forming his hand into the shape of a teardrop rather than a balled fist. He informed the children that this was much easier.

Abels told the students that "fisting" is not about forcing your hand into somebody's "hole, opening or orifice" if they don't want it there. She said that "usually" the person was very relaxed and opened him or herself up to the other. She informed the class that it is a very emotional and intense experience.

At this point, a child of about sixteen asked why someone would want to do that. He stated that if the hand were pulled out quickly, the whole thing didn't sound very appealing to him. Abels was quick to point out that although fisting "often gets a really bad rap," it usually isn't about the pain, "not that we're putting that down." She informed him and the class that "fisting" was "an experience of letting somebody into your body that you want to be that close and intimate with." When a child asked the question, "Why would someone do this?" Abels provided a comfortable response to the children: in order to "put them into an exploratory mode."

- **Rubbing each others' clits**

Gaucher presented the next question, "Do lesbians rub their clits together?" Gaucher and Abels asked the kids if they thought it was possible and whether someone would do a "hand diagram" for the class. No one volunteered, but a girl, who looked about fifteen or sixteen, stepped up to the board and drew a three-foot high vagina and labeled the labia and clitoris. She put up, "inside the 'G'-spot." While drawing, Gaucher told her to use the "pink" chalk, to which Abels responded, "Not everyone is pink, honey." All the children laughed.

After the chalk vagina was complete, the children remarked on the size of the "clit," and the presenters stated that that was a gifted woman. Then Abels informed all the young girls that indeed, you can rub your "clitori" together, either with or without clothes, and: "You can definitely orgasm from it." Gaucher told the kids that: "There is a name for this: tribadism," which he wrote on the board and told one girl who looked about fourteen to "bring that vocabulary word back to Bedford [a town in Massachusetts]." Netherland informed the children that it wasn't too difficult because: "When you are sexually aroused, your clit gets bigger."

- **Should you spit after you suck another boy (or a man)?**

Gaucher read the following from a card: "Cum and calories: Spit versus swallow and the health concerns." He informed the children that although he didn't know the calorie count of male ejaculation, he has "heard that it's sweeter if people eat celery." He then asked the boys, "Is it rude not to swallow?" Many of the high school boys mumbled

"No," but one about the age of 16 said emphatically, "Oh no!" One boy, again about the age of sixteen, offered his advice on avoiding HIV/AIDS transmission while giving oral sex by not brushing your teeth or eating food for four hours before you "go down on a guy, because then you probably don't want to be swallowing cum."

• **Is oral sex better with tongue rings?** Another question asked was whether oral sex was better with tongue rings. A sixteen-year-old student murmured, "Yes," to which all of the children laughed. Gaucher said, "There you have it" and stated something to the effect that the debate has ended.

• **Use a condom?** It's your decision, really. Although all of this was supposed to be part of an aggressive HIV/AIDS prevention campaign, the session ran 55 minutes before the first mention of "protection" and safer sex came. Even in the context of the "safer sex" discussion, it was pointed out that these children could make an "informed decision" not to use a condom. Outside in the conference hall, the children could easily obtain as many condoms, vaginal condoms, and other contraceptive devices as they wished from various organizations which distribute such.

Pinch Approved What Happened at Fistgate

Pinch Sulzberger had his people in place at the time of the Fistgate mess. Gilman had been Publisher since 1999 and Renee Loth had just been installed as editor of the opinion page. Their main object was damage control, how to keep the "homophobes" from endangering the "progress" that had taken place in the schools under Weld and Cellucci (and later Jane Swift when Cellucci resigned so she could become Governor).

They didn't lose any time. Renee Loth wrote an editorial about Fistgate on May 20. The headline made it clear what she thought about Camenker and Whiteman: "Attack on sex education."

There was really no problem with Fistgate, she wrote: "They [the teenagers] were asking the sorts of things teenagers ask every day ..."

Many immediately wondered, where had she grown up? Did she really ask about "fisting" when she was a child? Had she asked whether "lesbians rub their clits together," "should you spit after you suck another boy or man," "whether oral sex was better with tongue rings," etc.?

Regardless of where she had lived in the past and with whom she had associated, she was happy that the children now were getting "accurate" information instead of "inaccurate or dangerous answers from their peers." But this information that was presented by the Department of Education was about as dangerous as it can get, particularly with the presence of AIDS. As a person who has been many places in a long lifetime and seen many things, I'd much rather put my trust in the "inaccurate and dangerous answers" from my peers than I would from these dirty, old men and women from the state.

Loth denied that the session could lure children into homosexual sexual activity. But in the next sentence, she said, "To judge from the questions, most were already sexually active." But if "most" had already been corrupted by previous sessions, that means there must have been some who had not been. In fact, some students were obviously not yet into this behavior because they asked why anyone would want to do some of those foolish things. How many students were hearing this dangerous instruction for the first time? It could have been one, three or ten students. We don't know and she doesn't either. But she agrees there were some.

Before she came to the *Globe*, Loth had been political editor at a free alternative newspaper in Boston, the *Phoenix*, which earns a large part of its money from advertisements aimed at homosexuals. If one needs advice in the future about policies on the Middle East, nuclear weapons or whether we should raise the interest rates, remember you can always discover what Pinch's person in Boston thinks. Just read the editorial page at the *Globe*.

Unable to Contain Citizen Outrage

Pinch's people in Boston were unable to control the outrage that resulted. Talk show host Jeanine Graf picked up the story from *Massachusetts News* and spent three hours every evening for two weeks on the issue. The Deputy Commissioner of Education, Alan Safran, apologized on her show. Thereafter, Pinch's paper went on a **personal** attack in a news feature on June 1, not an editorial, that Graf was suspected of being — a Christian!!

It wrote, "Already, protesters ... are commenting on Graf's background." What was that dangerous background? The *Globe* provided the answer. "About ten years ago, she did in fact work for a Christian station, Salem Broadcasting's WEZE-AM (590) in North Quincy."

The paper couldn't confirm that she actually is a Christian. But it did express its concern that she might be. The headline on the story was, "Graf must be accountable, too."

They also revealed that her reporting of the Children's Sex Conference Scandal was very successful and reached a lot of parents, or else they would not have written their story.

There were other glitches in the very long article:

• It said the taping by parents of the explicit sexual meeting was done "illegally." But no one knows the answer to that question. It's whatever the courts want to decide.

• The *Globe* did not report that many homosexuals called Graf and agreed that Fistgate should not have happened.

• The goal of the meeting, according to the paper, had been to "lower the rate of teen depression and suicide." But the *Globe* never revealed how explicit sexual instruction in "fisting," "oral sex" and such topics would prevent depression or suicide. In fact, many persons have pointed out that such instruction will increase the incidence of AIDS and other STDs and depression.

• According to the reporter, she spent "a few nights" listening to the Graf show and found a "disturbing" fact: many listeners believe the purpose of the session was to encourage children to experiment in homosexual sex. "It's a specious idea that comes up repeatedly," she said. She complained that: "Graf does not contradict or correct her callers." But anyone who listens to the tapes or reads the transcripts can quickly see that the purpose of the meeting *was* to encourage the children to try the sex. Nevertheless, the *Globe* went on to attack Graf: "It's an idea rife with homophobia that can be used to rationalize all kinds of bigotry, including violence. Although Graf won't speak for her callers, she says she is not homophobic."

• There's a serious problem with the way the article closed: "Whether or not she agrees with the callers who go on air with hate-filled rhetoric or homophobic fables passed off as fact, she ought to take responsibility for what her listeners hear. To let lies go uncorrected is to be complicit in the bigotry they spread, which damages rather than promotes her legitimate discussion about the rights of parents. She's the adult here. She should recognize the implications of context as well as content." But Graf never aired "hate" or "fables" and the *Globe* never cited any. The only hate was at the *Globe*. And that was exhibited not in an editorial or a column, but in a news story.

Globe Wasn't Concerned with Freedom of the Press

When a gag order was slapped on everyone as to what had occurred in that session of teenagers, by a compliant state judge, Allan van Gestel, who was friends with the homosexual lawyers, this violation of Free Speech did not cause any concern among Pinch's people. But it did trouble other people as the entire country laughed at the Massachusetts court. Fox News lawyers came to Boston to instruct Judge van Gestel. Even the homosexual lawyers at GLAD advised Van Gestel he couldn't violate the Constitution in this manner.

Liberal lawyers Alan Dershowitz, Harvey Silverglate and others denounced the judge's Order, but the *Globe* didn't care.

The state Senate wasn't bothered by the Order either. It agreed that because of the Order, it was unable to debate whether it should discontinue funding of homosexual programs in the state schools.

On May 25, van Gestel finally realized he had become a laughing stock. He released the press from the order but continued it against the two whistleblowers. Nevertheless, he cautioned the homosexual plaintiffs that if he released the press from the gag order, the tapes would then be available to everyone. As the case has languished, the temporary order has remained in place except for the press. Meanwhile Camenker and Whiteman continue to pay lawyers as the suit slowly moves forward.

The *Globe* didn't understand the legal problems or else it distorted and lied on purpose. For example, on June 2 it wrote, "A state Superior Court judge has since barred the group from distributing the tapes, ruling at the request of a gay advocate that they were made in violation of wiretap laws."

If the judge had made that ruling, the suit would be over. That is what the suit will decide. All he had ruled was that he likes to help his friends. So he had made an unconstitutional order, which he later rescinded, that the plaintiffs might prevail at trial and therefore the tapes could not be distributed by anyone. Because the two whistle-blowers are only "little people," he has not yet rescinded his order against them. But he has never ruled that they were made "in violation of wiretap laws."

Margot Abels told the *Globe* on June 2, "This is absolutely sanctioned by the department [of education]. It's standard. There's nothing we did that was a secret. The department has always given us its full support-until now."

The scandal went right to Governor Cellucci's office but he refused to acknowledge that Fistgate had ever occurred even though his personal staff had terminated three state workers as a result.

It came back to haunt Cellucci a year later when he was almost denied confirmation by the U.S. Senate as Ambassador to Canada because of angry Massachusetts citizens. It took a hurried telephone call by President Bush and an unusual agreement with Sen. Jesse Helms to get the confirmation of Cellucci. The Governor agreed with Helms that he would sign a written document to follow the President's directives in all matters and not allow his personal beliefs to enter in.

Many in Massachusetts blame the appointment of Cellucci on Bush's Chief of Staff Andrew Card, a professional politician from Massachusetts, who is seen by many here as just another liberal politician that they hope does not try to return here. The new Governor, Jane Swift, was impressed by what happened to Cellucci and told the *Boston Herald* that she would oppose gay marriages and domestic partnerships. But she soon began to waffle, lost everyone's respect and, as a result, did not even run for Governor in 2002.

Camenker Vindicated by Reinstatement of Fistgate Teacher

A year later, Margot Abels was "thrilled" to be reinstated in her job by an arbitrator and reimbursed for her lost pay during that year.

But Camenker said this only proved that he was correct in what he had been saying all along.

"I believe Abels absolutely," Camenker told *Massachusetts News* when she first filed her suit against the state. "She is being used as a scapegoat," he said. "There's no question about it. For them to claim this was an isolated incident is completely disingenuous."

Camenker now said that the fact that an arbitrator came to the same conclusion that he did, does not make Abels a heroine. "Just because her superiors at the state approved her talking 'dirty' with children is not to her credit in any way," he stated. But, she told the *Globe*: "I do feel vindicated." And it was obvious that the *Globe* agreed that somehow this made what happened at Fistgate appear to be "okay."

Camenker told the *Globe* that he agreed with the arbitrator's decision, to a point. "No question about it: Her supervisors knew what was going on and encouraged her to do it," he said. "But this woman should not continue to be paid by the state to have contact with vulnerable children."

Observers were puzzled about the statement by arbitrator Marc Greenbaum that there were blank spaces in the tape that was recorded by Scott Whiteman. They could not understand how the arbitrator could have obtained a copy of the original tape which was still in the possession of someone unknown. (They were also puzzled that the *Globe* was so inaccurate as to report that Brian Camenker was involved in the actual taping.)

Greenbaum wrote in his report, "The blank spaces left by the PRC tape were filled in with important messages about AIDS prevention, abstinence, postponement, alternative forms of sexual intimacy, and the need for students to enforce their own boundaries of personal security." But Scott Whiteman, who attended the entire conference, has reported that no such messages were ever given during the entire workshop.

Fistgate made homosexual activists more cautious across the entire country, according to Abels. She told the *Boston Herald* that she was concerned that her firing triggered a dumbing-down of sex education and HIV prevention work. "I think a lot of programs around the country and the state have scaled back and gotten the message there are things to be afraid of. Now you can't just be about effective practices because it all became so political."

Governors Cellucci and Weld were happy the day that Justice Roderick Ireland was appointed, but Ireland went against the wishes of most blacks when he voted for gay marriage. He would have changed the decision if he had voted against it.

But Camenker says that she is wrong. He says that Fistgate got the program out of politics when the people found out what was happening. He says that Governors Weld and Cellucci and other politicians were keeping it quiet for as long as they could because the homosexual lobby was an excellent source of votes and money for them. But after Fistgate broke, they were forced to make some concessions and look like they were correcting the problem. The firing of Margot Abels was one of those concessions.

Camenker said at the time of the scandal that Governor Cellucci's office was well aware of what was happening because Camenker had personally told them.

Camenker commented, "Bill Weld decided, when he beat John Silber in that close race, that he was successful only because of the help and money given to him by homosexual activists." It was a political decision, he says. "Therefore," according to Camenker, "Weld repaid those activists by allowing them access to our public schools and even giving them the money to indoctrinate our kids."

By the time Cellucci was appointed Ambassador to Canada, the scandal about Fistgate had become so bad that President Bush had to make the personal telephone calls to get him confirmed. Most people in Washington now know about Fistgate.

Governor's Commission Lies Continually About 'Safety' and 'Suicide'

The Governor's "Commission for Gay and Lesbian Youth" is constantly talking about the "safety" and "suicide" of homosexual students in the Commonwealth.

SAFETY

In a speech on March 5, 1995 by the founder/director of GLSEN, who was in charge at Fistgate, Kevin Jennings revealed how he used "safety" to delude Gov. Weld and the state legislature into adopting his homosexual agenda for the schools of Massachusetts. The speech, titled "Winning the Culture War," was given at the Human Rights Campaign Fund Leadership Conference.

Jennings said: "If the Radical Right can succeed in portraying us as preying on children, we will lose. Their language 'promoting homosexuality' is one example. It is laced with subtle and not-so-subtle innuendo that we are 'after their kids.' We must learn from the abortion struggle, where the clever claiming of the term 'pro-life' allowed those who opposed abortion-on-demand to frame the issue to their advantage, to make sure that we do not allow ourselves to be painted into a corner before the debate even begins.

"In Massachusetts the effective reframing of this issue was the key to the success of the Governor's Commission on Gay and Lesbian Youth. We immediately seized upon the opponent's calling card, 'safety,' and explained how homophobia represents a threat to students' safety by creating a climate where violence, name-calling, health problems, and suicide are common. Titling our report: 'Making Schools Safe for Gay and Lesbian Youth,' we automatically threw our opponents onto the defensive and stole their best line of attack. This framing short-circuited their arguments and left them back-pedaling from day one.

"Finding the effective frame for your community is the key to victory. It must be linked to universal values that everyone in the community has in common.

"In Massachusetts, no one could speak up against our frame and say, 'Why, yes, I do think students should kill themselves.' This allowed us to set the terms for the debate.

"In Massachusetts, we made creating an environment where youth could speak-out, our number one priority. We know that, confronted with real-live stories of youth who had suffered from homophobia, our opponents would have to attack people who had been victimized once, which put them in a bully position from which it would be hard to emerge looking good. More importantly, we made sure these youth met with elected officials so that, the next time these officials had to vote on something, there would be a specific face and story attached to the issue. We wanted them to have an actual kid in mind when they had to cast their votes. We won the vote in the Senate 33-7 as a result."

SUICIDE

"It's a 'statistic' that's been repeated innumerable times: A gay teenager is some three times more likely to commit suicide."

That was the first paragraph in an article in the *Boston Herald* in 1997 by the Newhouse News Service. It pointed out that nearly ten years after the original publication of the widely discredited statistic by Paul Gibson, a social worker in Chicago, the figures were still being used even though many organizations had stated that there is no evidence that they are true.

Those organizations include The Center for Disease Control, The National Institute of Mental Health, the American Association of Suicidology, the American Psychological Association and some gay advocacy groups.

Even Joyce Hunter, the one time president of the National Lesbian and Gay Health Association, has said it is unknown if there is a connection between homosexuality and teen suicide.

Peter Muehrer, chief of the Youth Mental Health program in the Prevention and Behavioral Medicine Research branch of the National Institute of Mental Health and recent winner of the Secretary of Health and Human Services Award for Distinguished Service, analyzed the original studies on which the Gibson review was based and determined that the conclusions can not be supported by the data.

He wrote, "There is no scientific evidence to support this data." Joyce Hunter said she agrees with mental-health researchers that most gay and lesbian teens, like teens overall, are emotionally resilient people who "go on to develop a positive sense of self and go on with their lives."

Nevertheless, the scientifically baseless claim was the catalyst for the creation of the Commission on Gay and Lesbian Youth and the Gay/Straight Alliances in the schools. William Weld claimed that this suicide figure was a clear indication that our schools are unsafe for homosexual youth. Since the creation of the Commission, schools have been encouraged to start Gay/Straight Alliances, again under the presumption that schools are currently unsafe for homosexual students.

Fistgate Tapes Still Available

The original Fistgate story was in the May 2000 issue of Massachusetts News and a complete wrap-up was in the issue of July 2000, both of which are available free at www.massnews.com.

The edited tape which the Parents Rights Coalition is still not permitted to distribute is also available for our costs of $10 from Massachusetts News, P.O. Box 812844, Wellesley, MA 02482-0026. No telephone orders are accepted. You are cautioned that it has very coarse language and is not enjoyable listening.

You can contact Brian Camenker and the Parents Rights Coalition, a volunteer organization, at 781-899-4905 or P.O. Box 1612, Waltham, MA 02454. They are not allowed to sell tapes because of the court order. Their website is www.parentsrightscoalition.org.

Approximately 5,000 teens commit suicide in a year. There is no evidence to link those suicides to homosexuality.

25

Pinch Got Huge Victory in Massachusetts Gay Marriage Case . . . Or Did He?

Pinch obtained a huge victory in Massachusetts on November 18, 2003, when gay marriage was imposed by Margaret Marshall, Chief Justice of the Massachusetts Supreme Judicial Court — who also happens to be the wife of one of Pinch's employees, Anthony Lewis, the premiere columnist at the *Times* for years, now semi-retired. Lewis has the run of the *Times* building, including Pinch's office.

The most disturbing part was that we had <u>won</u> back in July 2002 when the legislature violated the state Constitution. We had put so much pressure on Pinch that his people broke the law. But nobody seemed to understand that.[1]

Marshall Unhappy that Three Justices Voted Against Her

It was disturbing to Marshall that the final vote was a tie. She had convinced only three judges to vote with her for gay marriage. The other three voted against her. This particular group of judges always

---

[1] All the leaders of our movement went running off the field after the vote on July 17, 2002. We had forged a shaky coalition which was successful, but they couldn't grasp the dynamics of what was happening. Massachusetts Citizens for Marriage stood all alone after that.

MCM had agreed to have the local Focus on the Family group and the Catholic Church do all the lobbying. The Focus group went flying off to a meeting at headquarters in Colorado Springs the day after the vote and never returned to the battlefield. They were thinking about other things. They basically had a three person staff with a receptionist and two other employees, who did everything, including lobbying. The Catholics, who have 80% of the legislators in the state as nominal members, were so preoccupied with the pounding that Pinch had administered about molestation by priests that they were terribly distracted and unable to focus on the Amendment as they had during the petition drive.

I understand that Margaret Thatcher has written a book in which she says that it is not your enemies who do you in. It is your friends.

likes to do things unanimously, and it was a pleasant surprise to us that the vote was as close as you can get, 3-3, with Marshall casting the tie-breaking vote.

I have to take some credit for the closeness of that vote. Although I did not discuss the issues of the particular case before them very much, they could see that those on the side of traditional marriage were responsible, rational people.

Although it appeared to be a victory for Pinch, it may, in the long run, prove to be his undoing. He's already in trouble across the country over Jayson Blair. When everyone discovers how he engineered this newest "victory," it may be his demise.

Pinch has had this moment in mind for many years, and I don't know why I wasn't perceptive enough at the beginning to see what was happening. But I was new and I bowed too much to the experience of others, both here and on the national level. When Pinch's father bought the *Globe* in 1994, the son was already publisher of the *Times* and was looking ahead to use this liberal state as the means to impose gay marriage on the entire United States. Bill Weld was Governor here and totally comfortable with that idea.

The legislators could be and were, easily bought with the huge quantities of money that were pouring in from homosexual activists and others from outside the state. The big unions were important supporters. Before the legislature voted to *not* vote on the Marriage Amendment, the union lobbyists visited every legislator. During the vote, there was a low chant, "This is a union vote. This is a union vote."

The main problem that Pinch faced back when he first thought about it was that at least 60% of the people in the state were not behind his idea. But if he could only get a Chief Justice of the state's Supreme Judicial Court appointed who would be on his side, it would not be necessary to win the people or the Legislature. The court could just mandate it.

Therefore, he reasoned: Why not put Anthony Lewis' wife on the Supreme Judicial Court? Pinch was good friends with the couple. Once he had accomplished that goal of installing her as Chief in 1999, it was just a matter of time before they would get it done together. There was no opposition in sight except the voters, who appeared quiescent.

Although these three homosexual couples appeared ecstatic after the vote on November 18, 2003, they may have a surprise when they stop and realize that three judges voted against the ruling calling it an "aberration," among other things. The dissents weren't given much publicity by the press but this could be the final highpoint of homosexual activism if the citizens become angry enough about the SJC decision.

Suddenly, out of nowhere, appeared naive Sally Pawlick in the spring of 2000 with Massachusetts Citizens for Marriage[2] and a plan for a Constitutional Amendment. Pinch knew he would lose a referendum, as did Sally, which would forbid Marshall from imposing gay marriage. Pinch became angry and determined. He used the *Times* and the *Globe* to bully and libel in an attempt to stop the citizens from enthusiastically supporting the Protection of Marriage Amendment, and also he gave "cover" to the legislature. When the citizens remained unfazed by his effort, he continued the bullying and libel but also began to urge the legislature to just forget what the Constitution said.

That violation on July 17, 2002, resulted in Senate President Birmingham losing his bid to become Governor, as did Shannon O'Brien. She was able to easily defeat Birmingham in the Democratic

---

[2] It was known as Massachusetts Citizens Alliance until the signature gathering started when the state required it to begin a new legal entity, which was called Massachusetts Citizens for Marriage.

primary because voters were hostile over his illegal conduct on the Marriage Amendment. Then O'Brien waffled on gay marriage and domestic partnerships. As a result, Republican Mitt Romney was able to be elected.

If the legislature had been allowed to vote in 2002 and 25% had approved the Amendment, the measure would have been sent to the legislature for its approval, with a vote scheduled at the ballot box in November 2004. It would have passed at the ballot box and this decision would be nullified. Marshall would not have been able to do what she did. (You can read an interesting colloquy about that between Mary Bonauto and Justice Greaney in the transcript of the oral argument on our website, the one where he assured her she was going to win.)

The reason that a majority of the legislators were able to thwart a vote is because only 25% are necessary to send the measure on to the ballot box. Even though the legislature is *required* to take a vote, no one can force the majority to do anything, not even the SJC, if they refuse to do so. Margaret Marshall's court made that decision in 2002 in Sally's suit.

With his big megaphone, Pinch may be able to continue dominating the scene as the *Times* has done for over a century. He may be able to "spin" his way out of this one. Only time will tell what impact this will have on his subscribers, many of whom have blind loyalty.

This is not a matter of gay marriage. It is whether we still have a democracy in Massachusetts.

Homosexuals Have the Money and the Power

The homosexual activists have the passion, money and power. They have the law firm of GLAD, based in Boston with five, fulltime lawyers and eleven other staff members with an estimated budget of $1 million. It was started back in 1978. They also have a fulltime staffer of the National Gay and Lesbian Task Force, founded in 1973, living and working in Cambridge. That was the group that trained people to battle the Marriage Amendment. The Massachusetts Lesbian and Gay Bar Association has about fifty lawyer/members. They have a permanent seat on the governing body of the Massachusetts Bar Association. There is not enough space to mention all the activists working here.

Governor Mitt Romney never has understood why he became Governor in 2002. It was because Massachusetts Citizens for Marriage, under the leadership of Sally Pawlick, so damaged Senator Thomas Birmingham for his illegal actions that the people rejected him in the primary. Romney still doesn't understand that the voters do not want domestic partnerships either. Romney continues to use Washington consultants who give him the wrong messages.

Against that array, there is not one lawyer anywhere in the state working on the side of marriage, only a few volunteers do so in their spare time. The largest family organization, the Focus group, has about three staffers, who handle a myriad of matters, not just the homosexual threat. They are always strapped for money and are a semi-religious group with a minister as the director.

Even the family groups on the national level do not have the firepower of GLAD, and they also carry a "stigma" with many citizens of being the "religious right." As one listens to focus groups and analyses surveys, it becomes immediately apparent that about half the citizens believe this should not be a "religious issue." Therefore, the family groups are immediately losing 50% of the people before they start. It makes it difficult to win. The church groups should alert their members, if they wish to be active, but not try to convince the secular people, who often go the other way just because they don't like a preacher lecturing at them. By the same token, the Massachusetts Catholic Conference, the lobbying arm of the church, has excellent people, but they should be behind the scenes, not out in front leading the charge.

Even Justice Sosman, who voted against gay marriage, urged Bonauto at oral argument to argue that traditional marriage violates

Julie Goodridge, left, and Hillary Goodridge, right, of Boston go to a news conference in Boston, Tuesday, Nov. 18, 2003, after learning of the Massachusetts Supreme Judicial Court's ruling that same sex couples are legally entitled to wed under the state constitution. They are one of seven couples who sued to win the right to wed.

the First Amendment because it's essentially derived from religion. That argument is raised by a lot of people, although it would appear that if we follow that argument, we will have to stop punishing murderers. After all, the Ten Commandants also forbids murder, as do all religions. Does that mean we can no longer have any punishment for murder? What Sosman's remarks do mean is that those in favor of traditional marriage should hesitate in making any inference that the decision is only for the religious to decide.

Pinch Saw an Obvious Pushover

The state of Massachusetts was an obvious pushover for Pinch, until Sally came in with her organization in the spring of 2000, a secular group which does not have to convert anyone to Christianity or Orthodox Judaism in order to get their support. Most persons are able to see the matter as an issue of strong families and healthy children. Although churches are very helpful because those people also see the need for strong families, it is not necessary that anyone be religious in order to support traditional marriage.

The people at MCM had from four-to-eight fulltime workers until 2003 when they went to one worker because they were waiting to see what would happen after the Legislature refused to vote on their Amendment.

It will be very difficult for anyone to put the pieces together at the *Times* even if they do get rid of Pinch. There are going to be many angry readers once they learn about the *Times'* involvement. They are going to lose both subscribers and advertisers. In today's world with unions and government watching everything an employer does, it will be impossible for anyone to quickly gather an unbiased staff, even if they have the desire to do so.

Margaret Marshall's Hearing Was a Sham

I did not participate in the gay marriage lawsuit because all anyone can do is to file a brief and hope someone reads it. Instead I was _personally_ before the Supreme Judicial Court four times from October 2002 to May 2003, looking them in the eye and asking for fairness — for the people to be allowed to vote on the issue as the state

Constitution mandates.

All the leaders of traditional marriage except Sally thought they were defeated in July 2002 when the Legislature violated the Constitution. But that wasn't the time to quit. **They had just won a tremendous victory by forcing Pinch and his crew to violate the law.**

The people understood, but they were confused. Everyone was tired and dispirited.

I started a lawsuit for MCM a few weeks later, telling the SJC there had to be some remedy when the Constitution was broken. The entire state was looking to the Governor and the SJC for leadership. Sally and others from MCM started a polite picketing effort outside Governor Jane Swift's office, but Swift didn't care what happened as long as she was taken care of. Finally, after months of being sweet, I sent the Governor a "lawyer letter" by FedEx to her home the day before Thanksgiving, sternly telling her that if she didn't do her duty and call the Legislature back for a vote on the Amendment, we would be suing her *personally* for violating our Constitutional rights. That did it. The Governor immediately sent a request to the SJC, asking for an advisory opinion as to her duties.

Her request arrived on the same day I was appearing before the entire court, December 3, 2002, to argue the case I had filed in July. I told the SJC that if they couldn't think of any other remedy, they could just send MCM's Amendment to the next session of the Legislature which would assemble in January.

That was a silly move on Jane's part. She did my work for me. Her request was exactly what I was asking the Court to do, i.e., tell everybody what their duties were. On December 20, they gave Jane her answer. Yes, the Legislature had violated the Constitution. Yes, she had also violated the Constitution. She was now required to call the Legislature back before the end of the year. They were required to vote.

But the *Globe* wrote exactly the opposite in its story on December 21. Nobody had time to read the full text of the opinion. Christmas Eve was coming in three days. They believed the *Globe*. The required vote never took place.

On January 2, 2003, Sally was back at the Court House, filing another suit asking the SJC to move this suit to the new Legislature because the old one had forfeited its right to vote. A snowstorm postponed the first hearing before a single justice from February 18 to February 25, at which time Justice Greaney dismissed our lawsuit. An appeal was immediately filed for the whole Court to hear the case, which they did on May 9. We have still not received a decision from that suit. While we do not expect a favorable ruling, it is odd that they have delayed that decision beyond the normal time limit. They could have easily thrown the case out months ago with a single sentence: "Judgment of Single Justice affirmed." Instead, they sent me a special notice in September that they were extending the time for them to answer our suit.

Women Pass "Civil Union" Bill for Homosexuals

In the Vermont legislature, it was the women who passed the civil union bill, and they did so, enthusiastically. The bill would have died if only men were allowed to vote. The same dynamic may be true in this state.

Although the bill was passed by the Vermont House on March 16, 2000, the men voted to defeat the bill with only 41 in favor and 60 against, while the women voted for it by a four-to-one margin of 35-9. The final total was 76 to 69 in favor.

The supporters were 57 Democrats, 14 Republicans, 4 Progressives and 1 Independent. Voting no were 50 Republicans, 18 Democrats and 1 Independent.

All but one of the 32 female Democrats voted in favor of the bill, while four of 12 Republican women voted for it. More than half of the Democrats voting yes were women and more than a quarter of the Republicans voting yes were women.

The bill was seen as a civil rights issue and a vote for "families" by those legislators who approved it. Some of their comments were:

"I will not be silenced by hatred and intolerance." Rep. Marion Milne, R.

"No one should ever be treated as a second-class citizen. No one." Rep. Bob Kinsey, R. A 72-year-old native whose great-great-grandmother was an Abenaki Indian and whose daughter is a lesbian.

"My roommate by choice was a black. I don't feel it is right to treat anyone differently than you would want them to treat you. I don't understand homosexuals, but I can be tolerant of them." Rep. Dick Marron, R., a 62-year-old Catholic owner of a resort in Stowe.

"Their pain and their inability to fit the mold [when speaking of her two lesbian daughters] has been our pain as well. Please help to remove the stigma. Make Vermont a leader in the preservation of family life." Rep. Mary Mazzariello, D.

"It would have been so easy to vote 'No' and avoid facing the issue. Are people going to shake my hand or are they going to throw something at me?" Rep. Jack Anderson, D.

"Those of you who will vote "No' on this bill, I'm sorry for your fear because we as gay and lesbian people, gay and lesbian couples, we are not a threat. We're not a threat to you, your relationships, your committed marriages....We are your neighbors. We are worth loving and we will love in return." Rep. Bill Lippert, the only gay member of the legislature.

"It may have to do with the fact that women traditionally focus on family and nurturing and relationships, that women's identity comes from connecting." Rep. Anne Pugh, D.

"For whatever reason, I feel there's more fear among the male gender. Men seem to be more critical of people. It's just our species, probably." Rep. Michael Vinton, D., a retired state trooper.

26

Marshall Would Not Allow Discussion at Oral Argument

Little discussion was allowed by Margaret Marshall at the oral argument about gay marriage in April 2003. Only about 15 minutes was given to the attorney for the state to explain why Marshall could not impose gay marriage. The Chief Justice really didn't want to hear any of that and rudely stopped all discussion at the end of the exact time allotted.

It wasn't surprising, therefore, that in her November 18 decision, she lectured us in this manner: "[Our law] works a deep and scarring hardship on a very real segment of the community for no rational reason."

No rational reason! ? !

Marshall first arrived here from her native South Africa in 1968, two years out of college, and is now lecturing us that our history for hundreds of years is without "rational reason?" Who told her that, her husband?

She's probably having a good time down at Times Square, laughing with Pinch and her husband, Anthony Lewis, about what they have accomplished here in Massachusetts. They may even be discussing how they're going to have her appointed to the U.S. Supreme Court. They are undoubtedly already talking with Hillary Clinton about arranging that when Hillary becomes President in 2004 or 2008. The two women were apparently at Yale Law School at the same time even though Marshall is older. Hillary was in the class of 1974, while

Marshall graduated two years later in 1976. It is a very small, intimate school.

Marshall's husband, who was the premiere columnist for the *Times*, first started as a reporter in 1948, left for four years with another paper, and then returned for good in 1955. He became a columnist until Pinch got so much grief about his columns on Afghanistan, which many thought were threatening our troops there, that they agreed in 2001 that the *Times* would retire his column.

Lewis told the *Globe* at the time it was a "joint decision" between Pinch and him. He is still prominently listed with his picture on the paper's website, "The New York Times News Service," as a columnist whose columns other newspapers can purchase, but apparently the *Times* itself no longer wants him. He has been allowed to "save face." He told the *Globe*: "The last few weeks of overreaching by George Bush and [Attorney General] John Ashcroft will no doubt leave me frustrated at not being able to knock them."[1]

When Marshall and Lewis traveled to Australia in 2002, he was introduced there as a columnist for the *Times*. Never known for humility, Marshall also lectured that country and its Supreme Court. She told them that their judges "can, and should, tolerate a great deal more criticism of judges and of the judiciary." Some wags wonder if the Assistant Attorney General, Judith Yogman, who opposed the gay marriage lawsuit, would have been allowed to quote that statement back to Marshall at oral argument.

It's also interesting to note that Lewis was one of two non-lawyers, since the inception of the award, to be awarded the prestigious "Henry Friendly Medal" in October 2002 from the American Law Institute in Philadelphia. A strange coincidence is that Margaret was already in Philadelphia that day. She is a member of the Institute's governing council.

I wrote in a story just before oral argument: "She [Marshall] will

---

[1] Some of Lewis' wisdom over the years have included:
- "Mr. [David] Duke was only following in the footsteps of respectable politicians. [Such as] Ronald Reagan [and] George Bush."
- "If the official Republican platform is carried out, a 13-year-old girl who becomes pregnant as a result of being raped by her father and has an abortion could end in the gas chamber."
- "People across the country, opponents and supporters both, are learning something that Massachusetts has understood for some time. Never underestimate the intelligence or determination of Michael Dukakis."

Margaret Marshall received fame as a young woman in South Africa for her civil rights advocacy, but she wouldn't let anybody in Massachusetts approach her lofty perch to discuss gay marriage. The only person representing the people, Asst. Attorney Gen. Judith Yogman, got 15 minutes to talk against gay marriage. How can such a stupid procedure be tolerated? Does Marshall really belong on Mt. Olympus by herself?

instruct us in history and sociology and advise us that the romance we have seen in love and marriage since our country began is not real. She says that marriage is really about 'economics,' and no woman likes marriage." That was certainly prescient on my part. Does it reveal a lot about her marriage to a man who is now 77 years old?

Thirty-Seven Minutes for Both Lawyers

The oral argument on March 3, 2003, was a farce. Only two people were allowed by Marshall to have any dialogue with her or any of the other six judges. Other than those 37 minutes, it would have been highly unethical for any judge to discuss the case with anyone, to see what others thought. We don't know if the judges did that, of course, but how were they to decide what to do if they couldn't discuss it with *anyone*?

Of course, the answer as far as Marshall was concerned is that she didn't have to discuss it with anyone. She had made up her mind a long time ago. She knew the opinions of the other lawyer, Mary Bonauto, and those at the Massachusetts Lesbian & Gay Bar Association.

The two people that the judges were allowed to talk with on March

3 were both lawyers, of course. They were given a combined time of 37 minutes and 11 seconds for both of them to address the judges. No other testimony was ever given to any judge by anyone at any time, unless someone violated the ethics code. No one knows how many judges ever read any of the written briefs.

Justice Marshall first interrupted Assistant Attorney General Yogman after she was only eight seconds into her allotted time of fifteen minutes. Marshall consumed 56% of Yogman's time, never allowing her to present her case and also preventing the other Justices from asking questions. At the end, after she had just told Yogman she could have a "a few minutes" to sum-up, Marshall closed down the charade after the attorney had spoken for only 28 seconds.

Some, who want to be nice, have wondered, after reading that Yogman had politely requested an additional 30-seconds in order to finish a portion of what she had been trying to say and Marshall snapped, "I'm afraid your time is up," whether Marshall suddenly had to go to the bathroom. In any case, Yogman could do nothing but say, "Thank you," and everyone stood while Marshall fled the courtroom.

Attorney Yogman did an excellent job of arguing against the lawsuit and that is why Marshall filibustered and would not let her speak. That was the only input the judges got from anyone except in briefs. It was the only chance for the public to see what was happening.

Marshall and John Greaney together took 82% of Yogman's time,

John Greaney and Marshall were most strident and discourteous. They took the bulk of Yogman's 15 minutes while she was forced to listen to them. Everyone should read the transcript of the hearing which is posted on our website, the only place I know of in the country that has it.

not giving her any chance to present her case as she had planned. But they were in for a surprise because she answered their questions in a superb manner, making them afraid to let her continue talking.

Mary Bonauto Was Appealing Superior Court Decision

The case was before the SJC because Mary Bonauto and her four associates were appealing a ruling of Superior Court Judge Thomas E. Connolly. He had dismissed the lawsuit on May 2, 2002, saying that it was the Legislature which should resolve this question.

The trial judge had ended his 17-page opinion with this sentence: "While this Court understands the plaintiffs' efforts to be married, they should pursue their quest [at the Legislature] on Beacon Hill." Instead, the plaintiffs appealed his decision, as expected, to the Supreme Judicial Court, where they had many friends, but not as many as they had thought.

Although the colloquy with Yogman may be a trifle boring for some and appear ridiculous to all, it exquisitely shows the absurdity of allowing lawyers to make this basic decision. They all think they are such clever debaters, but this is not a question for a "debating club." If it were, Attorney Yogman would have won hands down. One has to wonder what kind of grades Marshall had at Yale Law School.

Marshall's intent became clear when she questioned Yogman about why marriage was established in the first place. Marshall denied that marriage was established to protect children. She believes that marriage is about "property."

"Let's go back to the original marriage acts where I think it would be a stretch to say it was for procreation," Marshall intoned at Yogman, who continued to remain civil. "One way to look at it is that marriage is always a property relationship and if there were offspring, certain properties follow as a consequence, certain rights, certain obligations towards the offspring. If, in fact, there were offspring outside marriage, they were dealt differently. What the Commonwealth seems to be saying, and it's not unreasonable, is that you have cut off the first piece of the history and picked up just at the procreation point."

But Attorney Yogman could not let that pass and retorted: "No, Your Honor. Although the concept of marriage has changed, it hasn't

changed to be purely an economic partnership. It's still based funda-
mentally . . ."

At which the Chief Justice interrupted again: "No, no. I'm not suggesting it's only an economic partnership, but one of the original bases
was to recognize that two people in a certain kind of union brought
with them certain economic benefits to that, and if there were offspring
as a consequence of that union, that the benefits flowed in a particular
way."

But Yogman could not agree to that. "I beg to differ. I think it was
the other way around, that the reason that economic benefits are con-
ferred on married couples is to encourage this setting for procreation
and childrearing. It's not the other way around."

To which Marshall responded, "It's part and parcel of the same
thing, correct?"

The Assistant Attorney General attempted to conciliate this powerful figure, while keeping her strong position. "Well, the benefits that
flow from marriage, that the state has attached to marriage are because
the state wants to encourage this model of marriage where there are one
parent of each sex and the legislature might conceivably believe still
today that that is an optimal setting for procreation and childrearing."

Justice Greaney joined Marshall by asking Yogman to "reconcile"
the "paradox" that the SJC has created. "The state acknowledges," said
Greaney, "that same sex couples with children, who are permitted,
obviously, to adopt children under the *Tammy* decision constitute a
family, but they don't constitute a family for purposes of being married?
Are those ideas somewhat at odds?" (The *Tammy* decision came from
the SJC in 1993.)

Attorney Yogman replied: "Not at all, Your Honor. The idea that
same-sex couples can adopt on a case-by-case basis is not at all incon-
sistent with the idea for the legislature or the Court to say that they're
required to permit marriage. Adoption is one thing, marriage has many
other responsibilities and benefits associated with it other than child
rearing."

But Greaney warmed to his attack on marriage. "You would agree
with me, however, that there is no firm definition of family. There is
the idea of family, according to our decisions and other thinking that's

gone far beyond the notion of two heterosexual people married, having children?"

Yogman valiantly fought these people who are supposed to be entitled to respect. "That's correct, Your Honor, but there's never been a suggestion that there was a constitutional right to that. To the contrary, the Court said that while foster parents share a lot of the attributes of a family, there is no fundamental right of foster parents to adopt. They have said that while some of the interests associated . . ."

At that point, Margaret Marshall was unable to contain herself. "That's an interesting distinction because we haven't said that everybody has a right to adopt." When the Assistant Attorney General quickly agreed, Marshall continued: "But we have said that a group of people that hitherto fore were not permitted to adopt are permitted to adopt."

Yogman countered that that did not involve the Constitution. "But that was by interpreting a statute. The Court didn't suggest that that was constitutionally required and other Courts that have considered it have said . . ."

But the Chief Justice interrupted again. "No, and it is a position that was interpreted by this Court and has not been changed in any respect by the Legislature."

The Assistant Attorney General stood her ground. "That's correct. But adoption, again, is something very different than marriage. There is nothing, and in fact, the plaintiffs in this case have all the benefits associated with childrearing. They all are the adoptive or natural parents of their children and so the issue of the right to control the upbringing of the children is not an issue in this case because they have all the rights of parents and the children have all the rights of children."

At this point, an unidentified male Justice took the attack. "What would you identify as the top — the most important reasons for the state justification for excluding these kinds of marriages?"

To which Yogman responded. "The most important justification is that limiting marriage to opposite-sex couples furthers this state's interest in fostering the link between marriage and procreation."

That is one place where I believe there was a better answer. The simple answer was that homosexuals have not been excluded anymore than other groups. No matter how you define "marriage," there will always be some group complaining. Homosexuals are not the only group. The only other rational decision would be to eliminate marriage completely. But what the state does now is not "irrational," and to say that it is, as Marshall does, is in itself "irrational." (This is like going back to law school where most of the class are "C" students.)

A male voice then asked: "How — let me interrupt you for just one moment. How would prohibiting same-sex couples from getting married further that link between marriage and procreation?"

The answer came back: "Marriage, procreation and childrearing. They are all related and same — the idea of the Legislature could conceivably believe — this is what I believe is the strongest argument. The Legislature could conceivably believe that encouraging same-sex couples to marry would not be a beneficial thing in terms of childrearing."

But the unidentified male responded with a ridiculous non sequitur: "Because they would not be available to marry people of the opposite sex?"

Attorney Yogman hastened to straighten out this confused Justice. "No. No, not at all. No. Because the Legislature could conceivably believe that an optimal setting for childrearing and procreation is a family where there are one parent of each sex because mothers and fathers, the Legislature could believe, and there is literature to support it, that mothers and fathers each make unique contributions to the upbringing of a child. Just as this court said in *Blixt*, there is a possibility that children would benefit from having a parent of each sex. It's possible that many children do very well with a parent of one sex, but nevertheless the court said . . ."

But Yogman was interrupted by Margaret Marshall yet again. "Ms. Yogman, I well understand the argument. When you link marriage, procreation and childrearing and say that the legislature could well believe that optimal setting is with heterosexual — two parents — to what extent does recognizing that single-sex couples, as in *Tammy* [the 1993 SJC case], which the Legislature has not sought to amend in any way, is not a powerful recognition that childrearing in fact with single-sex couples is optimal for certain children?"

The attorney repeated Marshall's words back to her. "'For certain children.' That's the difference, Your Honor. Adoption is on a case-by-case basis. Every family . . ."

But Marshall was not going to allow Yogman to talk. The lawyer was too good and was making serious inroads into Marshall's arguments. "I understand, but if you make the link between marriage, procreation and childrearing, what you are saying is when you go backwards you make the case for childrearing, procreation, but not for marriage."

Yogman attempted to explain. "I'm saying across-the-board and that's the difference between marriage and adoption. Marriage, if it's permitted, would be for any same-sex couple and then . . ."

But she was interrupted again by Marshall. "The State is free to say, for example, after a heterosexual couple has been married for ten years and has produced no children, unless there is evidence that both parents are infertile that they should be divorced so that the other parent — so the parents can be free to marry to try and procreate with another couple?

The attorney responded, "No, Your Honor. First of all, for the state to draw the line that way would be an impermissible intrusion into the private lives of the people involved."

Enough already! Do we really need to listen to Marshall's attempt at intellectualism to know whether children need a mother and a father?

Marshall Should Have Recused Herself

Margaret Marshall should not even have been sitting on this case. She is in charge of all the judges in the state. As such she was responsible for Suzanne DelVecchio, the first woman in history to be Chief Justice of the state's trial court, the Superior Court where this case was first heard.

DelVecchio has never attempted to hide the fact that she is clearly in favor of homosexual marriage. She attended a meeting of the Massachusetts Lesbian & Gay Bar Association in 2000. She is an extremely enthusiastic person and told the group: "Vermont recognizes same-sex couples. And here we are in Massachusetts. Would you please? It's embarrassing. Could we get with the program a little bit? ... The only way gays and lesbians in this state are going to achieve what has been achieved in Vermont is to say who you are, apply for the [important] jobs and demand to be seated at the table ... Nothing is easy. Do you think getting my hair this color is easy?" Also at that meeting with DelVecchio were two lesbian lawyers who were honored for their role in the Vermont marriage case.

Marshall would not censure DelVecchio because she was deeply involved herself. The year before, Marshall had appeared at the same homosexual group where she noted "with pride" that her native land of South Africa was the first country to write sexual orientation protections into the national Constitution. The group reported: "Marshall read excerpts from the stirring decision [which struck down sodomy laws in South Africa]. The Justice encouraged those lawyers in attendance to pay attention to the growing body of gay-friendly international jurisprudence."

In October 2000, Marshall attended, as an honored guest, the Annual Gala of the Women's Bar Association, a political organization which lobbies in the courts and the legislature. The featured speaker was Dee Dee Myers, former Press Secretary to Bill Clinton, who told the crowd to resounding cheers that Al Gore would win by a large margin and to even louder cheers that Hillary Clinton would win in New York. Myers warmly welcomed Marshall and noted that both of them were married to the *New York Times*, because they both had husbands who worked there. At that political event, Mary Bonauto, the lawyer who would argue the gay marriage case before Marshall, was honored. (We were told that Bonauto made derogatory remarks about *Massachusetts News* at that event, but we were unable to discover exactly what they were.)

After listening to a tape of the oral argument of the gay marriage case, Sally was so upset that she filed a Complaint against Marshall for violating the Code of Judicial Conduct in that judges are required to uphold the "integrity" and "independence" of the judiciary, and to avoid anything that even gives the "appearance of impropriety." The homosexual group where Marshall spoke in 1999 was one of the primary supporters and activist groups in the gay marriage opinion of November 2003.

Sally's complaint before the Commission on Judicial Conduct was filed on March 18, 2003, requesting that Marshall be removed from the case. Because Marshall is essentially the chairman of the Commission, we didn't expect much to happen, but we wanted to let her know that someone understood she was violating the Canons of Ethics. The lesbian lawyers that she had helped to honor had many cases pending in the courts of the state, over which she had supervisory responsibilities.

Mary Bonauto Is "Special Friend" of Justices

When most lawyers address the Supreme Judicial Court, they are very formal. This was a serious occasion, but not for Mary Bonauto.

Mary opened by saying, "It's Mary Bonauto here..." whereas Judith Yogman opened in the traditional manner: "Judith Yogman, Assistant Attorney General ..." It was apparent from the very first word that Mary was up there with old friends.

We don't know how many other Justices were among the 1,600 people who honored Mary at the political dinner on October 5, 2000, where she was praised and flattered, but we do know that Margaret Marshall was. The Chief Justice was an honored guest who was acknowledged and applauded at least once.

Mary's special treatment at the oral argument didn't end with the opening salutation. She was allowed to speak without interruption and was treated graciously, but Judith Yogman was not. She was constantly interrupted and badgered by Marshall in particular. John Greaney also harassed her, along with other unidentified Justices.

Marshall's Courts "Mired in Managerial Confusion"

Margaret Marshall's courts are "mired in managerial confusion" and in need of "sweeping changes" a scathing report by a panel of eight business and academic leaders reported to the Chief Justice on the same day she held the marriage hearing.

Marshall herself had appointed the committee the previous August. The panel found the court system to be "dysfunctional" with only pockets of excellent performance. "The existing organization of the courts is unmanageable, inefficient and lacks accountability," it said.

Due to inequalities in the system, "some citizens receive better justice than others." Also, "morale is near the breaking point, and there is little concern for customer service. Employees cry out for leadership. The public wants reasonably priced, quick, and courteous justice, but often receives the opposite," the report stated.

It stated further, "These shortcomings affect a broad range of constituents, as well as court personnel. Taxpayers bear the burden of an unreasonably expensive system, witnesses and police officers are away from other responsibilities as they wait to testify, and litigants wait years for justice."

Marshall spun the report by saying that the panel recognized the "excellence" of the *decisions* of the courts. She said the judges must now "elevate management in our courts to that same level of excellence."

What does that mean? Everyone knows that the way that lawyers and citizens are treated in our courts is a disgrace, with everyone wanting to avoid them. Many trial lawyers are giving up trial work. They can't stand it any more. Why does Marshall dismiss that so lightly and pretend she's going to fix it quickly?

In addition, she wasn't telling the truth when she said that the leaders, whom she had appointed, recognized the "excellence" of the *decisions* made by the courts. The *Globe* accepted her spin without question, but when questioned by *Massachusetts News* whether they had studied or measured the quality of judicial decisions, and if so, by what means, spokesman John Lamontagne of Morrissey & Company, told us that the panel was mainly going by the long history of the Massachusetts courts.

"The committee was not asked by the Chief Justice," he says, "to look at the quality of decision-making. In the report, the committee makes reference to the court system's longstanding 'reputation' for sound decision-making and the fact that high-quality decisions are often undermined by slow action, high cost and poor service. The committee did not specifically review decision-making practices, nor was it asked to do so."

Justice Greaney agrees with the panel about the public perception of the courts. He told a group of judges from the Superior Court on Nov. 1, 2002: "Unfortunately for us, this cynicism has seeped into the judicial system. We are now part of the crisis in public trust and confidence in governmental institutions. A considerable number of citizens

Marshall gestures in November 1999 on her first day as Chief Justice, when her plan was just coming together for gay marriage in the state. Pinch Sulzberger had lobbied heavily for her appointment and confirmation without revealing that he had a conflict of interest in the appointment, due to the fact that her husband worked for him.

now think that judges are nothing more than politicians in black robes; that the court system utterly fails to protect the rights of the poor and minorities; and that the law is a mass of unpredictable outrageous decisions. The average citizen, if called upon to give an example to justify the latter point, would probably refer to three cases: the O. J. Simpson trial; the McDonald's coffee cup spill case; and *Bush v. Gore.*"

I included that statement in one of the briefs I gave to the SJC in 2003. I told them: "Most citizens would respectfully disagree that the 2000 Presidential election was in any way unfair, particularly with the hindsight that was available in the fall of 2002. But they would not be surprised that even our most respected judges in Massachusetts have a strong liberal bent. And those citizens are quick to point out the plaintiff's naiveté for believing she will find justice anywhere in Massachusetts."

But poor Judge Greaney appeared bent on proving that what the people believed about the courts was true. For example, he was not bothered in any way that both the Legislature and the Governor had intentionally violated the state Constitution. He also didn't understand that his remarks to the Superior Court judges about "politicians in black robes" included him. It was not cynicism that the public had, it was the truth. How could any judge make derogatory statements about the President or the U.S. Supreme Court, as he did, in such a manner? He actually assured Mary Bonauto during the oral argument that she was going to win. He and she discussed what she should do if the Marriage Amendment passed in 2004.

Pinch Lobbied Heavily to Have Marshall Appointed

Pinch pulled out all the stops to have Marshall appointed to the SJC in 1996 and then appointed as Chief Justice in 1999.

He did not reveal that she is married to his employee who is twenty years her senior. She apparently has no children and some say that as a result, she has no appreciation for the feelings of women who have. They say she has never had any experience with a family and has focused only on her career. She was on the board of directors of a Boston home for unwed mothers that performs abortions, and some speculate may have had one herself. Psychologists are reporting nowadays that this often causes permanent distress.

She may be bitter that *she* never had children. For twenty years, since she was 37 and he was 57, she has been married to Anthony Lewis

The *Globe* lobbied heavily for her in both editorial and news stories, never revealing its conflict of interest. In one of its "news" stories on October 12, 1999, titled "Rulings show nominee a moderate jurist with progressive views," the first sentence was: "Sex offenders have rights. ... Modern families no longer mean just mom, dad, and the kids."

The paper then cited some of those "moderate" rulings:

• The *Globe* wrote: "When the SJC last August ruled that anyone convicted of a sex crime is entitled to a hearing before being listed on the state's sex-offender registry, Marshall wrote: 'The burden will be on the sex offender board to establish at the hearing that the offender poses a risk to vulnerable populations.'"

• Concerning an opinion where Marshall struck down a Boston ordinance creating domestic partners because it was clearly forbidden by state law, the *Globe* wrote: "Marshall urged state lawmakers to craft legislation that acknowledges the place of nontraditional families in modern life. 'We recognize that . . . [a] "family" may no longer be constituted simply of a wage-earning father, his dependent wife, and the couple's children.' Nonetheless, 'Adjustments in the legislation to reflect these new social and economic realities must come from the Legislature.'" (The foregoing text appeared in the *Globe* exactly as printed here.)

So Marshall promised that she would not do what she did do on November 18. She said the Legislature must make the decisions about marriage. Perhaps she would claim that is what she is doing.

The *Globe* "news" article also claimed: "An examination of her rulings and the comments of colleagues indicate a moderate jurist who tempers some of her progressive views with judicial restraint and an awareness of the powers and limits of the courts. In the tradition-bound court that convenes in a high-rise on Pemberton Square, Marshall, the controversial chief justice nominee, has also added energy and spice to a frequently bland bench."

It's always nice to have "spice" in your Supreme Court.

Marshall graduated from college in her South African homeland in 1966 and came to the United States two years later for a master's degree from Harvard. After Yale Law School, she became a partner in the prestigious firm of Choate, Hall and Stewart, leaving there to become General Counsel for Harvard University. She was appointed to the SJC in 1996 and then elevated by Gov. Cellucci to Chief in 1999.

After reading the transcript of the gay marriage case (which is printed in full on our website), I wrote the following headline for the print edition: "Supreme Court Planning New Type of 'Relationship' to Replace 'Failed' Institution of Marriage; Extreme Feminist Scheme Makes Children Secondary to 'Partners,' Marshall Will Be Feminist Heroine, Mass. Will Be 'Leader' of Nation."

Free Transcript Available on Website

The written transcript of the oral argument is extremely help-ful in understanding what happened there. It would be impossible for any reporter, no matter how excellent, to write a good story without it. All that is furnished to the press after such a hearing is a tape recording about an hour after the event. But it does not begin to give the insight that the transcript does. It cost us quite a bit to have the session transcribed, but it was well worth it. You can print the transcript from our website at www.massnews.com by searching for: "full text of oral argument before sjc." It will be the second article down on the screen.

Even better is watching the transcript while listening to a tape. That allows you to hear the intonation of Marshall as she is snap-ping at Yogman. However, we have not made copies of the tape and have no desire to do so, but we will oblige you for our costs if someone really wants one. If you are a member of the press, the court might furnish it to you free-of-charge.

27

Everyone Who Disagrees With Chief Justice Marshall Is a "Prejudiced" Bigot

When Margaret Marshall saw the opinions of her fellow justices about gay marriage, she must have cringed. The judges have prided themselves upon working as a body, with few dissents. It now appears that those days may be over These were not the words of "right wing kooks" in those dissents, but her fellow Justices.

• "Today, the court has transformed its role as protector of individual rights into the role of creator of rights, and I respectfully dissent." Justice Francis X. Spina

• "[T]he case stands as an aberration. To reach the result it does, the court has tortured the rational basis test beyond recognition." Justice Martha B. Sosman

• "Whether the court is correct in its assumption is irrelevant. What is relevant is that such predicting is not the business of the courts." Justice Robert J. Cordy

Courtroom for seven Justices of the Supreme Judicial Court.

All the pundits appear to have missed the significance of the above quotations. But, then again, it's almost impossible for any newspaper reporter to have grasped this significance within their deadline. This insight does not come when you're in a frenzy to make "deadline."

The words of the dissenters show that we finally have an "intelligent discussion" in process in Massachusetts, which is what I have been attempting for five years. This should have a profound effect upon what happens here in the next six months that the court has given the Legislature to do something. The only problem will be informing the citizens about what these Justices have said. Obviously, The New York Times Company, including its two subsidiaries in the state, the *Boston Globe* and the *Worcester Telegram*, will be working to see that they *never* discover the truth. In their story written in the *Times* on November 19, 2003, our old friend, Pam Bullock, did not go into any depth.

If Pinch was angry to see Sally's referendum come out of nowhere, think what he will do when he discovers this book you're holding.

One's heart must go out to Margaret Marshall. When you look at the picture of the idealistic young woman who arrived here in 1968 eager to help the world, it is sad to see her going down the road that many seem to follow when they become entwined with the *Times*. Although Pinch will do his best to keep her reputation intact, for a while, he will not care when she no longer serves his purpose. Her dream of a happy SJC working together under her leadership has been shattered. That might explain her uncivilized behavior at the oral argument last spring. She knows she is not making sense.

When I first appeared before the seven judges in 2002, none of them seemed interested in listening to me. They were occupied with other things. It was readily apparent and discouraging that no one had had the time to read my briefs. Now it appears that we may finally have a court that will forego consensus and debate issues contentiously, but with respect, which is why they are there. But it seems doubtful that Margaret Marshall will be able to do that.

Cordy Was Fired Up

Justice Cordy wrote the longest opinion of all and Marshall felt compelled four times to answer him, only him, by name in her opinion, which is highly unusual. She obviously realized the sagacity of his remarks. Justice Cordy was so passionate about the matter that he wrote 9210 words, as compared to 9021 for Marshall.

If lawyers in other states or academics want to understand this issue, the three dissenting opinions are the place to begin. They are better than any law review article will ever be.

I knew at the end of my last session before the SJC in May 2003 that I had gotten Justice Cordy's attention. He asked Assistant Attorney General Peter Sacks if it was correct that the only option that Massachusetts Citizens for Marriage had was to spend another $1.7 million, try again and hope that someone in the Legislature would follow the Constitution the next time. Attorney Sacks, who is only a "hired gun," as is every attorney and is required to represent his client whether they are right or wrong, replied with some skewed information and I was not allowed any time to respond. However, it appeared to me at the time that Justice Cordy had been awakened.

Here's a short sampling of Cordy's opinion. (If you wish to read more, the entire opinion is easily found. If you do not know where to go, you can use the website of the legal newspaper I used to own at www.lawyersweekly.com. All three dissenting judges joined in each other's opinion, so all three agree with what you are reading.)

Justice Cordy Explains Why We Have Marriage

"[T]he institution of marriage has existed as one of the fundamental organizing principles of human society. ... Marriage has not been merely a contractual arrangement for legally defining the private relationship between two individuals (although that is certainly part of any marriage). Rather, on an institutional level, marriage is the 'very basis of the whole fabric of civilized society,' ... and it serves many important political, economic, social, educational, procreational, and personal functions.

"Paramount among its many important functions, the institution of marriage has systematically provided for the regulation of heterosexual behavior, brought order to the resulting procreation, and ensured a stable family structure in which children will be reared, educated, and socialized. ... [A]n orderly society requires some mechanism for coping with the fact that sexual intercourse commonly results in pregnancy and childbirth. The institution of marriage is that mechanism. ...

"The marital family is also the foremost setting for the education and socialization of children. Children learn about the world and their place in it primarily from those who raise them, and those children eventually grow up to exert some influence, great or small, positive or negative, on society. The institution of marriage encourages parents to remain committed to each other and to their children as they grow, thereby encouraging a stable venue for the education and socialization of children. ... More macroscopically, construction of a family through marriage also formalizes the bonds between people in an ordered and institutional manner, thereby facilitating a foundation of interconnectedness and interdependency on which more intricate stabilizing social structures might be built. ...

"It is difficult to imagine a State purpose more important and legitimate than ensuring, promoting, and supporting an optimal social structure within which to bear and raise children. At the very least, the marriage statute continues to serve this important State purpose. ...

"Taking all of this available information into account, the Legislature could rationally conclude that a family environment with married opposite-sex parents remains the optimal social structure in which to bear children, and that the raising of children by same-sex couples, who by definition cannot be the two sole biological parents of a child and cannot provide children with a parental authority figure of each gender, presents an alternative structure for child rearing that has not yet proved itself beyond reasonable scientific dispute to be as optimal as the biologically based marriage norm. ... Working from the assumption that a recognition of same-sex marriages will increase the number of children experiencing this alternative, the Legislature could conceivably conclude that declining to recognize same-sex marriages remains prudent until empirical questions about its impact on the upbringing of children are resolved. ...

"As long as marriage is limited to opposite-sex couples who can at least theoretically procreate, society is able to communicate a consistent message to its citizens that marriage is a (normatively) necessary part of their procreative endeavor; that if they are to procreate, then society has endorsed the institution of marriage as the environment for it and for the subsequent rearing of their children; and that benefits are available explicitly to create a supportive and conducive atmosphere for those purposes. If society proceeds similarly to recognize marriages between same-sex couples who cannot procreate, it could be perceived as an abandonment of this claim, and might result in the mistaken view that

An Intelligent Discussion About Homosexuality
Will Massachusetts Listen?

We're teaching a lifestyle in the schools of Massachusetts which is deadlier than cigarettes.

In homosexuality, 30% of our young men will be dead within ten years or they will be HIV positive.

And yet, a serious discussion is not allowed.

Hate is spewing forth from a small group of homosexual militant "activists" in an attempt to stop any conversation except their agenda. They dominate *The Boston Globe* and the other media which strive so hard to be "inclusive."

We also see hate from uninformed, judgmental persons. But mostly we see apathy from an unknowing citizenry.

Part I. Massachusetts' Policy on Homosexuality Is Damaging Our Children

By J. Edward Pawlick
Publisher, *The Massachusetts News*

We're teaching an addictive lifestyle in Massachusetts schools where:

- 30% of homosexual men will be dead before age 30 or they will be HIV positive.[1]

- If they survive the age of 30 **and** *never* get AIDS **and** have a stable relationship, they'll still live 30 years *less* than married men.[2]

This lifestyle is being taught *by us*, especially to the most vulnerable of our boys. These children are the most vulnerable because of many factors, often including a poor relationship with their father. Instead of helping these children when they need it most, we send them off

This 1999 pamphlet by me calling for An Intelligent Discussion About Homosexuality was finally answered in November 2003 by the three dissenting Justices. I was finally hearing a coherent, intelligent discussion of the subject.

civil marriage has little to do with procreation: just as the potential of procreation would not be necessary for a marriage to be valid, marriage would not be necessary for optimal procreation and child rearing to occur. In essence, the Legislature could conclude that the consequence of such a policy shift would be a diminution in society's ability to steer the acts of procreation and child rearing into their most optimal setting. ...

"The court recognizes this concern, but brushes it aside with the assumption that permitting same-sex couples to marry 'will not diminish the validity or dignity of opposite-sex marriage,' and that 'we have no doubt that marriage will continue to be a vibrant and revered institution.' Whether the court is correct in its assumption is irrelevant. What is relevant is that such predicting is not the business of the courts. A rational Legislature, given the evidence, could conceivably come to a different conclusion, or could at least harbor rational concerns about possible unintended consequences of a dramatic redefinition of marriage. ***

"The Legislature is the appropriate branch, both constitutionally and practically, to consider and respond to it. It is not enough that we as Justices might be personally of the view that we have learned enough to decide what is best. So long as the question is at all debatable, it must be the Legislature that decides. ...

"While the courageous efforts of many have resulted in increased dignity, rights, and respect for gay and lesbian members of our community, the issue presented here is a profound one, deeply rooted in social policy, that must, for now, be the subject of legislative not judicial action."

Justices Sosman and Spina Disagree with Marshall

Both Sosman and Spina also used tough language in their opinions.

Sosman wrote: "Today, rather than apply that test, the court announces that, because it is persuaded that there are no differences between same-sex and opposite-sex couples, the Legislature has no rational basis for treating them differently with respect to the granting of marriage licenses. Reduced to its essence, the court's opinion concludes that, because same-sex couples are now raising children, and withholding the benefits of civil marriage from their union makes it harder for them to raise those children, the State must therefore provide the benefits of civil marriage to same-sex couples just as it does to opposite-sex couples.

"Of course, many people are raising children outside the confines of traditional marriage, and, by definition, those children are being deprived of the various benefits that would flow if they were being raised in a household with married parents. That does not mean that the Legislature must accord the full benefits of marital status on every household raising children. Rather, the Legislature need only have some rational basis for concluding that, at present, those alternate family structures have not yet been conclusively shown to be the equivalent of the marital family structure that has established itself as a successful one over a period of centuries. People are of course at liberty to raise their children in various family structures, as long as they are not literally harming their children by doing so. ... That does not mean that the State is required to provide identical forms of encouragement, endorsement, and support to all of the infinite variety of household structures that a free society permits.

"Based on our own philosophy of child rearing, and on our observations of the children being raised by same-sex couples to whom we are personally close, we may be of the view that what matters to children is not the gender, or sexual orientation, or even the number of the adults who raise them, but rather whether those adults provide the children with a nurturing, stable, safe, consistent, and supportive environment in which to mature. Same-sex couples can provide their children with the requisite nurturing, stable, safe, consistent, and supportive environment in which to mature, just as opposite-sex couples do. It is therefore understandable that the court might view the traditional definition of marriage as an unnecessary anachronism, rooted in historical prejudices that modern society has in large measure rejected and biological limitations that modern science has overcome.

"It is not, however, our assessment that matters. Conspicuously absent from the court's opinion today is any acknowledgment that the attempts at scientific study of the ramifications of raising children in same-sex couple households are themselves in their infancy and have so far produced inconclusive and conflicting results. Notwithstanding our belief that gender and sexual orientation of parents should not matter to the success of the child rearing venture, studies to date reveal that there are still some observable differences between children raised by opposite-sex couples and children raised by same-sex couples. ...

"As a matter of social history, today's opinion may represent a great turning point that many will hail as a tremendous step toward a more just society. As a matter of constitutional jurisprudence, however, the case stands as an aberration. To reach the result it does, the court has tortured the rational basis test beyond recognition. I fully appreciate the strength of the temptation to find this particular law unconstitutional, there is much to be said for the argument that excluding gay and lesbian couples from the benefits of civil marriage is cruelly unfair and hopelessly outdated; the inability to marry has a profound impact on the personal lives of committed gay and lesbian couples (and their children) to whom we are personally close (our friends, neighbors, family members, classmates, and co-workers); and our resolution of this issue takes place under the intense glare of national and international publicity. Speaking metaphorically, these factors have combined to turn the case before us into a 'perfect storm' of a constitutional question.

"In my view, however, such factors make it all the more imperative that we adhere precisely and scrupulously to the established guideposts of our constitutional jurisprudence, a jurisprudence that makes the rational basis test an extremely deferential one that focuses on the rationality, not the persuasiveness, of the potential justifications for the classifications in the legislative scheme. I trust that, once this particular 'storm' clears, we will return to the rational basis test as it has always been understood and applied. Applying that deferential test in the manner it is customarily applied, the exclusion of gay and lesbian couples from the institution of civil marriage passes constitutional muster. I respectfully dissent."

Justice Spina wrote: "What is at stake in this case is not the unequal treatment of individuals or whether individual rights have been impermissibly burdened, but the power of the Legislature to effectuate social change without interference from the courts ... The power to regulate marriage lies with the Legislature, not with the judiciary. ... Today, the court has transformed its role as protector of individual rights into the role of creator of rights ...

"The court has extruded a new right from principles of substantive due process, and in doing so it has distorted the meaning and purpose of due process. The purpose of substantive due process is to protect existing rights, not to create new rights. Its aim is to thwart government intrusion, not invite it. The court asserts that the Massachusetts Declaration of Rights serves to guard against government intrusion into each individual's sphere of privacy. Similarly, the Supreme Court has called for increased due process protection when individual privacy and intimacy are threatened by unnecessary government imposition. ... The statute in question does not seek to regulate intimate activity [behind closed doors] within an intimate relationship, but merely gives formal recognition to a particular marriage. The State has respected the private lives of the plaintiffs, and has done nothing to intrude in the relationships that each of the plaintiff couples enjoy. ... Ironically, by extending the marriage laws to same-sex couples the court has turned substantive due process on its head and used it to interject government into the plaintiffs' lives."

Anyone Who Disagrees with Margaret Is "Prejudiced"

Margaret Marshall made a donkey of herself in her opinion which is easily discernible to those of you who have been following along.

<u>Marshall is not interpreting the state Constitution. She is writing a new one.</u> (However, she does not have the authority to do so and she knows it.) <u>The legal way to change the Constitution is to have the Legislature initiate a referendum or for someone like Sally to get enough signatures to require that a referendum be held.</u>

Marshall wrote: "[The state] has had more than ample opportunity to articulate a constitutionally adequate justification for limiting civil marriage to opposite-sex unions. It has failed to do so."

Ample opportunity?!? Seventeen minutes is an ample opportunity?!?

It took Marshall 9000 words to explain her ruling, yet she had expected the Assistant Attorney General, Judith Yogman, to explain the subject to her in only 17 minutes and a few seconds.

She cut off Yogman in a disgraceful manner when the lawyer requested only thirty seconds more. No person, much less a judge, should ever treat anyone in such a discourteous manner.

Then Marshall wrote that those who do not believe we should have homosexual marriage are "prejudiced." She started that paragraph at the very end of the opinion with this: "The marriage ban works a deep and scarring hardship on a very real segment of the community for no rational reason." She continued: "[This] suggests that the marriage restriction is rooted in persistent prejudices against persons who are (or who are believed to be) homosexual."

There you have it, you prejudiced bigots, including the three dissenting Justices. Your only salvation is to move to Cambridge, the homosexual capital of Massachusetts, where Margaret and Tony live and join in the party.

Marshall Kept the Opinion for Herself

The writing of court opinions is always assigned by the Chief Judge to different judges so that they all have an equal workload but Justice Marshall kept the gay marriage case all for herself. After all, she and Pinch had worked hard and long for this. It was not just another boring case. She was not a judge here, she was an advocate in another "civil rights" cause. She would not let go of this one.

Marshall obviously thought this would make her famous and improve her chances of being named to the U.S. Supreme Court. It certainly made her a heroine to Pinch. If he continues to be the President of The Company, he will be able to continue the publicity he has given her in Massachusetts.

The reporter for the *Christian Science Monitor*, Sara B. Miller, said that Marshall's ruling was a "pen stroke heard around the world" and "this relatively unknown Massachusetts jurist ... has thrust herself into the middle of the nation's culture war. ... While she is not expected to become a national lightning rod, her recent decision is likely to catapult her onto the national stage, putting her both in the spotlight and the limelight." That made Margaret smile.

I hate to say I told you so. That needn't have happened; she could have had someone else write the decision. She could even have helped them write it if she wished. But if she had done that, she wouldn't be famous.

"Civil Rights" Champion

Marshall likes to tell reporters that she is merely a civil rights advocate, as though she is unique in that quest. She doesn't realize that what may be her "civil right" will almost always be a grievous interference with the civil rights of someone else. But "civil rights" is a magic phrase today. She must have told Sara Miller about her "courageous" stands for civil rights because the first paragraph in the article says:

"Margaret Marshall likes to say she's lived through two revolutions — the overthrow of apartheid in her native South Africa and the advancement of women in the U.S. Now the chief justice of the Massachusetts Supreme Judicial Court is on the forefront of a third: the redefinition of the family. ... Marshall was raised in South Africa and came of age fighting against systematic segregation, which many say has formed her notions of freedom and fairness as a judge."

Another paper, the *Berkshire Eagle*, used the same theme in its headline and in its lead paragraph:

"**Gay-marriage ruling: Echoes of apartheid fight.** In 1966, while South Africa was under the grip of apartheid laws that denied black people the right to own land or vote, Margaret H. Marshall led a group of 20,000 student activists protesting the regime's racial discrimination. ... Legal professionals focused on those sentences, especially the use of the words 'second-class citizens,' to illustrate the South African born Marshall's strong belief that the rule of law in this country should prevail over prejudice." (It would be interesting to see proof of that "20,000 student" claim.)

One would assume that if we were to search more stories in more newspapers, we would discover that the Chief gave the same story to every reporter. One must wonder how black people feel about being compared to homosexuals when polls are showing that most blacks are not supportive of gay marriage.

Started Out Totally Wrong

Marshall started out totally wrong in her opinion. In the very first paragraph, she said the question before them was whether the state could "deny" marriage to homosexuals.

But the simple answer to that — Judith Yogman would have told Marshall the answer if she had been allowed to talk — is that Massachusetts does not deny marriage to anyone, except for laws prohibiting polygamy, marriages of brother and sister etc., ones where there is communicable syphilis or, in some cases, if the person is under eighteen-years-old.

There are no laws that "deny" homosexuals from marrying. And there is no definition of marriage in either the Constitution or laws that the Legislature has passed. Everyone has always assumed that we all know what marriage is. There hasn't been a need for a definition.

Marshall's good friend, Mary Bonauto, urged the court to just go ahead and say that the Department of Health had made a mistake. Bonauto pointed out that there was nothing anywhere that "denied" the Department the right to issue licenses. But if Marshall did that, she wouldn't become famous, would she? The whole world wouldn't be bothered reading her opinion.

Of course, we knew that the next thing Marshall would do was to say this is not a religious issue, because by so doing she would thereby make it into a "religious issue." Attorney Yogman never said it was a religious issue, but Marshall put it right at the top of her opinion with this: "Many people hold deep-seated religious, moral, and ethical convictions ... but our concern is with the Massachusetts Constitution ..." But we know that is not the truth because she has no concern at all for our Constitution, except to twist it for her own special goals.

And besides, everyone has known for hundreds of years that marriage is a secular institution. Does she think she's the only one who knows? As she said later, "In Massachusetts, civil marriage is, and since pre-Colonial days has been, precisely what its name implies: a wholly secular institution."

The judge went into a lengthy description of the seven homosexual couples and what outstanding people they are. That may well be true, and it probably is, because they were all carefully chosen by the 16-person staff at GLAD. She told us "they include business executives, lawyers, an investment banker, educators, therapists, and a computer engineer."

But what exactly does that prove? There are many other fine people who are not included in marriage as we know it. How about mothers who have children out-of-wedlock? Should we have marriage for them also, with the Secretary of State appointed as their spouse? Or how about widows? How about those three lesbians who truly love each other and have children who are dependent upon them? How about the two women who truly love the same man? What harm will it do to let them marry? How about two sisters who live together because their husbands have died. Must they have sex in order to get the benefits of marriage?

The simple answer is, there is no answer. Any system you establish will not be "rational" in every situation. The only really fair alternative is to just abolish the institution of marriage, which is the true aim of extreme feminists.

The truth about why Marshall wrote only about state law and never cited the U.S. Constitution is because she knew that she would have serious problems under the federal Constitution because there are judges there who still look at that document fairly. In Massachusetts, the state Constitution means anything she says it does. What she did here was to favor one group, homosexuals, and give them benefits that other groups do not receive. Most lawyers believe that would violate the U.S. Constitution. That would allow federal judges, like the dissenters in her own court, to show her duplicity.

Family and Children Not Important

She said that the state argued that it had two reasons for "prohibiting same-sex couples from marrying." The reasons were to have a favorable setting for procreation and to ensure the optimal setting for child rearing, which she says the state defines as "a two-parent family with one parent of each sex."

It was embarrassing to read her language about procreation. She filled it full of statements like this: "Fertility is not a condition of marriage, nor is it grounds for divorce." She would get an "F" in law school for an answer like that, which was totally unresponsive. She does not even grasp what Justice Cordy meant when he wrote that procreation was an important reason why society would favor marriage.[1]

It was also embarrassing watching her squirm around the truism that children do much better when they have a mother and a father to help and protect them. She wrote: "Protecting the welfare of children is a paramount State policy. Restricting marriage to opposite-sex couples, however, cannot plausibly further this policy." But that's only a matter of opinion. Where does she find that she has the power to make this earth shattering change to our society simply because of her opinion? The truth is that as an extreme feminist she believes that marriage is deleterious to women, and she must remove that institution, whether she can justify it or not.

It now becomes clear why she waited so long to issue her opinion. She was desperately trying to write something that would make sense. But she couldn't do so.

Her final absurdity is that her ruling, if implemented by the Legislature, would not destroy marriage as we know it. She wrote about her ruling: "But it does not disturb the fundamental value of marriage in our society."

---

[1] I entered Yale law school in 1958-1959 for the beginning of my second year after having attended night school at George Washington University in Washington D.C., but I was forced to leave after running out of money. I gained instant notoriety as the guy who left Yale even though he was somewhere in the top of the class. I quickly learned while there that they were training people only as Wall Street lawyers or academics. I wanted to work with the "working poor" in farming communities, working in a small firm on the problems of normal people. While at George Washington, I had been employed as a clerk by the firm of Lloyd Cutler, the lawyer who later bailed Bill Clinton out of trouble in the 1990s. I noticed that while the graduates of Yale always talked about the poor, they usually worked for someone like General Motors.

28

All Lesbians Not Sweet and Kind as Marshall Says

Although Margaret Marshall gives the impression that <u>all</u> lesbians are wonderful peace-loving people, that's not the reality, according to a mainstream group of the women's movement in Boston.

The news that women are as violent as men when relating to their "partners" comes from the "Network for Battered Lesbians," a group formed in 1989 to protect the state's women from such abuse. The group is recommended by the Massachusetts state government on the Department of Revenue's website under "Domestic Violence." (That's where we discovered it.)

The Network is particularly interested in making "outreach to youth" because "many women are battered in their first lesbian relationship."

Many others have observed that lesbians and extreme feminists in Margaret Marshall's courts are hostile and nasty to men, to their children and to straight women when they get sucked into the family courts. The problem is so blatant that many conscientious lawyers have gotten totally disgusted and quit that type of work. They simply cannot stand it anymore.

The sad fact is that all lesbians, by definition, are unable to have meaningful relations with half the population: men. The lesbians are proud that they are dysfunctional about an intimate relationship with any member of the opposite sex. That characteristic does not appear to be true with male homosexuals. As a matter of fact, the majority of

These pictures were taken at a gay pride parade in Amherst. This young girl rides in the back of a pickup with the sign, "My Dad is trans and I am proud of her."

Children of homosexuals are forced to fight the battles of their adults even though we are constantly told how terrible it is to be a homosexual in our society. This young boy did not look too happy riding in a Jeep with a red boa around his neck and signs saying, "We're Here, We're Queer" and "Drag Queen."

This young woman was encouraged to march with only tape over her breasts, although it was unclear what the message was supposed to be.

A homosexual "Pride Bear" greeted all the young children and posed for pictures with them.

High school students from Northampton joined in the parade.

Amherst High School is where the new Principal was terminated this year because he made a sexual advance to a teenage boy. He also had a very young boy living alone with him but the boy was removed by DSS. The school officials were keeping all of this a secret until one parent made the scandal public.

them appear to have good relations with women on a surface level.

The hostility of lesbians in the family courts has become a serious problem in Massachusetts. Although many children are often raised without a mother and father, this is not the preferred model, certainly not if the children were allowed to choose. In almost every divorce, they want both their parents, even when they have been mean to them. For lesbians to be active in the family courts in an aggressive hostile manner is doing great damage, but Margaret Marshall apparently condones it. She chatted with our reporter, Ed Oliver, a year or two ago, but never got back to him as she had proposed. One must assume that she approves what is happening in the courts. Does she accept the feminist belief that the institution of marriage must be abolished?

All homosexual activists talk constantly about the terrible problem it is for "homosexual" children to be taunted and even beaten by haters. If that is really true, how could they subject an innocent child to a lifetime of that? All children when they become teenagers do not want to be different. Do they believe that having two women for their parents would not make that child totally "different?" Are they merely using these children as pawns to fight for them?

Women As Violent as Men, Say Boston Lesbians

The Network For Battered Lesbians does not tell at what age the "first lesbian relationship" happens or when their "outreach" would occur. However, based upon what occurred at Fistgate and elsewhere, it is apparent that both would take place when the girls are in high school or earlier. This indicates that many girls are in danger of being molested by older women.

This interest in teenagers causes many to wonder whether the Network itself is a method for female batterers to become acquainted with a cadre of young girls with whom they can play sex games.

The Network says that the threat of violence among lesbians is so strong that many hesitate to go to gay meetings. One of them explained the fear they feel. "I recently attended a queer progressive activists retreat and organizing school. I was impressed by honest comments people made about not feeling safe at the retreat or other queer organizations." She says she was "frustrated that issues of safety surrounding domestic violence were not addressed."

Lesbians as a group were among the most vocal opponents of the Protection of Marriage Amendment. They were being pushed out front by the extremist feminists at the *Globe*, NOW and others.

Butches and Femmes

The world of lesbians is divided into two parts, according to the Network. One is the "butches." These women look and act like men. (However, no one believes that all women with that body type enjoy sex with other women.)

The other type of lesbian is "femmes," who look like all other women. For some reason, they are sometimes attracted to other women for sex. These are the ones who will go from men to women and back again, and are classified as bi-sexual.

In 1997, the Network began to welcome "bisexual women" into their organization.

The Network wrote at that time, "One thing we've done to be more inclusive ... is [to] refer to 'woman to woman battering' rather than 'lesbian battering,' in recognition that not all women who have intimate relationships with or are battered by women are lesbians."

It's tough to identify the batterer when it is a woman, we are told. When you have a man involved in domestic violence, it's easy — you always blame the man. But, cautions the Network, this does not apply when two women are involved. Therefore, they warn that the programs which protect battered women should screen their clients very carefully.

"We would suggest to programs who are reluctant to screen that they view the issue in the context of safety. Screening is not about identifying battered women and screening them in, but identifying batterers and screening them out — and battered women's programs do that all the time.

"It's just that when working with straight women with male batterers, the process is much simpler. By only giving out shelter and support group locations to women and being wary of men who call the hotline or show up at the office, support groups, etc., batterers are effectively screened out — men are an easily identifiable group to be cautious around.

"Screening out female batterers is not as simple, because they are not easy to distinguish as a group. They look like us, they act like us (at least on the surface), and there's no clear way to automatically tell who they are."

The Network says that lesbians are just as dangerous as men. "The implication is that lesbian/bisexual women batterers are not so bad, that they're safe to be around, that they may even be indistinguishable from their battered partners. Again, this is a dangerous message to put out, because lesbians/bisexual women who batter do everything that heterosexual male batterers do, from subtle manipulation to murder, and are equally unsafe."

In addition to the domestic violence that is found among lesbians, there is sadomasochism. This unusual practice makes it a game to be violent to each other. It is often confused with domestic violence, says the Network.

"Simply defined, s/m is a particular kind of sexual activity that takes place in a determined time and place, or 'scene,' with the limits and roles of each partner clearly defined. Any violence, coercion, or domination in s/m takes place in the context of the consensual scene. Both of the partners agree on a safeword, so that if someone changes her mind about her limits or wants to stop the action part way through for any reason, she can.

"The argument that s/m is battering because one person uses physical force against another leaves out what we know about the importance of the context of violence in battering. Battering is a pattern of violent and coercive behaviors that one woman uses to maintain power and control over her partner. Battering does not take place in a limited, predefined setting; it affects the entire relationship. Battering is not consensual; no one asks to be abused."

Explains Why Fathers Cannot Obtain Justice in Marshall's Courts

These statements from the Network reveal why the taxpayers of Massachusetts fund nineteen centers across the state to house battered women and give them free legal assistance, while there is no help at all for men who are falsely accused or who are battered themselves.

The centers are a part of the Legal Assistance Corporation, which is run by Margaret Marshall as part of her duties at the SJC and is popularly known as "poverty lawyers." The organizations which receive this money from the SJC are as numerous as sand on the beach. Possibly, the Network is one. It is impossible for a citizen to trace all the recipients of the largesse. Marshall really doesn't want us to know.

Many children of straight fathers are being treated in an arbitrary, irrational manner in Massachusetts by the Department of Social Services (which appears to attract lesbians and extreme feminists as social workers), by judges who were social workers themselves or closely allied with them, by poverty lawyers who are lesbians, and others.

Massachusetts News has recounted the suffering of countless fathers *and their children who feel abandoned as a result* in stories about Ken Newell, Harry Stewart, David Luisi, Edward McLarnon, Bill Leisk and many others whose families have fallen into the clutches of lesbians and extreme feminists who are given enormous power. It truly brings tears to your eyes as you see what these families endure.

We've also written about straight mothers who were warned they would lose their children if they didn't leave their husbands. They refused to leave and their children were snatched from their families, often by the local police — just as the DSS social workers had promised. That brings terrible trauma on the children. This included the children of Nev Moore and Heidi Howard, among many others. There were too many for us to write about. We could only scratch the surface of a few of their tragic stories.

If a man is only <u>charged</u> with domestic violence, whether he is guilty or not, he is immediately placed in a batterer's program which he must attend and do what he is told, or he may end up in jail.

The most famous case was Harry Stewart, a father who was sent to jail for six months in 1999 for refusing to sign a **false** statement that he had abused his wife. All fathers are forced to sign such statements. If they do not do so, they are considered to be in denial, which is the worse sin, and threatened with removal from programs of the private organization, which is usually owned by former social workers. If these former social workers remove a man from their program and tell the judge the man is uncooperative, he faces a jail sentence as happened to

Harry Stewart. All the fathers eventually get this message.

Judge Eileen Shaevel made a ruling vindicating Stewart two years later after a trial in the Dedham court. She found there was "no evidence" at all that Harry Stewart ever threatened or harmed his wife since their separation in 1995.

We could fill volumes with similar tales of Margaret Marshall's dysfunctional courts, but she is coldhearted and unmoved. If you're interested, you can find many such stories in the archives on our website.

Lesbians Have Most 'Domestic Violence'

In Rhode Island, nearly 1 in 10 of the domestic violence cases in 1999 involved same-sex partners, the *Providence Journal* reported. Since less than 3% of the population is homosexual, they have three times more violence in Providence than do heterosexuals.

A majority of the homosexual domestic violence cases in Rhode Island involved male couples, but only by a small majority of 55.4%. Since the number of male homosexuals is more than twice that of lesbians, the number of domestic violence cases involving male homosexuals should have been about 66%. It would appear as though lesbians are the most violent group of people in Providence.

Some 50% of the violent crimes against all homosexuals were the result of "domestic violence," according to a *Boston Globe* report about arrests in New York.

Heidi Howard

During emails with Joan Lukey, President of the Boston Bar Association, she asked why I am so critical of the poverty lawyers that she funds with our tax dollars sent to her by Margaret Marshall. She wondered: "Did you consider yourself to be 'tolerant' of those in need of assistance, in your criticism of the BBA's plea for greater funding for the delivery of legal services for the poor?"

I wrote in the paper:

I've no doubt that Atty. Lukey would shed tears, as I did last month, if she could hear the struggles of Heidi Howard's children as she strives to keep her family together in the face of unethical, illegal attacks from DSS that are never-ending.

But Lukey will provide no lawyers or other help for Heidi Howard with the tax dollars which we have entrusted to her. Why? How can Lukey be so hard-hearted? Isn't that what those lawyers are for — to protect us when state bureaucrats are breaking the law in their torture of a citizen? (And my use of the word "torture" is not overstated in this case.)

Doesn't she know what is going on in the courts or doesn't she care?

The answer is that Atty. Lukey's help in such disputes is extended only to *single **women***. It *never* goes to women who are still with their husbands. And it *never* goes to any man.

How can this be? Why won't she give help to the man, Ken Newell, whose family has been severely damaged by the Boston Bar lawyers . . .

. . . or to David Luisi, whose children have been hounded and destroyed (no exaggeration), by the poverty lawyers from Hale and Dorr (of which Lukey is a Senior Partner) . . .

. . . or to Harry Stewart, another man who finally triumphed over five lawyers from the prestigious firm of Foley, Hoag and Eliot by defending himself without a lawyer (but only after he had spent six months in jail on false charges).

We don't have space to name all the good people that the Boston Bar refuses to help because they don't fall into the status of "politically correct."

It's too bad that there is no lawyer anywhere in Massachusetts who has the time, the desire and the money to challenge this feminist, legal aid system which is so grossly unfair in its application.

Every citizen should criticize the Boston Bar system which selectively helps only a limited group of "the poor."

I publicly advised Atty. Lukey that we would print in full any response she had to this editorial, but I didn't hear from her. I didn't hear because there is nothing she can say.

I have no idea about Lukey's personal life but I do know that many, probably most, women-lawyers establish a home for their children when they begin to have babies. The ones who continue in practice, and speak for "all women everywhere," are those who do not enjoy being a fulltime mother. The women who are home with their children are simply not represented.

The Howard Family Was Almost Destroyed By Marshall's Courts

What was the crime of Heidi Howard?

She refused to destroy her family. That has become a crime in Massachusetts. For violating that crime, she and her husband, Neil, were arrested, handcuffed and shackled. Here is how it happened.

The employees of the state, who were either lesbians or extreme feminists, demanded that Heidi leave her husband. They wanted her to get a free divorce from Margaret Marshall's poverty lawyers at Greater Boston Legal Services. She refused because she loved her husband and children. As a result, the bureaucracy became very hostile and tried to destroy her.

Town police were instructed by state employees to come to her home at a time when they knew she would be alone. They wanted to separate her from her husband and children. She was taken to a mental hospital in a police ambulance and kept in the hospital against her will, under the supervision of state employees, for over two weeks. It wasn't until she agreed to leave the area, go to a "shelter" in Springfield in the far corner of the state and not return to her home, that they released her. When she left the shelter without permission after a few days, she committed the ultimate sin.

Records from her medical file at the hospital, Emerson Hospital in Concord, show that the social workers were in charge and told the hospital what to do.

Because she was enthusiastic about breastfeeding her children and did so until the child no longer desired it, the state employees filed a formal complaint against her for that.

State lawyers spent hundreds of hours of work in court fighting Heidi and her husband.

The obvious object was to simply wear them down and make it impossible for them to respond.

The state even demanded that a busy judge decide whether she

The trauma brought to this young family, the Howards, by lesbian and extreme feminists is so heart wrenching as to be unbelievable, just because Heidi Howard would not move away from her family. It was the children who suffered the most after they were dragged by town police, kicking and screaming, from their happy home. You should go to our website and read about this family.

should be allowed to nurse her two-month-old baby.

When she and her husband hired a lawyer in an attempt to respond, the state's lawyers went to court and demanded that Heidi have her own lawyer because there was a conflict of interest between her and her husband.

The only thing that saved the Howards, they say, was that Atty. Chester Darling volunteered to represent her for free or else the state would undoubtedly have been successful in keeping and putting their children up for adoption.

The attempt to wear them out went on for a year with their lawyers being forced to attend 30 hearings, many times having to wait for hours, before the case would be heard.

There is always talk of settlement in any lawsuit. Judges always require such talk, but not when an unlimited amount of money from the state is funding their lawyers to fight these troublesome parents. That becomes the tactic, to just destroy and punish the other side with paper and hearings. There will be no settlement.

Innocent parents, such as the Howards, have no idea that as soon as they enter any maternity ward in any hospital in the state, they have been engulfed by a network of snooping, prying persons, many of whom have rigid personalities. They like to dominate others. The Howards were apparently engulfed by such unknown, faceless persons at Spaulding Rehabilitation Center, Boston.

Heidi's independent, inquisitive nature had drawn such ire from state employees that their desire was to keep taking any more babies she could produce. This would give them more clean, white children that were easily adoptable, which would, in turn, give them more money to hire their friends for all types of consulting, visitation centers, batterer courses, etc. This all takes millions of taxpayer dollars a year, but it is worth it to the consultants, many of who now drive expensive sports cars.

A parent must be very careful because if the children are forcibly taken away, kicking and screaming by a stranger, for even one day, just that short separation from the home is serious trauma. This is true, even if the foster parent is perfection itself, although in most cases they are not. The children often suffer serious abuse at those homes, just as Christopher and Ethan Howard did in this case.

The Howards were joyfully reunited in January 2002, after two years of separation and thirty (30) hearings with Atty. Chester Darling and Greg Hession representing them. The grueling ordeal finally ended happily when retired Judge Robert Belmonte had the courage to stand up to the system and send the children back home.

But this will never end. The nasty social workers appeared at the Howards' door again in the beginning of 2003 as the result of an **anonymous** tip. They were back banging on the door demanding to "interview" Heidi again, when they knew she was home alone.

If there is one thing Heidi had learned the hard way, it was, "Always say 'no' when a DSS worker wants to enter your home, and always take their threats very seriously." So she did not answer the door when they appeared without warning.

On Monday they returned and banged some more. This time they left a legal notice that an anonymous violation had been received against the Howards and the social workers would be back the next day

One would expect after a lawyer won a 9-0 decision at the U.S. Supreme Court that he would be welcomed as a hero back home. But not Chester Darling! After 17 different judges and administrators in state and federal courts had heard his case, only one had voted for him. They were terribly embarrassed. When the Howards were in trouble, Darling got not one penny from the state money distributed by Margaret Marshall.

at 1:30 for an interview. But Neil Howard called and told them not to come. He informed them that if an interview were scheduled, it would include Atty. Hession, a reporter from *Massachusetts News* and a tape recorder.

Such an interview did take place but the charges disappeared into thin air with the lawyers present.

What bothers observers in 2003 is that the Howards will never know whether an anonymous complaint really was filed, and if so, what the alleged tip was about. Is there some snoopy neighbor who dislikes them that much? What looms large is whether there are social workers who are lesbians or extreme feminists who will always be angry because she returned to her home and family.

The Howard family will never know the answers to those questions and Margaret Marshall will never be able to relate to that anguish. It is difficult for any of us to relate to that fear that still exists of having the town police drag your children away again because of an anonymous tip. It is particularly difficult for Margaret Marshall who has no idea what it is like to be a mother. That statement may sound harsh, but it is a fact which cannot be ignored, try though we may, if we are to be fair to the Howard children and the lack of response to their plight.

Our stories received wide circulation and were picked up by Fox News, among others.[1]

---

[1] If you are interested, these are the stories we printed about the Howards.
March 2001
Newborn Snatched from Parents by DSS

Harry Stewart Goes to Jail

Harry Stewart was convicted in Quincy District Court in 1999 for a technical violation of a restraining order by a hateful wife. The violation occurred when he opened a heavy, metal outside door at an apartment house for his little boy after they returned to the apartment from a visit. Before opening the door, he waited ten minutes in the car honking the horn for the mother to let the boy in as the child struggled to enter.

Stewart waited for ten minutes because his wife had a history of putting him in such positions. He finally got out of the car because the boy had to go to the bathroom.

Judge Joseph Welch, the presiding judge at Stewart's trial, told the jury that they were not to confuse the issue by looking for any "abuse" by Stewart. The jury was instructed to return a guilty verdict if Stewart had violated the court order by getting out of his car.

Stewart was convicted and given a six-month suspended sentence on condition that he attend a batterer's program called "Common Purpose." In order to enter the program, Common Purpose wanted him to admit that he was there because he had abused his wife. He

---

Why Was Mother Shackled? (Detailed history of case.)
Did SJC Chief Margaret Marshall Approve Shackling?
Hospitals Monitor New Mothers for DSS
Neighbors Speak Well of the Howard Family
April 2001
Mother's Hearing Delayed . . . Again
Breast-Feeding of Baby Became a Legal Issue
State Tried to Disqualify Father's Lawyer
DSS Tells Howard Child Before Any Hearing That He Will Be Adopted
Embarrassing to be a Lawyer in Massachusetts
Howards Ask for Help in Paying Attorneys
May 2001
State Moves to Destroy Howard Family; Adoption Is Imminent
June 2001
Howard Children Slowly Reuniting With Parents
August 2001
Baby Returned to Mother Who Was Shackled in Lowell Court
September 2001
Fox News Picks Up MassNews Story About Howards
February 2002
Howard Family Is Together Once Again
Why Was Heidi Howard Arrested?
First Class Family
Why Were Social Workers So Nasty?
What We Did to Bring Our Children Home

refused to sign the false confession and was jailed for six months.

"How can a judge send me to a batterer's program for men that abuse women if he's saying there are no abuse charges there?" Stewart said to MassNews. "I wasn't even accused of abuse."

He said that many fathers are faced with that dilemma. "Either you lie and sign a false confession and attend a batterer's program, or you are going to jail for six months for violating parole. That's coercion."

Stewart said his wife attacked him with knives and cookware and uttered death threats. He said there aren't any

Although Harry Stewart never battered his wife, he was sent to training school and told he had to sign a confession. He refused because it would be a lie. He was sent to the county jail for six months as a result.

batterer's programs set up for women to deal with their violence. The programs are all set up for men. "That clearly demonstrates how biased the system is against men and fathers," he says.

Stewart, acting as his own lawyer, got the restraining order against him vacated two years later after he battled his former wife's free team of lawyers from the elite law firm of Foley, Hoag and Eliot. The former wife, who evidence shows was the abuser in the family, kept renewing the restraining order against him and was seeking a permanent one.

Massachusetts News called several of the embarrassed lawyers at the time to find out why they made such a production of going after an innocent man, but they did not want to comment. They also would not answer questions about what sort of criteria they use to choose clients.

"Why did it take six years before I finally had an evidentiary hearing?" asked Stewart.

Stewart said that is a big problem. Men are not given an evidentiary hearing where any testimony is heard. "They are given a restraining order. Ten days later, you are supposed to have a hearing. But it's not an evidentiary hearing. You stand before the judge and she stands before the judge. Most of the time it is a he-said, she-said. She says, 'I'm afraid of him.' He says, 'I haven't done anything to her.' And then BAM, he gets a restraining order."

Stewart said if there is no other evidence than someone's word, the case should be dismissed. He said judges say it is only a civil law, there is nothing to worry about. "I say, if she can lie to get the restraining order, she can lie to say I violated it when she puts me in jail."

In an evidentiary hearing, said Stewart, the judge has to produce findings of fact and actually prove his decision. "What the judge does instead at the ten-day hearing is take the woman's affidavit and magically make that evidence. He calls it an evidentiary hearing but it's not one."

Stewart said former District Attorney Bill Delahunt (now a Congressman) teamed up with a former judge and another to set up Norfolk County as a so-called national model for combating domestic violence.

"All three of them, Delahunt, Black and Klein were taking equal credit almost in a competitive way. They were on *60 Minutes* for having such a great domestic violence program. The show was even repeated a few different times. But what *60 Minutes* failed to see was something the fathers in front of the courthouse were pointing out. The state office that checks out the courthouses on a yearly basis gave the Quincy District Court an 'F' rating.

"Our point was, how can a court that got so much national attention just two or three years ago — over three hundred courts have modeled themselves after that courthouse — how could the state commission give them an 'F' rating?

"We were trying to show the public that the more Quincy District Court handed out restraining orders to law-abiding men — they had a larger amount of orders per capita than any other courthouse — the more successful the program was going to look because these law-abiding citizens were not going to violate them for the most part, although

Lesbians and extreme feminists have been abusing fathers and their children at the Norfolk County courts in Dedham and Quincy for years, but Margaret Marshall still doesn't care.

sometimes there are very vindictive women who try to put men in jail for technical violations.

"Quincy sent out tons of restraining orders to good men and not many of them violated them. It made Quincy courthouse look like a very successful courthouse. People would say, 'Look at all those restraining orders. Because of their great counseling programs they have in place, men are not violating them.' But it's not true. I never saw any counseling programs other than the batterer's programs that men are forced to go into.

"So, Quincy put out a lot of restraining orders on law-abiding men who didn't violate them and it made Quincy look good. That was the secret of Quincy District Court.

"Because the Fatherhood Coalition revealed things like that to the public, the DA's office went after us like a rabid dog.

"Quincy was our headquarters. The head of the South Shore chapter of the Fatherhood Coalition was a psychiatric worker called John Daniels. He went to jail. The leader of the chapter after Daniels was a Weymouth School Committee member. He was thrown into a mental institution. I was the last leader of that chapter. After I went to jail, everybody was afraid to do anything with the South Shore chapter of the Fatherhood Coalition. Since me, there hasn't been any South Shore chapter."

Stewart says Daniels had a restraining order and was supposed to call his children certain days of the week. His former wife would not let him talk to his children. She'd hang up the phone or not answer it at all at his appointed call-in times.

After two or three months, the mother got an answering machine. Daniels left a message to her telling her it is not good for the children to not have both parents in their lives. "And then he said in the message, besides, you can get into real deep trouble because you are in contempt of court for not letting me talk to the children," according to Stewart.

Stewart said the former wife took the tape to her attorney and said that Daniels threatened her. "Somewhere between the attorney and the judge the tape got lost," says Stewart. He said the judge sent Daniels to a batterer's program although Daniels never had a record of abuse. The wife just told the judge she was afraid of him.

The batterer's program dismissed Daniels and wrote to the court that he was inappropriately placed and didn't belong there. But the judge said he would find a place to send him. Daniels participated fully in a program where he was placed except he wouldn't stand up and admit he was a batterer. Judge Black sent him to jail, says Stewart.

"After Daniels, Paul Corey took leadership. The man is a genius, very intelligent. On his own, he had written proposed legislation before he ran into us at the Fatherhood Coalition. He would leave food and clothing at the end of the driveway because his kids would call him and say they didn't have any food.

"While they tried to prosecute him for that, he didn't participate because he thought the whole thing was ludicrous. While he was doing this passive resistance, he was reading a book by Handy on non-violent resistance; they brought in a psychologist to analyze him because he wouldn't talk to anybody except his attorney.

"They sent him to be evaluated at Medfield State Mental Institution. They were trying to put drugs into him. They were trying to say he had delusions of grandeur. They said that because they didn't believe he knew people up at the State House and was trying to pass these bills."

According to Stewart, even Corey's public defender telephoned him and asked what she should do for Corey because he was so delusional. Stewart told her Corey is telling the truth and to just call the State House and check up on him. She did make some calls and found Corey was telling the truth.

Stewart says he told a doctor about the drugs the hospital was giving Corey. The doctor replied that those drugs would make him delusional. He also told Stewart they couldn't give him drugs until after they had observed him for about fifteen days. Corey had only been in there a few days.

Stewart says he brought the doctor on a visit with him, and unannounced to the institution, the doctor did several tests on Corey and determined he was highly intelligent and other than being a little depressed, which was normal under the circumstances, nothing was wrong with him.

Stewart says he and the doctor finally caught the DA unprepared, went to a judge and managed to get Corey out of there.

Judge Coven Agrees

The judge who sent Harry Stewart to jail and is Chief in the troubled Norfolk County court revealed a month later that he was "burned out." As you read this, you must wonder where Justice Marshall was while the Chief in one of her courts was publicly complaining that he was burned out.

Judge Coven wanted to start sitting in other courts so that he could become "refreshed and renewed," he wrote in an article in the *Boston Globe*.

I replied in an editorial: "We couldn't agree more. That's why we've written many times that our judges should not sit in the same court for years — particularly in family courts."

Then I said:

He says he's overworked but he allows this tomfoolery to occur in his court every day of the year. The gravamen of Judge Coven's article in the *Boston Globe* was that he needed more money. But he wasn't so crass as to start his article that way. He started by saying he was worried about a judge who was leaving early:

"Her decision means the loss of a respected colleague and a dedicated public servant. This represents not only the loss of a dedicated judge, but an indictment of the entire system, emblematic of a system that has failed to retain the energy, excitement, and commitment of one of its best and brightest."

We couldn't have said it better. The judiciary in the state of Massachusetts is in a shambles. And Judge Coven personified the problem.

He finally got to his point at the end of his piece when he said, "[J]udges continue to be paid less than a first year law associate in a large law firm who might have just graduated from law school ..."

The problem with that observation is that Coven never qualified for such a lofty position. That's why he's never received that kind of salary.

Before he became a judge, Coven was a poverty lawyer for his entire career, working for much of that time as a Senior Attorney at Greater Boston Legal Services. This is the federal- and state-funded group which represented Ken Newell's wife. They represented her for nothing even though she clearly has too high an income to be eligible for free legal help. But those poverty lawyers, most of whom are women, totally refuse to help any men.

How could Judge Coven possibly say he is unbiased and fair when it's always his old lawyer-friends who are appearing before him? Do you think they get a little better treatment than most do?

But we're happy to see that he is finally acknowledging the

"failure of the judicial system" of which he is a "leader."

The Batterers "Re-education Training"

Ken Newell didn't want to end up in jail like Harry Stewart. Therefore, when he was forced by the courts to attend three programs for men who are "batterers" of women, he tried to stay out of trouble.

These programs were all run by private companies. One of them was "Common Purpose" in Quincy. This is the company that received national attention when it expelled Harry Stewart from its program because he wouldn't sign a statement that he had battered his wife even though he had never been violent to her.

Newell was also pressured to admit he was an abuser, solely because of his wife's accusations. He refused to admit to the charges even though he was told he would have a hard time seeing his children if he were dismissed from the program. All the while, "Common Purpose" was in constant contact with his wife, he says. Documents shown to *Massachusetts News* confirmed that "Common Purpose" assumed Newell's guilt and said he was in denial. Newell says that he was kicked out of the program after he had been attending for 35 weeks. The director testified against him at his divorce hearing, saying Newell was a "dangerous man."

It is one of many such private companies that are licensed and funded by the state and receive fees from clients also. It is a non-profit corporation that was bringing in $600,000 annually. Men in domestic violence disputes and in DSS "Service Plans" are frequently required to attend for at least 40 hours of classes.

One father in the program told *Massachusetts News*, "You have to say that you did [the violence]. If you were accused of it, then you did it, and it doesn't matter what the truth is."

This explains why the programs were compared to the "re-education camps" that were operated in Cambodia and China, where the government attempted to control the minds of its citizens. The Fatherhood Coalition describes the programs as "Orwellian," and the father's story from inside a Common Purpose program invokes images from George Orwell's 1984, where a man is forced by an overpowering government body to declare that two plus two is not four.

These programs are only for men, even though the U.S. Department of Justice reports that "similar proportions of men and women admit to engaging in violence against their partner."

Newell also attended another program at Brockton Family and Community Resources that was run by Patricia Kelleher. "My wife had me arrested twice while I was in there and Kelleher came up with a report saying that I was 'an extremely dangerous person.'"

Feminist Theory Requires 'Admission of Guilt'

Batterers intervention programs, such as Common Purpose, were started in the 1970s and are based on a feminist model.

They claim that our society places value on male power and that this power structure makes men become batterers. Proponents of this theory contend that batterers are usually not violent in other relationships, but they are violent with women with whom they are expected to share power, i.e., their wives.

In order to stop the domestic violence, the men must be re-educated away from their current understanding of men, women and power. Further, since this patriarchal understanding is ingrained into the minds of men, then every man is guilty and he can confess to being a part of the patriarchy. The program's insistence on confession, even from the non-violent, comes directly from the theories upon which the program is built.

The feminist model employed by Common Purpose is "The Duluth Curriculum," which has not been shown to be an effective curriculum for making violent men less violent. Nor has it been shown to be an accurate portrait of why men abuse women, even if it could be proven that they are more guilty of abuse than are women. More and more information suggests that those men who are batterers are also violent in their relationships with other people, not simply with women, suggesting that the feminist model may not address the reason that some men commit domestic violence.

In the domestic violence industry, there are a number of competing theories about the roots of violence. Some suggest that the violence is a function of family dysfunction; others suggest that the violence stems from the batterer's psychological problems. Currently it is the feminist model that dominates, which may explain why any man, regardless of his history, may be considered violent and asked to confess.

In the feminist model, the violence of men towards women is a part of our culture, even though the evidence is pointing to the fact that women are more violent; and, therefore, men need to be re-educated. The confession is relevant for any man, because all men are a part of the system of hierarchical relationships between men and women, the very existence of which constitutes abuse towards women.

Saga of Ken Newell's Children

The worst family court in our state is in Norfolk County in Dedham. It has a high percentage of lesbians and other extreme feminists who dominate the court. I saw this firsthand as we did a series of stories on Ken Newell and his two children whom we helped by putting him in the care of Chester Darling, the lawyer who won the U.S. Supreme Court case by the vote of 9-0.

We have much more about the Lesbian Network in our issue of May 2002, which is at the MassNews website. The website for the network is www.thenetworklared.org.

29

Tragedy of Jayson Blair Exposes Decay at Times

Tons of paper have been used to tell the "meaning" of the Jayson Blair tragedy, and it was a tragedy. That young black man fell into the arms of the destructive *New York Times*, just like the members of the Sulzberger family we have read about. He was lucky he got out when he did.

Despite all the efforts of the pundits, no one appears to have stumbled onto the truth.

The story of Jayson Blair is not about eliminating discrimination. It's about Pinch's inability to relate to one particular class of people: white males.

That's not my spin. That's what Pinch himself has said and demonstrated many times. It's best exemplified in a statement made during a party at the Metropolitan Museum of Art after an historic Pinch failure in 1992, which was about a new section in the *Times* called "Styles of the Times." The new section demonstrated in the first issue that it was written largely for homosexuals or for immature young people who were still trying to shock their parents.[1]

A dignified older man approached Pinch at the party and said he

---

[1] The first edition of "Styles of the Times" on Sunday, May 3, 1992, had a front-page picture of a muscular bare arm and fist. That night Punch and Carol were dining with friends when the friend said he had been startled to see "The Arm Fetish" in the morning paper. The Sulzbergers looked puzzled. "It has to do with fist fucking," they were told, apparently a reference to what teenagers were taught at Fistgate in Massachusetts a few years later. A couple of weeks later, the *Village Voice* had a parody of the *Times* with an aroused hunk in his underwear under a headline, "The penis fetish." Reproductions of the *Times* cover sold briskly among gays. Abe Rosenthal commented at a birthday party for a staffer where Punch was in attendance: "I knew we were in a new age when I saw the first edition of Styles of the Times. Not only did it give New York the finger, it gave it the whole arm." Punch managed a weak smile even though his son had embarrassed him once again. But that type of article didn't end with that issue and the section was finally killed by Punch in June 1994 to the disapproval of Pinch.

thought the new section was "un-*Timesian*." Pinch thanked him but told a crowd later that alienating older, white male readers meant: "We're doing something right."

What Pinch is attempting to accomplish is to gather everyone in the country into one large group to discriminate against white males (or should we say white males who are also straight?) It still appears that Pinch is not able to accept people <u>as individuals</u>, *not* by their race, sex, religion, whatever. He appears unable to conceive of the idea that he is allowed to accept people by their own inherent qualities, which is known as being "color-blind."

What happened to Jayson Blair is a sad validation of my 1998 book, *Freedom Will Conquer Racism*, which shows how the Civil Rights Act of 1964 is continuing to damage the very people it is intended to protect.

Despite what blacks believe today, the Act was <u>not</u> passed because of Democrats like Pinch. (Does anyone remember Robert Byrd, Democrat of West Virginia, who filibustered all night in an attempt to defeat the Act? Yes, that Democrat is still in the Senate in 2003, isn't he? Anyone remember his filibuster?)

When the law finally did pass in 1964, the House rose in a rare standing ovation to the leadership of the man who had steered it through the House, a Republican from Ohio, William McCulloch, who didn't have enough black voters in his district to fit into a telephone booth. The opponents were largely in the South and were all Democrats. The Republican minority leader in the Senate, Everett Dirksen, also was very important in its passage. It passed there by a vote of 63% of the Democrats and 82% of the Republicans. I don't believe that is a cause for rejoicing among Republicans because I believe it has created terrible problems for black people, but if we're going to say who was responsible for its passage, we should get it right.

The subtitle of my book is: "The Civil Rights Act is damaging everyone in America, especially blacks and women." What has transpired as a result of that Act has done cruel things to Blair because people like Pinch use people like Blair only to gain more power and to assuage the guilt they feel because they are so rich.

As for the loss of manufacturing jobs that the Democrats are blam-

ing on Bush today, anyone can see that that began when the manufac-
turers began to flee America in droves in 1975 when the Act was
unfairly and strictly enforced by Gerald Ford and then Jimmy Carter.
By the time Reagan got in, it was too late. That loss of manufacturing
jobs has hurt black people and caused a loss in self-esteem more than
anyone can imagine.

The simple fact is that studies show that one of the largest factors
in any person's success today is vocabulary, which is a measure of one's
ability to express himself clearly. The only measurable difference
between those who reach "success" and those who remain as a part of
the pack, or behind it, is their vocabulary. If two people have the same
aptitudes, the one who becomes the manager will always be the one
with the higher vocabulary.

The people with the largest vocabularies are not lawyers, doctors or
college professors. They are the presidents of corporations. They have
risen to the top because their vocabulary has given them the ability to
express themselves.

What's That Have to Do with Jayson Blair?

One of the great tragedies of life is a person with *high* aptitudes and
low vocabulary.

It applies to poor Hispanics. We see the hostility of the *Times* to
English immersion in schools, where Hispanic children discover that a
knowledge of English, as soon as possible, is vital to their confidence
and their eventual success. They *can* learn to speak and write well.

Pinch will tell them: "It's okay to talk or write any way you want.
You let them guess what you mean. You have a right to be here."
Baloney! You can be sure he doesn't tell his own children such non-
sense.

This also applies to poor blacks like Jayson Blair who, by their interest in things like Ebonics, are given an excuse for not knowing English
and not having a good English vocabulary. You can be sure that the
Jews among Pinch's ancestors did not learn Yiddish to the exclusion of
the language of the country in which they had settled. His mother,
Barbara Grant and her family, of course, also used English to speak
their first words.

A random study of 18 black, inner-city children in Washington, D.C. showed that <u>those children had the same aptitudes as the overwhelmingly white, middle class people that the Laboratory usually tested</u>. But the *vocabularies* of those children were pathetically low. The good news was that their vocabulary is not an aptitude which is genetic and cannot be changed. Indeed, it *can* be changed because it is merely a measurement of their learning. The bad news is that no one is doing anything about it. Three specific children were mentioned:

• *<u>Fifteen-year-old boy</u>*. High inductive reasoning, high foresight, a tasker's personality. This combination strongly suggests law as an optimum profession. The practice of law, however, requires a large and exact English vocabulary. Without it, the boy, who scored at the fifth percentile in vocabulary will never become a lawyer.

• *<u>Seventeen-year-old girl</u>*. High ideaphoria, high graphoria, extremely people-oriented. Teachers score this way. She could potentially be a fine teacher if she dramatically improves her vocabulary.

• *<u>Fourteen-year-old boy</u>*. High structural visualization, high finger dexterity, high inductive reasoning. A natural pattern for scientific research or medicine. How many scientists have a five-percentile vocabulary?

The researchers expressed their own frustrations this way. "Put yourself in the position of a man or woman who is capable but lacks expression for that capability because of a low vocabulary. Imagine the profound frustration and raging bitterness such an intolerable situation can provoke. If a person senses that his talent, his very reason for existence, is being squandered, denied acceptable fulfillment, is it any wonder that he turns to illegal or violent modes of expression for his thwarted aspirations?" They even believe that when people think, they use words to do so. Therefore, the higher the vocabulary, the deeper the thought.

Professor Thomas Sowell of the Hoover Institution at Stanford University, a black man, may have an answer as to why people like Pinch an interest in Ebonics. Professor Sowell says that the common thread of group activists around the world who wish to retain their political power is "separatism." Therefore, group activists often seek separate languages, separate institutions, and even separate territories. Even where most of the group already speaks the language of the surrounding society, as among the native people in New Zealand, group activists seek to artificially reconstruct a separate language community.

As a person who was born in New York City at the same time as Punch and raised in South Orange/Maplewood, New Jersey, a very fine community when I was growing up, I have always rejected much of the New York City lifestyle. I fled it after World War II because of a deep desire to live near the land, among farmers and others with the same instincts. I can empathize with those natives of this and other countries who say that this society, by which they mean those who live in and rule the nation from their perches in New York City, will never understand them.

People like Pinch say that natives who live near the land should have their own culture and language. But a look at the Indians here in Massachusetts shows that none of them really wish to return to life as it was before the Europeans arrived. In Connecticut, the Indians have become so wealthy with their gambling and liquor that they are despoiling the entire countryside with their garish monstrosities, a sprawl which is worse than that of the white man. So there is no reason not to include them in learning English. We have seen that they also want to "succeed."

Are We Still Talking About Jayson Blair?

For whatever reason, Pinch is a classic racist. He sincerely believes that Blair is inferior. Therefore, he must be treated like a person who cannot succeed without Pinch's help. Baloney. Just stay out of his way and watch him go.

But Blair does need good schools with discipline so that he is allowed to study. He must be allowed the opportunity to rise to his own level. He cannot go to Harvard unless his vocabulary is sufficient to sustain him there or he will surely fail. But there are plenty of excellent schools a rank or two below Harvard that will give him just as good an education, maybe better.

He cannot work at the *New York Times* at age 26. No person has ever accomplished that in the past. Why destroy this young man by pretending he can do so? You cannot assuage your feelings of guilt about your racism by this type of pandering. Pinch's friend, Howell Raines, who was terminated after the scandal, said many times that he had guilty feelings because of his bigotry as a youngster in Mississippi. Many liberals have guilt feelings like that and attempt to salve them by showing how tolerant they are compared to the rest of us "bigots." But what makes them think we are bigots like they are? Even Joe Lelyveld, the Executive Editor who had to be recalled after the scandal, believed in promoting blacks, gays and women, but he also thought that Pinch's diversity training was naive and degrading.

Who Is Jayson Blair?

For those few readers, who may still not know who this Jayson Blair person is, let's fill you in a bit.

<u>May 2, 2003.</u> The worst possible thing happens to the Sulzberger family. Their privacy curtain is torn apart. Everyone could see there weren't any wizards there at all! They were forced to announce that a young black man, Jayson Blair, 27, had made up stories that had been prominently printed in the *Times*. Grievous problems were found in 36 of the 73 columns he had written in the last seven months. The young man had been part of

Pinch Sulzberger told black journalists in Dallas in August 2003 about the Jayson Blair tragedy; it was all Blair's fault. Pinch had no responsibility, he said.

Pinch's affirmative action program.

Blair had been a reporter for the paper for four years, rising from a college intern to a staffer on the national desk. Numerous editors had quietly issued warnings about his sloppy reporting and irregular behavior from the beginning.

In April 2002, his supervisor, the metropolitan editor, had written two sentences in a memo: "We have to stop Jayson writing for the Times. Right now." But that did not stop his meteoric rise. Instead, Editors Raines and Boyd assigned him to two of the most important national stories of the day, the sniper attacks in Washington in October 2002 and then to developments on the home front about the war in Iraq.

June 6, 2003. The two top editors resign. One is the Executive Editor, Howell Raines, the white Mississippi liberal who had worked for the paper since 1978, and still was trying to atone for his early treatment of blacks as a teenager in his home state. The other is his black assistant, Gerald Boyd, who had been with the paper since 1983. For some reason, Pinch Sulzberger did not resign.

The *Times* itself reported it this way in a summary of the resignations:

> Howell Raines and Gerald M. Boyd resign as the top-ranking editors of the New York Times five weeks after resignation of reporter Jayson Blair set off chain of events that exposes fissures in management and morale of newsroom; publisher Arthur Sulzberger Jr. applauds Raines and Boyd for putting interest of newspaper above their own; says Raines will be succeeded on interim basis by Joseph Lelyveld, his immediate predecessor, who retired in 2001; says there will be no immediate successor for Boyd, who was managing editor; resignations set off wave of emotions, from sadness to relief, for staff members; news is shocking to others, who heard Sulzberger say during town-hall-style meeting on May 14 that he would not accept Raines's resignation if it were offered;
>
> Times's investigation into Blair's journalistic deceptions, including plagiarism, brought to surface long-simmering complaints about management-style of editors; some staff members

say top-down management style of Raines and Boyd contributed to gaps in oversight of Blair; some reporters and editors say they told Sulzberger that newsroom's disaffection with Raines is so deep as to be most likely irreparable; tensions were further inflamed when second controversy arose over use of freelance reporters by Rick Bragg, national correspondent close to Raines [Bragg used other reporters to write his stories for him]; Sulzberger, citing importance of newsroom morale, says he accepted resignations with great sadness.

<u>July 14, 2003.</u> The era of Bill Keller begins. A liberal columnist at the *Times*, he is named as Executive Editor, walking in the footsteps of Turner Catledge, Abe Rosenthal, Max Frankel, Joe Lelyveld, Howell Raines and those before them.

Keller quickly showed that nothing would change at the old gray lady. It would not be a balanced newspaper as Adolph Ochs had envisioned. Keller quickly announced he is a "collapsed Catholic" who is "well beyond lapsed." The August 2 edition had a front-page article attacking Mel Gibson, a conservative Catholic, for producing a film about Jesus that the *Times* hadn't seen, and on page seven, it tried to steer people away from attending a debate over homosexual marriage, by claiming that it is "politically toxic." In other words, they were saying the people should just let the lawyers and judges decide that issue. Do you think Pinch wrote that story?

One of Keller's first appointments was feminist Jill Abramson as one of his managing editors. She was coauthor of a book attacking Clarence Thomas. A *Times* review of the book said she is "as liberal as he is conservative," according to Cliff Kincaid at Accuracy in Media.

Did Blair Do This on Purpose?

Blair may have done this on purpose. He could see that Pinch and his minions were treating him like a pet, instead of a man. They were using him for their own purposes. They didn't really have any respect for him. They were merely trying to show how "tolerant" and "inclusive" they were. Blair saw this was a sham and that they had made *him* into a sham also. Their relationship had to end some time. It couldn't go on like this forever. Blair made many attempts to demonstrate this, each attempt becoming more ridiculous. But he only became more frustrated because Pinch could not understand that a pet could have a mind and soul of his own.

The fallout from the Jayson Blair scandal was enormous. The *New York Times* had to apologize. It had to grovel. This was unprecedented! Can anyone imagine Pinch's father, Punch, doing that?

After the first meeting about the scandal, a memo from Pinch, Raines and Boyd was sent to the staff, "We accept our responsibility for creating" an "atmosphere where people feel afraid or disenfranchised."

Please note carefully that the memo said, "*We* accept our responsibility." It continued, "We apologize and commit ourselves to fixing it." Both editors "resigned" a few weeks later on June 5, but Pinch is still there.

We're still in the shoe store. When Pinch said he took responsibility, he was only mouthing words; he wasn't taking any responsibility at all. He will not resign no matter how bad things are until he is forced to do so. Only the hired help are expected to resign and fall on their swords.

Pinch was quoted, about this debacle in the *Times*, in an early story: "The person who did this is Jayson Blair. Let's not begin to demonize our executives, either the desk editors or the executive editor or, dare I say, the publisher."

Most Perceptive Comment

The most perceptive pundit noted that the *Times* had stated in their front-page story about the scandal: "Mr. Blair repeatedly violated the cardinal tenet of journalism, which is simply truth."

Then the analyst noted: "The problem is that the *Times* doesn't believe there is such thing as truth — that is, absolute reality. In fact, probably no newspaper in America has been harsher on evangelicals and conservative Catholics for making truth claims or, as it has disparagingly called them, 'moral absolutes.'"

The commentator who wrote that was Chuck Colson of Prison Fellowship, who continued:

Truth is, by its very nature, an exclusive claim, that is, if what is being stated is true, something else cannot also be. And truth is true even if no one believes it, yet the *Times* and much of the academic establishment in America reject this proposition. In fact, so widespread is the postmodern philosophy today that 64 per cent of Americans believe there is no such thing as moral truth.

But now the *Times* finds itself caught in what has been called "the postmodern impasse." It may be fashionable to dismiss moral truth claims, but the absence of truth leads to chaos, and we find we can't live with it. The *Times* can't live with a reporter carrying its own philosophy to its logical conclusion. The editors want their people to report only truth, but they don't believe absolute truth exists.

Should we then be surprised that a twenty-seven-year-old journalist steeped in postmodernism and multiculturalis — points of view vigorously defended in the pages of the *New York Times* — doesn't believe "the cardinal tenet of journalism, which is simply truth"? If we say there is no truth, we shouldn't be surprised when people make up stories and pass them off as if they actually happened.

And this is one of those issues that we can use with our secular friends to show that the position of the secular world today, its belief system, is philosophically untenable. You cannot live with the logical conclusion of what they say they believe.

I respect the *Times* and its handling of this crisis. The problem is that the *Times* can't possibly solve its own problem. This is a crisis of truth that will be solved only when our elites, like the *New York Times*, reject postmodern relativism and once again commit themselves to the honest pursuit of *the* truth.

To which Adolph Ochs, the great grandfather of Pinch would say Amen and Amen.

Appendix

How the New York Times Pushed Us
Into Vietnam and Then Ran Away,
Creating the 1960's Generation

The book you are reading, *Libel by New York Times*, is not about the Vietnam War. However, it is apparent that some discussion of that war is unavoidable in light of the tremendous amount of nonsense out there. The American people clearly understood what was happening in the 1960s, but our leaders had no clue, especially those who were running the *New York Times*. They had the power to change the world, and they did, but in a terribly wrong direction, which is still very damaging to our country.

There's not much conflict in the facts, only the interpretation. Therefore, we first print a short summary of the facts by a conservative icon who wrote in 1983 a history of the world from the 1920s. Obviously, his report about Vietnam had to be succinct. Although his facts appear to be correct, his interpretations, I am sorry to say, are entirely wrong, but it is a good indication how much misinformation there is.

Then we cite a book from a liberal who was in Vietnam for over twenty years for *Time* magazine and the *Washington Post* and wrote a superb account of what he saw, which was the subject of a documentary for PBS.

Our Vietnam policy was a disaster from the beginning, starting with Franklin D. Roosevelt, who knew nothing about the country and offered it to China. Immediately after his death, the OSS (which was the CIA of its day) endeavored to establish a left-wing, nationalist regime. The person they picked and established there three weeks after the surrender of Japan, was none other than Ho Chi Minh.

From Modern Times by Paul Johnson

The following section is exactly as conservative historian Paul Johnson wrote it. I have not inserted any bracketed comments, ellipses or other additions except for bracketed numbers to indicate those portions about which I have comments at the end. I have left intact all of his British spelling such as "despatch" and "programme."

It is important to grasp that America never had any territorial ambitions in Indo-China, either as a base or in any other capacity. But its policy was usually muddled and invariably indecisive. In the first place it was entirely Europe-oriented. Truman, on taking office, was advised that Indo-China was secondary to the absolute necessity to bolster France as a stabilizing power in Europe and assist her 'morally as well as physically, to regain her strength and influence.' To feel confident again, France needed to get back her Indo-China empire (or so it was argued); and in December 1946 the French drove Ho into the jungle and brought the Emperor Bao Dai back from Hong-Kong. Reluctantly the Americans acquiesced in the French creation of three puppet nations, Laos, Cambodia and Vietnam, and gave them recognition as independent states within the French Union on 7 February 1950. At the same time Russia and China recognized Ho's regime. It was at this point that the struggle became an international one. Russia and China poured in arms. In May America did the same, and with the outbreak of the Korean War the next month the US aid programme accelerated fast. In 1951 it was $21.8 million in economic and $425.7 in military assistance. By next year the military aid had risen to over half a billion dollars: 40 percent of France's costs. [1] Dean Acheson was warned by State Department officials that America was 'moving into a position in Indo-China' in which our 'responsibilities tend to supplant rather than complement those of the French'. But he decided that 'having put our hand to the plough, we would not look back'. He argued that the situation in Europe was too dangerous for America to think of deserting the French in the east. By 1953-4, America was paying for 80 percent of the French war effort.

Then, on 8 May 1954, the French fortress at Dien Bien Phu surrendered. The defeat was made possible by the unexpected scale of the arms assistance now being provided by Russia and China to Ho's forces. The French asked for direct participation by American airpower, and when this was refused they formed a new government under Pierre Mendes-France to negotiate a French withdrawal and a political settlement. The cease-fire agreement, signed at Geneva in July, provided for a division of the country along the 17th parallel, the Communists keeping the North, the West the rest, unity to be brought about by elections in two years' time under an International Control Commission.

It was at this point that Eisenhower's customary good sense failed him: indeed, it can be argued that he was more responsible for the eventual mess in Vietnam than any other American. He should have signed the accords and compelled the premier of the South, Ngo Dinh Diem, to abide by them. It is possible Ho would have won free elections and become ruler of a united Communist country. Would that have been a disaster for America? Even Acheson, in his famous 'perimeter' speech of January 1950, had not considered a non-Communist government in Indo-China essential to American security. [2] George Kennan, in a memo dated 21 August 1950, argued that it was 'preferable to permit the turbulent political currents of that country to find their own level ... even at the probable cost of an eventual deal between Vietnam and Vietminh, and the spreading over the whole country of Vietminh authority.' [3] This was Eisenhower's own feeling. He said he could not 'conceive of a greater tragedy for America than to get heavily involved'. 'There is going to be no involvement,' he repeated. If America did go in, it would only be in agreement with her principal Allies and with explicit constitutional approval from Congress. He worked on the Chiefs of Staff and got from them the assurance (May 1954) that 'Indo-China is devoid of decisive military objectives and the allocation of more than token US armed forces to that area would be a serious diversion of limited US capabilities.'

But Eisenhower was in two minds. He popularized the theory that, if Vietnam was 'lost', the whole of Indo-China would vanish into Communist hands; and that if Indo-China was swallowed, other countries in South-East Asia must follow. He spoke of 'a cork in a bottle', a 'chain-reaction' and 'falling dominoes'. Not only did he refuse to sign the Geneva accords himself, but he acquiesced in Diem's refusal to submit to the test of free elections. That was a fundamental departure from American global policy in the Cold War, which had always rested on the contention that conflict between East and West should be decided not by force of arms but by the test of an honest poll. Diem was permitted to evade this basic principle and, indeed, was rewarded by American military and economic assistance, for the first time direct and not through a French intermediary. Thus it was Eisenhower who committed America's original sin in Vietnam. [4] In default of unitary elections, the Vietcong emerged in 1957 and a new war started up in the South. Eisenhower made America a party to that war, claiming, in his last major statement on the subject (4 April 1959): 'The loss of South Vietnam would set in motion a crumbling process that could, as it progressed, have grave consequences for us and for freedom.'

When Kennedy reached the White House, Vietnam was already one of America's largest and costliest commitments anywhere in the world. It is hard to understand why he made no attempt to get back to the Geneva Accords and hold unified free elections. In Paris on 31 May 1961, de Gaulle urged him urgently to disengage: 'I predict you will sink step by step into a bottomless military and political quagmire.' Nevertheless, in November that year Kennedy authorized the despatch to Vietnam of the first 7,000 American troops, for 'base security'. General Maxwell Taylor, who recommended the step, warned that, if things got worse, 'it will be difficult to resist the pressure to reinforce' and that 'there is no limit to our possible commitment.' Kennedy himself shared the unease. He told his colleague Arthur Schlesinger: 'The troops will march in; the bands will play; the crowds will cheer; and in four days everyone will have forgotten. Then we will be told to send in more troops. It's like taking a drink. The effect wears off, and you have to take another." That was an accurate prediction. Kennedy's instinct was either to stay out or bring things to a head by a direct American attack on Hanoi. An American invasion of the North, which would have been successful at this stage, would at least have had the merit of putting the clock back to 1954 and the Geneva Accords. There could be no fundamental moral objection to such a course, since by 1961 the North had effectively invaded the South. It must always be borne in mind, when analyzing the long tragedy of Indo-China, that it was the determination of Ho, his colleagues and successors, to dominate the entire country, including Laos and Cambodia, which was, from 1945 onwards, the principal dynamic of the struggle and the ultimate cause of all the bloodshed. America's errors were merely a contributory factor. Nevertheless they were serious. Unwilling to leave the country to its fate, or to carry the land-war to the North, Kennedy settled for a hopeless compromise, in which military aid, in ever-growing but never decisive quantities, was given to a client-government he could not control. Diem was by far the ablest of the Vietnam leaders and he had the great merit of being a civilian. Lyndon Johnson, then Vice President, termed him with some exaggeration 'the Churchill of South-East Asia', and told a journalist, 'Shit, man, he's the only boy we got out there.' But Kennedy, exasperated by his failure to pull a sounding success out of Vietnam, blamed the agent rather than the policy. In the autumn of 1963 he secretly authorized American support for an anti-Diem coup. It duly took place on 1 November, Diem being murdered and the CIA providing $42,000 in bribes for the soldiers who set up a military junta. This was America's second great sin: 'the worst mistake we ever made', as Lyndon Johnson put it. Three weeks later Kennedy himself was murdered and Johnson was president.

Some areas of disagreement in that summary by Paul Johnson are:

[1] Although Johnson states that our military aid was over half a billion dollars (40% of France's costs), he does not make it clear that this was before Eisenhower took office. The next year, 1953-4 it was 80% of the French effort, but it is not clear how much input, if any, Eisenhower had during that year. So we were well committed in Vietnam before Eisenhower took office.

[2] Whether Eisenhower should have signed the accords will always

be an open question to some, but citing Dean Acheson's speech as a way to find the answer is plain silly. That's the same speech in which Acheson told the world that Korea and Taiwan were not important to us either. In answer, Korea was invaded by the Communists six months later. We know that over a million boatpeople in Vietnam were so alarmed when we left that country that they exposed themselves to great danger by fleeing. Paul Johnson himself says that the Communists were committed to taking over all of Vietnam, Laos and Cambodia. How long would a joint government with them have lasted? It would have been constant chaos, just like telling South Korea today they have to unify immediately with the North.

[3] Johnson also quotes Truman's advisor, George Kennan, but that had nothing to do with Eisenhower, who didn't believe that we should leave South Vietnam all alone to deal with the machinations of the Communists. As Johnson himself correctly stated in the next sentence, Eisenhower never believed we should send our own boys over there to fight the war. _Never._ And Ike never did so, aside from a few hundred advisors, who I am sure were professionals, not draftees.

[4] Not signing the accords was not our "original sin," as Paul Johnson states. Most Americans agreed with Eisenhower that we should help those fighting for their freedom around the world but not send our troops to do their fighting for them. Paul Johnson himself said, "[I]t was the determination of Ho, his colleagues and successors, to dominate the entire country, including Laos and Cambodia, which was, from 1945 onwards, the principal dynamic of the struggle and the ultimate cause of all the bloodshed."

Also, Johnson is of the Catholic faith which was dominant in South Vietnam. The Catholics were naturally very interested in what was happening there, as they should be. It was said, however, to be a reason for JFK's interest. Much of that interest was kindled by a young American, Catholic doctor, Thomas A. Dooley, who spent several years there and made the Vietnamese people come alive to millions of Americans with his books and speeches which brought most people, including me, to tears with his tales. But it has been publicized lately that Dooley was dismissed from the Navy after having homosexual sex with an Admiral's young son before he journeyed to Vietnam. It is said he was an eccentric opportunist, or so we are told now. An excellent summary of Dooley can be found at the Culture Wars website, a Catholic magazine, at http://www.culture-wars.com/CultureWars/Archives/cw_feb98/Dooley.html

Vietnam, A History, by Stanley Karnow

A great book is *Vietnam, A History,* by Stanley Karnow who we assume would be classified as a liberal. The book was made into a PBS documentary by WGBH, Boston.

Karnow is a newspaperman who was in Vietnam, beginning in 1959, for more than twenty years for *Time* and the *Washington Post.* He was there. He watched everything happen. He returned for a visit in 1981 and then wrote this book. It is an excellent portrayal written by a newspaperman who knows how to tell a story. Karnow appears to give a dispassionate account without prejudices. No one can say that this is a rightwing, "kook" book. It comes from a liberal author and from the profoundly leftwing WGBH.

The author tells about the millions who were killed in what used to be French Indochina after we left. He explains that fighting between those in the north and south of what is now Vietnam is ancient in origin.

He shows that most Americans understood the truth even though they had to determine it themselves; the *Times* did not help. Although the polls showed in November 1967 that most Americans thought that we had made a mistake in committing combat troops to Vietnam, they believed that now that we were there, we should either win or get out. It was the second war, both in Asia, where our soldiers were not permitted to win, Korea being the first. Those polls were "often analyzed wrongly," as signifying "pro-peace" was Karnow's diplomatic way of putting it. A survey in November 1967 showed that 99% of the American people were unhappy and 44% wanted a withdrawal but 55% wanted a tougher policy. Even in 1980, 65% believed that "the trouble in Vietnam was that our troops were asked to fight a war that we could never win."

Obviously, no one would agree with everything Karnow wrote (he was fuzzy about the Harrison Salisbury report in the *Times*), but it was an honest attempt to give the real story about Vietnam. It is well worth the read for anyone.

Another interesting book was *A Vietcong Memoir* written by Truong Nhu Tang, who was the former Minster of Justice in North Vietnam, who became disillusioned and left for Paris in 1978. I am sure that many will say he was just a traitor to the cause. I have no idea about his character, but he does present a fascinating story of what it was like on the other side in a book published by Harcourt, Brace, Jovanovich.

Playbill

Index

Photo Credits